INDIANS

OF THE

UNITED STATES

—◆—

INDIANS

OF THE

UNITED STATES

◼—◼

CLARK WISSLER

REVISED EDITION

REVISIONS PREPARED BY

LUCY WALES KLUCKHOHN

ANCHOR BOOKS

DOUBLEDAY

NEW YORK LONDON TORONTO SYDNEY AUCKLAND

AN ANCHOR BOOK
PUBLISHED BY DOUBLEDAY
a division of Bantam Doubleday Dell Publishing Group, Inc.
666 Fifth Avenue, New York, New York 10103

ANCHOR BOOKS, DOUBLEDAY, and the portrayal of an anchor
are trademarks of Doubleday, a division of Bantam Doubleday
Dell Publishing Group, Inc.

Library of Congress Cataloging-in Publication Data
Wissler, Clark, 1870–1947.
 Indians of the United States
 Clark Wissler.—Rev. ed. / revisions
 prepared by Lucy Wales Kluckhohn,
 Anchor Books ed.
  p. cm.
 Originally published: Garden City, N.Y.:
 Doubleday, 1966.
 Includes bibliographical references.
 1. Indians of North America—History.
2. Indians of North America—Social life
and customs. I. Kluckhohn, Lucy Wales.
II. Title.
E77.W799 1989   89-17868
973'.0497—dc20   CIP
ISBN 0-385-02019-8

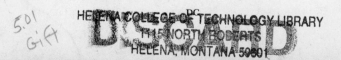

Contents

Part I
THE INDIAN IN PREHISTORIC AMERICA

Part II
THE GREAT INDIAN FAMILIES

List of Illustrations

Preface to the Revised Edition

Due to the increase in knowledge in the past twenty years, a number of changes have been made in the text as originally written. The greatest of these have been made in the first part of the book, specifically, in Chapters I and IV. The first chapter cites the new methods of dating finds and some of the many new and well-documented sites which have been found. The over-all outline of the chapter, however, is essentially as Wissler wrote it. In Chapters II and III, some more specific data—names—were added, but otherwise these chapters remain the same. Chapter IV has been rearranged to fit with current knowledge of the culture sequence, about which there is now much more information than was available a generation ago.

In the second part, concerning the Indian families, there have been far fewer changes than might have been expected in such a long time. The Indian languages have been classified and reclassified to the extent that controversy is the only certainty; for this reason Wissler's choice of the sixfold linguistic classification has been retained. In most instances, the bibliography has been increased, and includes specific titles on the various tribes. Information on the linguistic history and glottochronology is new, as is the treatment of the West Coast peoples and the Possible Relatives, the Salish. Additions have also been made in the sections on the Apache and Navaho, and other southwestern peoples. Those pages on which the tribes belonging to the different stocks have been listed have also been redone.

Concerning Indian Life in General, the third part, the major changes have concerned population figures, reservation life, and attitudes toward Indians. Indians are not in danger of dying out—on the contrary. Populations are increasing, but maintaining Indian identity sometimes poses problems. Just recently, for instance, the Miami tribe was awarded nearly five million dollars in three judgments, as settlement for lands in Kansas ceded to the government in 1854. The problem is that the Miami are split into two parts: one group constitutes a tribal entity, and now lives in Oklahoma; over three hundred thousand was awarded to them. An additional fifty-six thousand dollars was awarded to Miami Indians living in Indiana. The latter, however, is not an organized body: how should its funds be distributed? This must be done on a per capita basis, but the qualifications for this have yet to be announced.

Reservation life has changed greatly in the past generation, and now many Indians do not live on reservations at all. Material concerning these past twenty-five years has been added. The last generation has also seen a change in attitudes toward the Indians (except, perhaps, for the prejudiced), from "wards" of the government to citizens in their own right, and a number of misconceptions have perhaps been cleared up.

The reader should note that references in the book to "the writer" refer to Clark Wissler, rather than the editor of the revised edition.

It is with the greatest of thanks that acknowledgment is made to Miss Margaret Currier and the staff of the Library of the Peabody Museum of Harvard University, who patiently encouraged the use of, then reshelved, the many books; and to Richard Kluckhohn, whose encouragement and suggestions are an integral part of the revisions.

L. W. K.

Cambridge, Mass.
April 1965

Preface to the Original Edition

THE Indian of the frontier is the theme of this book. Many books there are which treat the Indian populations of the New World as a whole and some which, in more restricted fashion, review the Indians of the entire North American continent; but few books specialize in the Indians of the United States, portray their struggles to resist the advancing frontier, describe their mode of life and its modifications due to residing among white people, and finally, give some account of the Indian personalities of the time.

All this we have attempted to do in the succeeding pages. To this end the different tribes have been grouped by language families since that seemed to be the simplest mode of classification and the one most easily understood by the general reader. It is a curious circumstance that the tribes of these respective language families tend to be neighbors, thus forming geographical blocks. Frequently the main body of a language family occupies a geographical area, with a few outlying stragglers. It is by virtue of this that grouping tribes by language tends to classify them by geography also. Our hope is that this procedure will give the reader a general view of the Indian during the frontier period of United States history.

Finally, this book is the first in a special science series for general readers, to be known as the American Museum of Natural History Science Series. The books in this series will be written by members of the Museum scientific staff and others closely associated with the research and educational work of the institution. Since the present activities of the Museum staff cover in part the fields of astronomy, geology, the several divisions of biology and anthropology, it is anticipated that the series will ultimately comprise many volumes.

The author of this book on the Indians of the United States is under obligations to the Museum for permission

to use the plates borrowed from *Natural History* magazine and other of its publications, and to *Natural History*
for permission to reproduce the color plate on the jacket
of this book, Miss Maaron Glenby's portrait of Chief Eneas
Paul Koostatah of the Kutenai Indians. In preparing the
text, free use was made of information conveyed by the
exhibits in the Museum and their labels, an examination
of which should give a background to the meaning of the
text. It remains to make special acknowledgment to Colonel Theodore Roosevelt for constructive criticisms, to Mr.
Paul Richard for selecting illustrations, and to Miss Bella
Weitzner, Assistant Curator in the Museum, for important
revisions of the manuscript.

CLARK WISSLER
Dean of the Scientific Staff
American Museum of Natural History

1939

Introduction

THE way of life which is called American belongs to the frontier. It is hard for a loyal Englishman to understand why Americans face the West instead of the East, their acknowledged homeland, but it has been that way from the first. Opportunity and freedom lay in that direction. Even now, the tradition is so much a part of our hopes and our thinking that we look to the West with longing eyes when the going is heavy. At first the mountains of Pennsylvania and Virginia were the frontier; later, it shifted to Ohio and Kentucky; then to the Mississippi country; next, to the Missouri and the plains; then to the Rockies; and finally, to California and the Columbia. At all times, and even now, our first associations with the frontier are with the Indians. The European tourist still expects to meet them. Not so long ago, an Australian took the movies so seriously that he bought a ticket for Waco, Texas, expecting to see real fighting with Indians; and recently an educated Frenchman, who should have known better, purchased a dude-ranch outfit in New York, thinking that he was equipping himself for Indian fighting in the West.

Our wise men remind us that the frontier, as a reality, ended with the nineteenth century, and that what now plagues the White House and the Capitol in Washington is that there is no frontier for us to possess and enjoy. We still have the vision, but when we seek the reality, it turns out to be a mirage. The situation reminds us of a once-popular song, "All Dressed up but No Place to Go." We are told that life on the frontier gave the background and traditions which make old American families what they are. Families originating in the Atlantic coastal cities, long after the crest of the moving frontier had reached the Mississippi, and when the spirit of early America had become a tradition in the East rather than a reality, never quite understood what it was all about and so have drawn

apart rather than seek to participate wholeheartedly in the
veneration of old American ideals. Whatever may be the
truth about the old American spirit and the frontier, it
seems certain that the popular phrase "rugged individualism" characterizes it at the time when the adolescent and
the brave plunged into the retreating margin of the forest,
the prairie or the mountain country, according to the time
and place, striking out vigorously, often alone or at most
with one companion, to make a career for himself or go
down fighting. There were dangers, many of them, and
perplexing problems to solve, which, if surmounted, gave
increased strength and courage, but above all there were
freedom of action and independence of judgment. From
the first, the outstanding feature of the frontier was the
Indian, who was also something of an individualist; at
times, rugged enough to suit the most aggressive. The
frontiersman rarely had the Indian out of his mind and
frequently met him in person.

It is inevitable that acts of violence dominate the history
of the frontier because they are the climaxes in the adjustment of the Indian to the white. We think of the
Indian as always with a tomahawk in one hand and a
scalping knife in the other and of the white man as ever on
the alert, dodging from tree to tree, shooting Indians; but
this is again a matter of climaxes. More often than not,
Indians and whites were in friendly contact, exchanging
goods, information and knowledge of woodcraft, and were
occasional guests in each other's homes. Now and then an
Indian was offended by a white man, often justly enough,
and murdered him; perhaps more often a white man murdered an Indian. Now and then such incidents resulted in
retaliation by mob action, a band of Indians burning a
house or two, shooting livestock, murdering the adults and
carrying off the children. Again, a mob of whites would
murder an Indian family or two, perpetrating atrocities in
the hope that they would prove a deterrent to further
aggressive action. Many Indians were ambitious to collect
scalps but usually preferred Indian scalps. Yet occasionally
they sought a white scalp. All these were incidental to the

everyday life of both Indian and white; most of the time each was busy seeking food, providing shelter, clothing and other necessities. The climaxes came when organized pressure was brought by either group to retain or acquire more land and to limit hunting rights, as the case might be. The usual result was a war. Frequently the Indians struck first. The front-line whites and their neighbors in the rear often retaliated by attacking Indian towns when they could. In the meantime, the government continued negotiations for peace, which eventually resulted in a treaty and a brief period of peace. Occasionally, a great Indian leader agitated for war to check the advance of the frontier, resulting in more systematic raids upon a larger scale. In every case when the army took a hand the Indian lost the war, but usually he exacted more blood from the whites than he gave up.

Another point to remember is that France, England and Spain were intermittently at war over the possession of the country and that some of the Indian wars we read about were only fringes to these European wars. Most Indian tribes in the Ohio and Great Lakes area were friendly to the French, so when France and England went to war, these tribes would burn and murder on the English frontiers. The Iroquois usually favored the English, so Indians fought on both sides, which meant that they fought each other because their white friends were at war. Even when France and England were temporarily at peace, the French encouraged the Indians to raid the English settlements. After England took over Canada, some of the stronger Indian tribes raided and burned English settlements out of sympathy for the French. Later, the English of Canada encouraged the Indians to raid the rebellious colonists and, after independence, further to harass the frontier in the United States. We merely cite these few elements in the situation to call attention to the intricate way in which the life of the Indian is intermeshed with the American frontier and the large part he has played in the shaping of American life. Nor has he been merely the villain in the piece, though his methods were at times shocking enough, rather he was a friendly competitor with whom our ancestors were sometimes at war. His way of making war was original and non-European, so the English and the colonists made war upon the Indian according to his own pattern—surprise raiding, massacre and scalping. It does not sound nice these days, but then we hear on every hand that in the future the wars of civilized peoples are to be from the air, mostly by raids to burn, mutilate, kill and spread terror, with no regard for age, sex or condition.

However, the days of the frontier belong to history. The Indian now lives with us in peace; his numbers are increasing and intermarriage with whites is gradually narrowing down the racial cleavage. More and more he will live as do his white neighbors, but it will be a long time before he is absorbed into the white population and loses his community background and his tribal traditions. Yet the Indian of the past occupied the United States thousands of years before our ancestors knew there was such a country, acquired a store of knowledge as to the kind of life necessary to live in this country, domesticated the most promising of its wild plants, and thus, by experience, knowledge and achievement laid an economic foundation good enough for the building of these United States, so it cannot be denied that he has an important place in our history.

PART I
THE INDIAN
IN PREHISTORIC AMERICA

Chapter I

THE ABORIGINAL PIONEER

THERE was a time when no human foot trod the American continents. Yet it was not an empty world; the mammoth and the mastodon, great elephants of the past, the largest and strongest of American animals, roamed in the New World with little to fear. There were great cats who sneaked through the bushes and crouched in the tall grasses of the open country. The pasture lands were filled with herds of bison, elk and many now extinct ruminants. Even wild horses and camels were numerous. Among the curious beasts was the great ground sloth, bigger than a cow, who slept in caves and roamed abroad for his food. Whatever else may be said of this grand country, free from the intrusion of man, it was blessed with abundant wild life. It was a different world from that upon which Columbus gazed one October morning, several thousand years later, for great sheets of ice lay over eastern Canada and the northeastern United States. During the summer the melting along the edges of these ice fields sent flood-waters on their way to the sea, working out wide deep valleys and heaping up sand bars for the winds to scatter. Such is the picture of a more remote America, which no man saw, in a period of time spoken of as early Pleistocene.

What Columbus and his followers found was to them a new world, but different from that we have just sketched. Columbus found a man's world, populated from the arctic, on the north, to Cape Horn on the south. There were now no great ice sheets, except in the arctic, mere remnants of the once mighty provinces of the Ice King. There were now great forests and rolling plains where once ice prevailed. The animal life had changed, too, for neither

Spaniard, Frenchman nor Englishman saw the original wild horse, the sloth, the wild camel, the elephant or many other creatures familiar to the fossil hunters of our time. Nor did the living aboriginal Indian seem to know about them either. His astonishment over the European horse was great, and pictures of the elephant moved him to silent awe. He was woefully ignorant concerning his own past.

Thus it was left to the white man to recover this lost Indian history. Yet this was only one of many puzzles the New World offered as a challenge to European intelligence. On a more material level it offered opportunity, wealth and adventure. All the old families of white America, whose traditions made our culture what it is, are the descendants of explorers and adventurers whose legends are so deeply rooted in our scheme of life that the first thing one of us thinks of doing when he attains a little leisure is to go off on an expedition. Great popular award and acclaim go to the explorer who finds something new. To discover dinosaur eggs is more popular than to lead an army to victory. And how the mystery of the Indian stirs one! The first white scholars in Europe and America assumed that the Indian came from the Old World. After Russian explorers in the North Pacific Ocean made it clear that Alaska almost touched the mainland of Asia, wise men said the Indian came from that continent. You will find such statements in the oldest books upon the subject. In 1739 a great portrait painter named Smibert came to Boston to paint the colonial governors. He had painted at the Russian Court and so was familiar with the Siberians who appeared there from time to time. When Smibert saw Indians he pronounced them Mongolians. From that day to this, notwithstanding the intensive research of specialists, everything points to a Mongoloid ancestry for the Indian.

Many alternate theories have been proposed, however, including those of continental drift—separation of the Americas from Europe and Africa—those of peopling from lost continents, such as Atlantis or Mu. Some have preferred theories of crossing either the Atlantic or the Pacific by boat. Others have believed that the Indians were descended from the ten lost tribes of Israel. None of these theories has been accepted.

It is generally believed that the first men to discover America came from Siberia. Geology tells us that four times during the Pleistocene period, or Ice Age, glacial ice reduced the sea level, forming a land bridge across Bering Strait; here, even now, Asia and North America are separated by only fifty-six miles of shoal waters, a distance broken by steppingstone islands. It has recently been estimated that during the Wisconsin, or last glaciation, the sea level was reduced as much as 460 feet; such a drop would produce a broad plain more than a thousand miles wide. There would be ample room for crossings, imperceptible to the travelers themselves, which must have taken generations to accomplish. The narrows of Bering Strait itself would have been passable in winters in interglacial times, when the climate was much as it is now; the short distances across the ice between islands increased the feasibility of passage.

Remembering that we set out to recover the lost history of the Indian, the most intriguing question still remains: When was the first crossing from Asia?

This is a perplexing question. The ancestors of the Indians did not write books; nor did any of the early Indians keep records. So dates for this discovery of America must be considered in relative terms. The question may be phrased thus: Was aboriginal man here before the great ice sheets formed over eastern Canada and adjacent parts of the United States? Did he see the mammoth and the mastodon? The original wild horse? The camel? The sloth? The terrible saber-toothed tiger? For many years scientists and explorers have been searching in caves and elsewhere, seeking the remains of man and his works in such association as would prove beyond doubt that he lived here at the same time. There is a long, fascinating story in this scientific controversy; reputations were made and lost, friendships blasted in passion, experts accused of fraud and falsehood; a story which, once adequately written, would be an amazing ultrahuman document. But here we are interested solely in the answers to the above questions. What, then, is the story unfolding before us in the relentless advance of knowledge?

For a long time archaeology could offer no satisfactory evidence that the first "red Mongoloids" from Asia saw any of the known extinct animals, but within a decade the case became stronger. By 1940 at least five justly famous places had been found where early man left his card: on the campus of the University of Alaska, near Fairbanks; at Fort Collins, Colorado; Folsom, New Mexico; Clovis, New Mexico; Fell's Cave, southern Chile. Our frontier forefathers used to say, "Where there is a lot of smoke, some fire will be found." These five sites served as scattered markers for a trail beginning in Asia and ending at Cape Horn. Many sites have since been found which have shed additional light on this history; a recent discovery in the Valley of Mexico may radically change beliefs about the time when man first entered the New World.

New techniques of dating have also greatly increased our knowledge. One such technique, radiocarbon dating, involves the measurement of the amount of Carbon 14 (C^{14}), a radioactive isotope of carbon, in a given organic specimen. Present during the lifetime of every organism, C^{14} disintegrates at a known rate after death. Measurement of the remaining C^{14} yields an absolute, rather than a relative, date, accurate to within a few hundred out of many thousand years. By another technique, estimates are made of the time required for once-related languages to separate. In a step-by-step process, past relations can be shown between languages now totally separate. Such relationships have been shown for the Romance and other languages of the Old World; recent research has also revealed linguistic correspondences across Bering Strait.

Guiding our imagination by the facts at hand, we see a few adventurous aboriginals crossing from Siberia into

Alaska, where they find the hunting good. Some camped on what is now the campus of the University of Alaska. Examination of the chipped stone points and cutting tools found there revealed remarkable similarities to implements found in Mongolia. Unfortunately, the Alaskan artifacts were found in frozen muck deposits, and accurate dating was not possible.

We said that Alaska was rich in game. The students of fossils tell us that even while the great ice sheets lay over much of Canada and our own northeastern states, there was open grassland in the Yukon and Mackenzie valleys in Alaska and southeastward to the Gulf of Mexico. Forests now cover most of this area in Canada, but our forefathers found a great open country east of the Rocky Mountains extending down into Mexico. Following the warmer river valleys, they moved ever southward, hunting the many species of deer and bison, now extinct, which foraged before them.

It has long been imagined that these first immigrants from Asia started a great migration, as did the followers of Columbus much later. Band after band moved in. Those first on the ground disliked the intrusions of those who followed and, like Daniel Boone and his kind, sought the freedom of the wilderness. Research in linguistics has indicated a change in this theory, however. Work by linguists, especially Morris Swadesh, has indicated the peopling of North America by far fewer groups than had earlier been supposed; as few as four linguistic stocks have been suggested, and there may even be connections among them. This question has not yet been answered completely; time and more research will give us more clues.

However they came, eventually a group of these restless pioneers found the hunting good around Fort Collins, Colorado, and Folsom, New Mexico. The surrounding country was dotted with herds of bison, somewhat larger and perhaps more formidable than those pursued in the days of our forefathers and the contemporary Indians of the Plains. *Bison taylori* they are called by the scientists, as distinguished from the *Bison americanus* known to history.

Near Folsom, New Mexico, in 1926, excavators uncovered the skeletons of a small herd of the now extinct *Bison taylori*. In three years of investigation (1926–28) the bones of twenty-three animals were uncovered, all lying close together under many feet of clay and gravel, where they had obviously lain for a long time. Their position suggested that the herd had been cornered and struck down. Most tail bones were missing, hinting at the work of human hands that cut away the tails with the skins, a common practice even recently. Yet there was better evidence, for among the bones were a number of chipped dart points, most of them broken. One such fragment was found in the clay surrounding a rib of one of the animals; another piece found nearby fitted to form an obvious point. These were made by man, of course. The finding of another point embedded with a matrix of bones convinced even the skeptics that these were the instruments of death.

These chipped points were new to specialists. They were skillfully executed, after a unique pattern: a longitudinal flake was carefully removed from each face. Naturally enough, they were named Folsom points.

Near Fort Collins, Colorado, a camping place belonging to the Folsom hunters was discovered in 1924. Finds at Folsom had spurred the search for other remains of early man, and the Lindenmeier site, named for the owner of the land on which it was found, was excavated between 1934 and 1938. Many Folsom points were found, also in association with the *Bison taylori*. Many other stone implements of the everyday life of these people, such as knives, hammerstones, choppers and scrapers, were uncovered, as well as some tools of bone; refuse from a workshop gave clues to the manufacture of the Folsom points. But not until discoveries were made near Lubbock, Texas, was material found suitable for radiocarbon dating. Tests on charred bones found with four Folsom points yielded a date of 9883 ± 350 years ago. It is believed that the Lindenmeier site may be slightly older than the Lubbock site. In any event, it is safe to say that approximately ten thousand years ago the Folsom hunters inhabited the plains which are now part of the United States.

Some years after the discoveries at Folsom, road builders near Clovis, New Mexico, uncovered a deposit of fossil bones; in the subsequent excavations stone implements were found. These lay near bones of the same extinct bison as at Folsom. Stone points were also found in association with mammoth bones, one near a vertebra and another between two leg bones. Found *in situ* near the tusk of one mammoth was a bone shaft; this was thought to be the foreshaft of a spear, but a subsequent find indicates that this type may be a projectile point. In either case, the hunters here overcame bigger game. The position of the mammoth skull and the accompanying bones suggested that the animal had either mired down in a bog through his own carelessness or was stampeded into it by shrewd hunters. Although dates were not obtained at Clovis, stratigraphic evidence from other sites which have yielded "Clovis Fluted" points indicates that these people were perhaps a thousand or two thousand years earlier than the Folsom hunters. Nor is there reason to believe that this was the first meeting with the mammoth. Both mammoth and mastodon bones have been found elsewhere in the United States with stone implements suspiciously near them. Further remains of these extinct animals have been found in Asia, from which we surmise that the ancestors of our Folsom hunters had learned to slay them in their homeland.

Not long after these adventurous hunters feasted upon a mammoth at Clovis, the advance guard of this invasion passed into South America, eventually reaching the extreme southern tip of that continent. These may have been the last of the aboriginal pioneers to reach virgin country where no man had previously been. Here they made their last stand. Among the game they pursued were the now-extinct ground sloth and the original wild horse. Bones of these animals were found along with stone and bone tools in the Fell's Cave shelter and nearby Palli Aike Cave, near the Chile-Argentina border. Hearths were found, and many of the bones were burned; some of the implements found were in appearance not unlike those found in North America. Radiocarbon dates obtained from horse and sloth bones yielded a date of 8639 ± 450 years, thus establishing the appearance of early man in South America more than eight thousand years ago. Here, around their ancient campfires, gathered these first hunters, to rest in the flickering light, to retell the events of the day, how they waylaid the swift horse and by their superior intelligence brought him down. Perhaps there was a pessimistic note as the oldest man told how many horses one could see formerly, when looking out upon the grassland, but that yesterday he traveled far afield for a glimpse of a few fleeting animals. Probably he urged that more sacrifices be made to the angry supernatural powers and that greater care be taken not to offend them again. Possibly he complained that too many strange tribes were crowding into their country; that, as was their custom, they themselves should move on toward the south, but now they could not, for the sea, the big open water, made this impossible. Yet the cave was good, and if the unseen powers would be merciful they could doubtless go on as in the past.

This is but a bit of fancy and yet justified, for though we know so little of these adventurers, the outline of their achievements is recorded in their cave homes. Thus we can place them in the sequence of time and so follow these first Americans from Alaska to the southern Cape. They lived in a world somewhat different from the present; though many species of animals living then are still extant, others more picturesque are now extinct. Using all the evidence available, it seems safe to say that these early hunters spread through lands overrun by wild horses, camels and, here and there, herds of mammoths. Then the curious giant sloth should be included, not to mention a number of less impressive extinct species.

Just exactly when these travelers passed any specific

points on their way to Cape Horn is open to speculation. A recent find in the Valley of Mexico indicates that the journeys were earlier than ever before suspected. At a site near the town of Puebla, Dr. Juan Armenta Camacho found fragments of incised mammoth or mastodon bone, and other bone and stone implements, in geological deposits believed to antedate the Wisconsin glacier. Incisions on one six-inch bone fragment were believed to represent mammoths or mastodons, bison and a tapir. Material from the site was submitted for radiocarbon dating, hoping to confirm the pre-Wisconsin estimate of over thirty thousand years ago. A number of experts examined the site, and some believed the finds to be spurious—they believed that the incised bones had washed down from deposits more recent than those in which they were found. Nonetheless the handiwork of man was evident in the incisions; if the early date is confirmed, many ideas will have to be changed concerning the time of man's appearance in the New World. Whether the early hunters, who ate wild horses, reached Cape Horn before, during or after the Wisconsin glaciation we leave to those speculatively inclined; we do know that they reached the southern tip of the New World before the wild horse and the sloth were extinct. At least, it was so long ago that the historic Indians had never heard of it.

The next question is: What manner of men were these aboriginal pioneers? For a long time there were few skeletons found which would yield much information; for one reason, there were not many humans living thousands of years ago, by comparison to the number of animals. For another, perhaps these early hunters did not bury their dead but exposed them to the elements as did the Plains Indians. Much of the scant evidence which has been found was discovered under conditions which could hardly be termed scientific. Several finds, however, have gained the respect of the experts. On the shores of what was an ancient lake in Minnesota, highway workers unearthed the skeleton of "Minnesota Man," in fact a girl about fifteen years old, from deposits dated geologically at between eight thousand and twelve thousand years ago. The late A. E. Jenks, who examined the skeleton, stated that measurements and other observations proclaimed it to be "a primitive type of *Homo sapiens* of an early type of evolving Mongoloid suggesting American aborigines, especially the Eskimo, more than the present Asian Mongoloids."[1] Other skeletons were found in association with extinct animals in Florida, at Melbourne and Vero Beach; the conditions of the deposits and the damaged skulls have been the subject of a long and still unsettled controversy among the experts. Careful excavation and excellent documentation were achieved at a site near Midland, Texas, and the association of "Midland Man," also a female, with artifacts and fossil bones was recorded. The skull of "Midland Man" was relatively long and narrow, as were those of the three skeletons found with the already mentioned artifacts in Palli Aike Cave, in Chile. A tendency toward such dimensions, which have also appeared in skeletal material found elsewhere in the United States, has confounded the experts. This type of skull is not like the typical Mongoloid skull, which is more rounded in shape; nor is it typical of any specific group of American Indians. Boyd's research on blood groups among peoples of the New World has also yielded perplexing evidence. Boyd discovered that most South American Indians had type O blood, indicating the absence of either type A or B; as he moved north into the American Southwest, he found a predominance of type O, with a small percentage of type A, and further north, the Blackfoot Indians of the High Plains showed a predominance of types O and A, with a very small percentage of type B. Only the Eskimos (who are considered to be recent arrivals in North America) and groups with known white intermixing showed any appreciable percentage of type B, a type which is frequently found among Asian Mongoloids. Yet geological and archaeological evidence has not changed the belief

[1] H. M. Wormington, *Ancient Man in North America*, Denver, Colorado, 1957, p. 234.

that the ancestors of the present American Indians journeyed to the New World from Asia. The perplexing questions continue to appear; they may eventually be answered.

When we turn to mode of life, the general outlines of the picture are clear enough. The first immigrants were itinerant hunters. They left behind neither traces of pottery nor domesticated plants. Their shelters must have been crude, because no traces of them have been discovered. Being wandering hunters, forced to carry all their possessions upon their backs, their baggage was meager and simple. Their cutting tools were of stone, chipped, but similar to those of the middle cave period in Europe or even later. It is interesting to note that these New World hunters were as skilled as the best stone workers of the European cave period. Polished stone is scarcely present and ornaments are conspicuously absent. Of course, what they may have made of wood perished, but though they left behind many bones of the animals they killed for food, few of these were fashioned into even the crudest of implements. What we find, then, is a mode of life similar in general to the latest paleolithic cultures of Europe; in other words, the "Old Stone Age" of aboriginal America. We are not sure they used bows and arrows. There is good reason to believe that they all used the spear thrower to launch their stone-pointed lances against the bison and even the mammoth. Yet they were human enough, resourceful and brave, as becomes the ancestors of a virile people. There is no reason to believe that they tried to domesticate any of the animals they knew, for not even the dog has been certainly associated with them. Apparently their less nomadic successors, those who formed the settlements, so to speak, are the people who received or brought the dog from Asia.

The discovery of America by these early hunters was a great event, with consequences as momentous as those following 1492. At first the animals had the land to themselves. The largest animals had nothing to fear, but when man, the disturber and destroyer of nature, came, nothing was safe. He set fire to the grass and the forest to drive out the game. He dug pits, set traps and snares, shrewdly stampeded animals into bogs and over cliffs or pursued them relentlessly until exhaustion put them in his power. The abundance of game gave man the security and peace necessary to healthful family life, so his numbers increased rapidly, and he soon spread over the entire continent. When his advance guard reached Cape Horn the pioneer period entered into its decline, and with it passed the picturesque animals of Pleistocene time. After that, one period of aboriginal life passed slowly into another.

These early hunters did not pass into oblivion when the mammoths and their Pleistocene associates died off, for in certain caves near Cape Horn, five well-marked culture changes have been noted in the accumulated debris, representing as many thousand years or more, all the work of hunters, who made no pottery and left no other traces of anything more than the artifacts of the Stone Age. Even as late as 1750 the Indians of California and northward, across the plateaus, into the plains and far north into the forests of Canada, were merely hunters, most of them still dependent upon stone and bone tools. In a way, they can be considered as lineal descendants of the first hunters; but there were innovations in the way of living and borrowings from their more civilized neighbors, so that it is not far wrong to state that with the passing of the sloth, wild horse, camel and mammoth, the kind of hunting life we have described also came to an end; at least, this is what the diggings of archaeologists have revealed.

Students of climate tell us that many significant changes have occurred since the days of which we write. When the first hunters probably arrived the ice was slowly melting, receding toward the arctic, and is still melting. Some parts of the plains and plateaus were drying out, and the winds were whipping up great dust storms. In the cold belts along the margins of the ice sheets coniferous trees sprang up, thus causing the forest to follow the retreating ice toward the north. Coming behind and crowding out these evergreens were the deciduous forests which white men later cut away to make room for their farms. Scholars can trace these changes by several continually expanding methods, one of which is pollen analysis. This method depends on three basic principles: that large amounts of pollen are distributed; that pollen is very resistant to decay; and that pollen from different types is distinct and can be recognized. Pollen can be collected from ancient as well as modern deposits. In analysis, different types are identified and their frequencies noted; these data are arranged to show stratigraphic sequence, from which changes through time can be seen. Additional data on climate changes and the environment in which the early hunters lived can be obtained from geology, climatic history, paleontology, radiocarbon samples, or any of these and others in combination. All of these extend our knowledge of these fascinating early hunters.

So we take leave of these first of all pioneers. We do not know just how they looked, but whatever their facial features may have been, we can be sure of their general physique. There were no weaklings among them, for they ran down their game on foot and matched their wits against the fleetness of the wild horse and the might of the elephant. Yet a powerful spear arm, a sure and swift foot, a keen eye and a well-balanced nervous system were essential. Weaklings were doomed, for none but the fit could survive. Ignorant they were, judged by our standards, but wise in the ways of nature, and shrewd, far shrewder than any of the beasts around them.

Chapter II

RISE OF THE STONE BOILERS

SOME time after the hunters had spread over America a new people came upon the scene. They were hunters still, yet less roving, and had a higher standard of living, but their most outstanding peculiarity was to boil food with hot stones. For kettles they used vessels of wood, bark and skin and even closely woven baskets. Large pebbles heated in the campfire and handled with wooden tongs were dropped into the vessel. If the pebbles were hot enough the contents of the vessel soon began to boil. As a pebble cooled it was returned to the fire, another hot one substituted, and so on. All the cook needed to do was to sit comfortably near the fire, changing pebbles until the food was ready. These hunters lived in comparative luxury.

For all we know, the hunters of the extinct bison and the wild horse roasted meat over the campfire or ate it raw. Soup of any kind, hot or cold, had never been dreamed of, and hot water was to be had only on rare occasions, when a hot spring was discovered; but the stone boilers were aristocrats, they had all these luxuries, and their descendants were so well satisfied with this new way of cooking and the enjoyment of hot water that they went on improving their cooking baskets and wooden boxes—and have continued to do so down to our day. Their country was a wide province on the Pacific side of the United States and Canada, extending roughly from the Copper River, Alaska, to southern California, including the Plateau. We do not know whether in earlier days they spread over most of the United States and Canada, although in the Plains and Great Basin in the United States and in eastern Canada stone boiling was known to be one method of cooking. As pottery was not used early in North America, it is probable that stone boiling had a wider distribution than is now known.

Boiling water in a pot is such a commonplace matter that we fail to recognize it as a significant invention. Yet we can be sure that man did not always do it; he had to discover it. Like most inventions, it presupposes initial discoveries and long experience with the things and processes involved. To discover that water can be heated, soup made, etc., wooden bowls, baskets or other containers for water must be at hand. The effect of pouring water upon hot stones must be known. Then all we need is an observing person of more than average curiosity to wonder what would happen if the hot stone were dropped into a vessel of water. Once the heating of water was achieved, the boiling of food would follow. Yet it may have required several thousand years to achieve this epoch-making invention.

And what luxury this discovery brought to the hunters! There was now suitable food for young children, the aged and the sick. A new style in living came in, one to be copied far and wide. Yet this was not the only achievement of these stone boilers, for in time they came to make some of the finest baskets to be found in museums. Perhaps few who admire the beautiful baskets made by the Indians of California realize that many of them were intended for dinner pots. We suppose that even the first hunters knew how to twist hair and fiber into string; also that twigs, strips of bark, blades of grass, etc., could be interlaced, as our children learn to do with strips of paper in the kindergarten. From these fundamentals have come all the textiles the world has ever known, but countless minds and fingers have wrought to bring this about. The hunters did their part, no doubt, insignificant though it seems to us; they preserved the tradition if nothing more. Yet so far we find no evidence that they made baskets. In Fell's Cave, down toward Cape Horn, the hunters of the wild horse were followed by four successive hunting cultures before we find traces of baskets or any kind of textiles.

Many, many campfires were lighted during thousands of years, but no charred remains of baskets were left behind; once a bit of vegetable substance is charred in the fire, it becomes like charcoal and is practically indestructible. Of course this is negative evidence but, as an archaeologist would say, there are many indications to warrant the assumption that all the early hunters, from Alaska to Cape Horn, were pitiably weak in basketry. Anyway, we can be sure of one thing: a trip to a well-stocked museum will prove that in America the great basket makers were the stone boilers. For example, baskets made by the Pomo in California and the Tlingit around Sitka, Alaska, are often given the highest rating in beauty and precision of weave. We have known museum visitors to be shocked when told that even some of the finest of Tlingit baskets were used as common cooking pots. We remember once reading the narrative of a sailor, written more than a century ago, telling how, because these baskets had such delicate walls, the Indian cooks dug shallow holes in the sands of the seashore in which the baskets were set, then snugly banked up on the outside with sand. The water, meat and vegetables were then poured in, and a few hot stones did the rest. Weaving a basket closely enough to hold water sounds like modern efficiency, but not so long ago the Indian women from California to Alaska were doing it, as their ancestors had done for centuries and centuries.

Naturally there were other uses for baskets, nor was stone boiling always done in them. The Plains Indians sometimes took the paunch of a bison, hung it from wooden stakes so that it sagged in the middle, and put water, meat and hot stones into it. The writer saw it done once with a cow's paunch. Old Indians said that often the fresh hide of a buffalo was used, pushed down into a hole in the ground. A hunting or war party on the march sometimes killed a buffalo in the evening, turned the carcass on its back, removed the viscera, put water, blood and some soft parts of the animal into the cavity and then with hot stones prepared a feast, using the body of the unfortunate animal as a kettle in which to boil him. Maybe the hunters who first used stone boiling did it this way, but no one knows how this method of boiling began in America. It was known and practiced in parts of the Old World, and there are references to it in Greek literature.

Within the memory of persons now living, Indians around Puget Sound and northward made boxes of split boards in which hot stones were placed for boiling. Some of these same Indians made graceful canoes by hollowing out cedar logs and trimming the outside to the desired shape; but the graceful lines were secured by spreading the sides. To do this the canoe was filled with water, which was boiled by dropping in hot stones, until the wood became soft enough to bend into the desired shape. We mention these things to show that, after all, stone boiling is about as effective as any other kind of boiling. It may take longer but has some advantages—spreading the sides of wooden canoes, for example.

Everywhere primitive and civilized alike are prone to do as they have done. It is a fair guess that if iron or brass kettles came into the hands of stone boilers without a knowledge of how they were used by their makers, these kettles would be used to cook in with hot stones. Very likely most of the stone boilers never had an idea that boiling could be done in any other way. We suppose that if they saw people cooking with kettles hung over the fire they would be astonished that the kettles did not burn up as would baskets, boxes, etc.; but proving by their own observations that these new cooking vessels possessed such qualities, they would want to possess this novelty.

There has been some discussion among the professors of anthropology as to whether pottery was first made for cooking purposes or for use as containers for water and other materials. We suppose this is one of those puzzles for which positive answers are not to be expected. Yet if pottery vessels came into the hands of the stone boilers, we think it a safe bet that hot stones would be put into them instead of setting them on the fire. Archaeologists have often remarked that they find some pottery so crude that it would not stand setting on the fire. The present

Kutenai Indians of British Columbia claim that their mothers made pottery vessels until the late nineteenth century, but cooked in them only by inserting hot stones; they were not set directly on the fire. These Indians, by the way, lived on the edge of the area occupied by the majority of the stone boilers of America, and if they were stone boilers originally, it is easy to explain this way of using earthen pots in cooking. The skeptical may say that it could have happened the other way around; that the Kutenai may have been a pottery-using people who moved into the country of the stone boilers and, to be in style, used the much slower method of hot-stone boiling. However, they boiled in bark kettles and baskets more often than in clay pots. Since we can prove neither alternative, we leave it to the reader to decide which is the more probable.

So far as the data go, pottery was not made within the stone-boiling area when white people first arrived, nor have archaeologists found much evidence to show that pottery makers lived there at any time. The first white traders brought iron kettles and demonstrated their use. The stone-boiling Indians recognized their superiority at once, though there was one drawback—the food tasted different. Putting hot stones into the pot added something like seasoning, and we all know how particular we are that our familiar dishes have their customary taste. So at first they put hot stones into their newly acquired iron-pots. This may have some bearing upon the solution of the Kutenai puzzle.

While we are considering novelties, the Indians of the eastern Canadian woods command attention. They often cook in birchbark vessels. When on a trip they can get along without an iron kettle. Stripping a sheet of bark from the trunk of a canoe birch and folding it to form a seamless boxlike vessel provides a good substitute for a kettle; but the woman does not drop hot stones into it to boil water; she hangs it over the fire like an iron kettle. You may say it cannot be done, but these Indians do it. Bark will not ignite at the temperature of boiling water, and if the flame does not touch it, the bark kettle will boil as long as need be. Now how shall we explain this? Why did the stone boilers overlook so simple a thing? Perhaps it is not so simple. Would we have thought of it? These Indians were not stone boilers, nor did they make pottery, but their neighbors on the south used earthen pots for cooking. That may be the explanation. Knowing that boiling in earthen pots could be done over the fire, and having nothing but birchbark vessels, they experimented. That may not be the way it happened; it is merely a possibility. Travelers tell us that in winter these northern Indians melt snow for drinking water by hanging bark and skin vessels near the fire. As in the story of the steam engine young Watt got an idea from the teakettle lid lifted by steam, so some thoughtful Indian may have moved the bark kettle of snow nearer and nearer to the fire until the water boiled, thus making a discovery. But it is all a guess, because no historian was present to record the event.

The stone-boiling area, as white men found it, was distinguished for its specialization in two foods, salmon and acorns: acorns in California and Oregon; salmon in Washington, British Columbia and southern Alaska. If the history of these Indians were as important to us as that of the Egyptians, we should be writing that the acorn crop was the economic base of the culture of aboriginal California. For Egypt it was wheat, translated in the Bible as "corn." Thus, in so far as the civilization of Egypt and her ancient neighbors was founded on wheat, so the culture of aboriginal California was sustained by acorns. The important difference was that wheat was sown, whereas the acorns grew upon wild trees. The problems of the Californians began with the harvest, whereas the Egyptians had first to flood their lands, then plow and sow, tend the irrigation ditches and shoo the birds away. Perhaps this is what is meant by the biblical statement, "in the sweat of thy face shalt thou eat bread." Whereas the Egyptians sweated in the fields, the California Indians hunted and fished. Yet when the acorns were ripe the

Indian faced a real task. The whole village went to its favorite gathering grounds in the forest. Men and boys climbed the trees to knock or shake off the acorns; women and girls picked them up, carried them to the storage places and, ultimately, to the village. Since there was only one harvest a year, storage of some kind was necessary, as in the case of wheat. When the acorns were stored, the men and boys were through; they could go on with their hunting and fishing and occasional fighting.

As everywhere else, the woman was the feeder; she must transform these bitter, uninviting acorns into tasty food. This was a laborious process demanding many kinds of skill too detailed to be described here. First the acorns must be hulled by setting them up on their ends in shallow pits in flat stones and then skillfully pressing down upon them with a hammerstone. The kernels were tossed into a basket, the hulls thrown aside. In a way, this corresponds to threshing wheat.

With a basketful of hulled acorns before her, the woman prepared to make meal. She sat on the ground with a flat stone, a kind of mortar, between her knees, upon which she beat the acorn kernels with a stone pestle. As she pounded, the fine meal piled up in a ring around the striking place, the coarser particles rolled down the sides to be scooped up in her hand and cast under the pounder again. And so it continued, tap, tap, until all the kernels on hand were reduced to meal. Finally, a sifting basket was used to sort the coarse crumbs for a final pounding.

This process resulted in a basket of fine yellow acorn meal. The basket was likely to be a work of art, finely woven and bearing tasteful designs. Many such baskets may be seen in museums. But acorn meal is bitter because of the tannin in it, which is poisonous if taken in quantity. Yet long ago these Indian women found a way to eliminate the tannin. A shallow panlike hole was dug in sand. A dough was made of the meal and plastered over the bottom and sides of the hole, as when our cooks spread dough in a pan for a pie. Next, water was heated in a basket with hot stones and poured upon the dough. It soon seeped through the acorn meal, taking some of the tannin with it. Water had to be poured into the hole many times before the woman found the acorn dough sweet to the taste.

The cooking now began. If bread was desired, the dough was made into loaves and baked at an open fire. This acorn bread was a staple food and could be kept a long time. When callers dropped in, the thing to do was to offer them a chunk of acorn bread. On the other hand, if soup was desired, the soup basket was brought partly filled with water and some of the prepared dough stirred into it. Hot stones were next put in, which with some stirring produced the desired soup. Fastidious Indians dropped in a few mint leaves. After all, this sounds good enough for a civilized table, and many an Indian boy and girl, carted off to a white man's boarding school, furnished with what is called civilized food, may be excused for shedding tears because there was neither acorn bread nor the tasty soup mother made.

No doubt we have taxed the reader's patience in telling how one half of the stone boilers lived and shall now bore him further with some account of how the other half lived. For they fished for salmon, the fish that leave the sea at certain times of the year and crowd up the rivers and creeks to find room to lay eggs to perpetuate their kind. At such times fishing was easy; the Indian stood by the stream and scooped out or speared the fish as they passed. Here again the problem of storage arose. To be preserved, these fish were dried. We shall not go into the details of this process, but the methods used served the purpose. Among most of these fishers the custom was to pound the dried fish almost to the consistency of pemmican. This might be mixed with dried berries or pulverized roots. At the proper season, the villages in Washington and Oregon were noisy places. Lewis and Clark, the first efficient explorers of the region, said that the noise reminded them of a nail factory. In other words, the women were industriously filling their storage boxes and baskets for future use. These pounded materials, as in the case of acorn flour, were boiled in a basket or a wooden vessel by inserting hot stones. There have been cultures in which the symbol of feminine industry and efficiency was a spinning implement, but in the form of life we are now considering, the symbol should have been the homely stone pounder.

So we take our leave of these sturdy stone boilers. Simple folk they were, not striving to build empires or great cities, but skilled in their own crafts and arts. That they are of a respectable antiquity there can be little doubt; perhaps when Rome fell many of these women were pounding acorns and dried salmon in the same way as when Lewis and Clark made a surprise visit to their villages. The arrival of these white men must have been a sensation, but from what Lewis and Clark have written, we assume that these women stopped pounding but for a moment. The accumulated culture momentum of ages saw to that. The archaeology of their area suggests that the stone boilers were nicely adjusted to their environment and that serious famine rarely descended upon them. Had not the white man broken into their world, they would doubtless be stone boilers still.

Chapter III

THE FARMERS AND THE POTTERS

So far we have been looking at America in a time so remote that neither the making of pottery nor the raising of plants was known. Our own culture is based upon farming and raising livestock, so we take the garden and the pasture for granted; it may never have occurred to us that there could have been otherwise intelligent people in the world who never thought of planting something. But many such peoples are still to be met with in out-of-the-way places. We spoke of stone boiling as a wonderful invention; so it was in its day. No less significant was the discovery that plants could be made to yield more and better edible parts by tending them in a garden plot. Some scholars who consider the making of fire the greatest of all inventions place agriculture next. They are probably right.

Though we speak of agriculture as an invention, it is too complicated to have been the work of a single primitive Edison. Man must have slowly and unconsciously blundered into it by first protecting plants useful to him, noting that when he chose the best seeds for planting, the yield was greater. Finally, all this became formalized as knowledge in the heads of a few primitive philosophers who, by intellectual insight, grasped the true principles of plant growth. But here we are interested in the aboriginal or primitive hunters and gatherers of wild plants, who somehow seem to have stumbled into agriculture. They brought no seeds with them in their great migration from Asia; we know this because none of the plants cultivated by them were known in the Old World. The potato, tobacco, maize, tomato, chocolate, tapioca and a lot of other useful plants were cultivated in America long before

1492. All of which means that as farmers many of our prehistoric Indians were as good as any known.

We do not know which of the many early hunting tribes in the United States first took to farming, but the archaeologists are furnishing the information to reconstruct the picture. There are rock-shelter deposits in the Ozarks of Missouri and the rough country of Kentucky which tell us that most of the plants first cultivated there are still growing wild near these same primitive dwellings. It is surprising what a pile of debris in a rock shelter or the mouth of a cave can tell us about the lives of vanished peoples. For example, such debris in the Newt Kash Hollow shelter, Menifee County, Kentucky, when examined and analyzed from the bottom to the top, or from the earliest to the latest layers, showed first a period of Stone Age hunting, without agriculture, followed by hunters who took to gardening as a side line. Here and there appear the seeds and other fragments of many edible plants. That these formed a substantial part of the hunters' food was determined by analysis of some of the dried feces found in the debris. Some of the most common seeds in the debris, next above that belonging to the true hunters, are sunflower (*Helianthus annuus*), giant ragweed (*Ambrosia trifida*), pigweed or goosefoot (*Chenopodium sp.*) and marsh elder (*Iva ciliata*). In Missouri, people who have become known as the Ozark Bluff Dwellers also learned to cultivate these plants and either cultivated or collected many others including canary grass, wild seeds and many kinds of nuts and acorns. Animals, including bear, deer and elk, and particularly small mammals, were eaten, but proportions indicate that the diet was mostly vegetarian.

All of the plants mentioned still grow wild, but many of the seeds found in the rock shelters are much larger than those of the wild species. Botanists tell us that this means they were cultivated or domesticated. We should add that the gourd and the squash were present and so cultivated, but these do not grow wild locally. They were probably introduced from the south.

Now we see a people still hunters, sheltered crudely

under overhanging rocks, but rather sedentary in their habits, taming some of the wild plants whose seeds they had learned to eat and which they ground into some kind of meal. Gradually they improved the breeds of these plants and their methods of gardening, until the food supply from their gardens was sufficient to give them a feeling of security. Their principal danger was now from their own kind—hostile neighbors who coveted their store of food or their superior cave. Since no pottery has been found in this part of the debris, these old gardeners may well have been stone boilers, but we cannot be sure of that. They could have baked their seed meals in the ashes and roasted their game over the open fire. The gourds they raised would have furnished them vessels for most purposes; or they might have used woven baskets, although textiles but not baskets were found in the earlier deposits—actual baskets came later.

Judging by the thickness of the debris, which reveals little change in the methods of gardening, things were on an even keel for a long time, perhaps many centuries; but as we near the top layer, changes are evident. Some tobacco appears for the first time, then maize or corn, and pottery.

Corn must have come into the United States from the south long after it became the chief food plant in Mexico. Recent research has indicated that corn was first domesticated somewhere in southern Puebla, Mexico, at about 5000 B.C. The spread southward into Mesoamerica and northward to the people of southern Arizona and New Mexico probably occurred around 3500 B.C.; corn, radiocarbon-dated at this date, was found in Bat Cave, New Mexico. Later, a few centuries before the time of Christ, perhaps, varieties of corn spread north and eastward into other areas of the United States. One variety may have spread northward along the eastern coast of Mexico directly into Texas, and from there into the eastern United States. As a food plant, corn was superior to the domesticated weeds of our rock-shelter gardeners so that one demonstration of its use might have been enough; but it is more likely that the spread and increasing dependence on corn was gradual. The mythology of our living Indians tells us in poetic terms how corn was a gift from the gods. In the ceremonies of many tribes an ear of corn was used to symbolize Mother Corn, the source of life. In Utah, Arizona and New Mexico, corn is found in the simple little cliff houses of the Basketmaker periods, and later beans appear, also an importation from the south. The Pueblo Indians of later time depended largely upon corn, as do their modern descendants. They, too, speak reverently of Mother Corn; in fact, some Indians, especially the Navaho, speak of the growing corn in the field as if it were a living presence close to the gods. What we begin to comprehend is that these later Indian corn farmers were building up a mode of life, or culture, intimately adjusted to the cultivation of this grain. That they idealized the corn and their relationship to it is to their credit rather than otherwise. They even dramatized it, as in the Green Corn dance and other ceremonies.

We should pause a moment to catch the spirit of the corn legends, as in *Tales of the North American Indians*, by Stith Thompson.

The Origin of Corn

A long time ago, when Indians were first made, there lived one alone, far, far from any others. He knew not of fire, and subsisted on roots, barks, and nuts. This Indian became very lonesome for company. He grew tired of digging roots, lost his appetite, and for several days lay dreaming in the sunshine; when he awoke he saw something standing near, at which, at first, he was very much frightened. But when it spoke, his heart was glad, for it was a beautiful woman with long light hair, very unlike any Indian. He asked her to come to him, but she would not, and if he tried to approach her she seemed to go farther away; he sang to her of his loneliness and besought her not to leave him; at last she told him, if he would do just as she should say, he would always have her with him. He promised that he would.

She led him to where there was some very dry grass, told him to get two very dry sticks, rub them together quickly, holding them in the grass. Soon a spark flew out; the grass caught it, and quick as an arrow the ground was burned over. Then she said, "When the sun sets, take me by the hair and drag me over the burned ground." He did not like to do this, but she told him that wherever he dragged her something like grass would spring up, and he would see her hair coming from between the leaves; then the seeds would be ready for his use. He did as she said, and to this day, when they see the silk (hair) on the cornstalk, the Indians know she has not forgotten them.[1]

The intensity of feeling expressed in many versions of the corn legend and their intrinsic beauty all suggest the significance of corn to the Indian farmers of the United States. We feel sure that the core of the legend came from the south with the gift of the original seed. Perhaps the seed-raising hunters of the Mississippi Valley made many long and hazardous journeys to the southland and to the country of the cliff dwellers for some of this miraculous seed. To them it meant new life, a gift beyond price. The trip was dangerous, both in reality and supernaturally, and so was entered upon with elaborate purification and ceremony. In such a setting the return of the successful pilgrims could not be regarded as a commonplace matter, but one in which the gods were clearly present. We need not be surprised to note that, in the unwritten bible of the historic Indian farmers, the corn legend held a prominent place.

At the outset we spoke of these early people as farmers and potters. We have seen that the seed gatherers of Kentucky were without pottery for a long time and then learned to make it about the same time as they began to

---

[1] Stith Thompson, *Tales of the North American Indians*, Cambridge, Mass., 1929, pp. 51-2.

raise corn. Possibly pottery came from the south, as did corn. But however that may be, it too was a great gain. The precious corn could be much more easily boiled in earthen pots than by the older methods. Yet we note one distinction: whereas corn is still treated as a god among most living Indians, pots are relegated to the level of utilities. Their humble origins from the clay of the river-bank are neither heralded in myth nor regarded as in-carnations of a god. Possibly pots were looked upon as incidental to the gift of corn, an accessory as it were. We said above that many scholars consider fire and food grains as the two greatest inventions. However this may be, the Indian farmers seemed to think so, because they held special ceremonies to show their veneration for each. When we note that the use of fire came ages before the invention of agriculture, the significance of these cere-monies is enhanced.

Throughout most of the United States, except in the Southwest, the Indian women were the gardeners. Some scholars believe that in the transition from hunters to farmers woman played the chief role; many go so far as to say that woman invented agriculture, but archaeology is silent upon this subject. Granting the probability that the Indian woman did the gardening in all of eastern United States, we should then credit her with the invention of the hoe. Strangely enough, neither in our Southwest, nor Mexico, nor in South America, was a true hoe used. Yet the first white visitors to the Atlantic states tell how the Indian women heaped up the hills of earth around the growing corn with hoes, some with blades of wood, others with shell, bone and antler. Those early gardeners in Ken-tucky, whom archaeologists have made the heroes of the period, left some of their hoe blades in the debris in which the telltale seeds were found. Far to the north, in Dakota, the Indian women bound a buffalo shoulder blade to a handle; such hoes may be seen in museum collections. Along the Mississippi River and eastward, archaeologists find large broad stone blades which they think were used for digging, but whether these were mounted on handles as spades or hoes no one can tell, since they could have been used either way. But the known facts about the hoe excite our curiosity. Why should such an obviously practical and labor-saving device have been unknown to the clever ancients who built empires in Mexico and Peru? They were great agriculturists and credited with domesticating maize and many other plants we now cultivate, yet used simple spadelike tools. Then again the hoe seems to have been known and used in the Old World, especially in Egypt, but does not become conspicuous before the Iron Age. Such curious blindness on the part of tribes and peoples in some large areas, in contrast to the genius of many in other equally large areas, should set us thinking about the ins and outs of human behavior. Why should the whole of the two aboriginal Americas have been ignorant of the wheel? In the Old World its origin goes back so far that no one ventures to say when and where it was invented. If it is so much more difficult to think of a wheel than a hoe, then why should our eastern Indian have invented the hoe and not the wheel? And why did not the Maya or the Inca get the idea? Whoever finally answers these stubborn questions will make a great contribution to the science of human society.

Pottery is another invention whose geography puzzles us. Since so much pottery is found in Mexico and Peru, the tendency has been to suppose that the original invention was in that region, but archaeology helps little in deciding this point. In Arizona and New Mexico we find places where people lived who made no pottery; at other sites it is abundant. But because Mexico is not far away, many scholars have suspected that pottery came into the Southwest from that source. Others maintain that many peoples of North America obtained pottery from Asia; it seems probable that this took place after pottery was already in use elsewhere in the United States. In the Southwest, archaeologists have found what look like first experiments with pottery. Traditions support these finds: at Zuni Pueblo, F. H. Cushing reported some curious traditions about the origin of pottery, then a commonplace in Zuni

housekeeping. The Zuni tradition was, in substance, that
their forefathers made baskets and in time came to line
some of their basket trays with clay. In these trays corn
was parched by shaking the grains about among coals of
fire. What this implies is that the clay made it easier to
keep the basket from burning. By and by, so the story
goes, it was found that when the clay lining in a basket
tray became dry it could be lifted out and, with care,
used in the same way as before. Later, it was discovered
that these clay trays could be hardened by setting them
on the fire. All this sounds reasonable and natural enough.
It is a matter of history how we, in a few generations,
have passed from writing with goose feathers to the use
of fountain pens, a somewhat parallel case; but when
Cushing published this story, scientifically minded people
scoffed. They said that this was nonsense, merely a clever
Indian lie to please the white man. Well, they were right
in one way: the tradition proved nothing. It might have
happened that way, but if the reader will give his imagination freedom to soar, it will soon devise other equally
plausible ways in which pottery could have evolved. But
none of these can be proven either. Nor do we know of
anything that does prove it, though archaeologists have
found enough evidence to set the skeptic guessing.

In some parts of New Mexico and Arizona, in early
Basketmaker sites, many crude, heavy, sun-dried traylike
vessels have been found. Many of these vessels bear marks
upon the outside showing that they were molded in baskets. Further, the clay composing them is made stronger
by shreds of bark mixed into the wet clay. There may be
nothing unusual about this, for the makers of these earthen
vessels used similar reinforced mud to build the walls of
their houses and to hold stones in place, and what could
be more natural than for them to line baskets with similar
clay and eventually to make entire vessels of it? The vessels found in the earliest house sites were never fired, as
is the case with true pottery. In fact, they could not be
fired successfully with bark and other vegetable fibers in
their walls, but some of these vessels were found without

such tempering, as it is called, sand being used instead. Sand or shell, however, is the usual temper for clay used in vessels to be fired. Later, fired vessels appear in the same localities. Here again is something quite reasonable, natural and logical. In some such way pottery must have been invented. Perhaps the use of mud walls for houses led to the independent invention of lining baskets and eventually the making of unfired vessels. Such clay vessels could not have held liquids, but corn could have been parched in them, as noted above. Then it is possible that the knowledge of true pottery came from the south. However, this is all guesswork. All we know is that mud vessels shaped in baskets were known at the places excavated before fired pottery was known. We know this as we know that the first hunters to live in Fell's Cave, Chile, ate the wild horse, and that later the hunters who camped there used different kinds of stone tools and ate other kinds of game. And the earlier pottery tempered with grass and bark fiber reminds us that some very early Egyptian pottery is tempered with straw.

Now we must take leave of these aboriginal gardeners, some of whom finally rose to the level of farmers. The cultural history of North America, east of the Rocky Mountains, begins with the first hunters to turn agriculturists. All the great civilizations of the world have grown upon the foundations laid by farmers; in fact, farmers still carry the world upon their backs. This is why these first gardeners in the United States deserve a chapter in this book. They seem to have had some originality and perhaps independently recognized plant control as the way to achieve greater economic and social security. Anyway, they took the initial step and persisted in increasing measure, even down to the beginning of the last century. They deserve our respect and a place in the history of mankind.

It may be a good idea before we take leave of these early farmers to recall the geography of stone boiling at the time of Columbus. We saw how it was restricted to the Pacific side of the United States and Canada. Archaeologists have not devised a convincing technique for de-

termining the presence or absence of stone boiling by extinct peoples. So we must content ourselves with the observation that at the beginning of white settlement in the United States the stone boilers were not farmers, and apparently none of the farmers then living used that method, because they had pottery. It does not follow that all the non-farming hunters used stone boiling, because we have information that some of them used pottery before they became farmers.

Chapter IV

THE BUILDERS

THE tourist driving through the state of Ohio may see some of the world's finest prehistoric earthworks. The most unusual is the great Serpent Mound, a masterpiece in earth sculpture. More than a thousand feet of a sinuous serpent body extends along the backbone of a ridge ending on the brow of a cliff overhanging a small river. The serpent's head rests upon this cliff, its tail back upon the ridge, partly coiled; its long body is posed as if gliding along the crest of the ridge. The modeling is so good that the visitor can all but see the movement suggested. The enlarged head is an oval embankment, in the center of which is a heap of stones, possibly a fireplace and altar. On this oval embankment a fair-sized audience could gather round to take part in a ceremony or watch the officiating priests. What went on there we shall never know, since no traditions have come down to us, but we can feel sure that the procedure and the beliefs clustering around this earth sculpture were in keeping with its magnificence.

A much smaller and less artistic serpent is present in another part of Ohio, and we suspect that there were others, since most great structures are the culmination of many similar attempts. But there are other impressive earthworks in Ohio, and throughout the eastern United States. Within the last few decades, archaeologists have come to reconstruct a cultural sequence not only for the earthworks and the artifacts found within them, but for the peoples who inhabited the country many centuries ago. Sequences vary in detail from area to area, but a general pattern is evident. The farmers who inhabited the Newt Kash Hollow shelter may have belonged to the so-called

"Early Woodland" period, for the projectile points they left behind were similar in type to those of the Adena peoples, whose culture was characteristic of this period. That the Adena people themselves were farmers is probable, but definite evidence has not yet been found.

These people built mounds, but it is the Hopewell people of the next, or "Middle Woodland," period who became known as the great Mound Builders. Later, peoples living in an area with the Tennessee and Cumberland River valleys as its center also built mounds; these belong to what is known as the "Mississippi" period.

At one time, people believed that a race of Mound Builders invaded the country; for in the Ohio Valley, one of the centers of the Hopewell cultural development, the transition from the Adena to the Hopewell culture was marked not only by shared characteristics such as some burials, certain pottery types and ornaments, but also by biologically distinct populations—the Adena people were roundheaded, the Hopewell longheaded. Similar cultural transitions from Early to Middle Woodland took place in many areas of the eastern United States, however, without a change in population type. A new tribe may have moved in, but more likely the idea of building mounds came into the minds of a community of farmers already in the country. There is no reason to go outside of North America, to bring in a strange race and then assume that they died out without leaving any descendants. It is more likely that mound building ceased to be desirable and so passed away.

While the culture flourished, however, the manifestations were impressive. Hopewell builders created Fort Ancient, a series of earth walls skirting the rim of a small plateau. There is no good reason for considering the place a fort, but since it resembles modern fortifications served by artillery, the name came naturally enough. (The name should not be confused with that of the Fort Ancient Indians, who lived in villages in the valley below the hilltop enclosure; they lived many centuries later than the Hopewell Indians who built Fort Ancient itself.) That the enclosure had ceremonial significance is practically certain; in other words, it was a kind of temple. The size is impressive: the enclosed space approximates one hundred acres, the circumference is about three and one half miles, and the heights of the enclosing embankments range from six to twenty feet.

Inside the embankments is a moat from which the earth may have been taken to form the earth walls. It is estimated that the earth moved to form these embankments approximates 628,800 cubic yards. These statements should give some idea of the hugeness of this structure. Many other flat hilltops in the Ohio Valley are skirted by embankments, but the space enclosed and the size of the walls do not reach half the dimensions of Fort Ancient. So, with the great Serpent Mound, it stands as the last word in hilltop structures. Everyone contemplating Fort Ancient from a point of vantage upon one of its embankments is grieved that so much is silenced in obscurity. We should like to know what went on there, how many people toiled at carrying earth to the tops of these embankments, what they thought was its purpose and whether at times they doubted the justification for so much hard work. Yet somebody must have believed it the most important thing to do, somebody must have worked out the plan and superintended the work, and somebody must have felt that here was the greatest structure of its kind, the wonder of the age. No doubt speeches were made on successive occasions reminding those assembled there of the importance of their heritage and exhorting them to still greater efforts; however this may be, it seems to have been the last effort, or at least the one which reached the highest level of magnitude.

These Hopewell people made pottery, some of it rather artistic, some of it reserved for everyday use, and indications are that food was boiled in the latter type. Archaeological evidence suggests that they lived in crude cabins made of poles and bark, with earthen floors and the barest of furnishings. Corn seems to have been the chief crop and, among others, seeds of squash, gourd and beans give further evidence of agricultural development. Stone pipes abound, which means that tobacco was used and cultivated. The number of stone pipes found in some mounds is astonishing, but what is more significant is the attention given to their finish and decoration, many of them representing birds and animals so well executed that they can qualify as classic examples of the carver's art. There seems to have been a religious incentive in their carving, because one or two large groups of such pipes were found in settings which suggest offerings or sacrifices. To offer the finest one's culture can produce would be the last word in religious piety.

Sheets of mica were prized, perhaps as a mysterious, unusual substance of fine quality, a fit offering to the supernatural powers. Archaeologists have found caches of this material in mound burials. Many mica ornaments have also been found, some representative of human hands, or bird claws, or bears' teeth. Similar representations were cut from sheet copper; this material was also beaten into intricate shapes for ear spools, breastplates and headdresses, one of which was fashioned to look like deer antlers. Beads as ornaments were extremely common. These were cut to shape from shells, or made from stone, seeds, bone and copper. Pearls from the fresh-water clams of the tributaries of the Ohio River were drilled, and thousands were taken from a single mound near Hamilton, Ohio, not to mention large numbers from other mounds and burials. Many of these pearls were laid on the skeletons in such a position as to suggest necklaces; in some instances garments were covered with them. Fishing for pearls may well have been an important industry. Though we are now speaking of Ohio, pearls were known and treasured by the Indians of the Lower Mississippi—they have been found by archaeologists in other places in the Mississippi Valley—in Mexico and Central America, and even in South America. History tells us that in the early days of exploration the Spaniards seized all the pearls they could find, and shipped nearly a thousand pounds to Spain within a few years. Where the Indian custom for using pearls started we do not know, but that they made a strong appeal is evident.

South of the major Hopewell centers, other builders of earthworks also flourished, their cultures reaching greatest heights centuries after those of the Hopewell builders. There are thousands of mounds in the Mississippi Valley area and the eastern United States. Outstanding in size are certain flat-topped, terraced mounds, one good example being Cahokia, in East St. Louis, Illinois, built by people of the Mississippi period. The largest mound is about one hundred feet high, one thousand feet long, and a little over seven hundred feet wide, with a base of about sixteen acres; as approaches to the summit there are at least four terraces or platforms. The earth in this mound is estimated as three times that of all the embankments at Fort Ancient. It can therefore qualify as the largest single earthwork in the United States. The well-known Etowah Mound in Georgia, a center for the Buzzard or Southern Death Cult, is somewhat similar but much smaller, though still a large one as mounds go. Mounds of this type do not stand alone, but are usually in a group of conical mounds. At Cahokia the surrounding mounds number approximately eighty-five, some of which are distinctive in their class. The tendency is to look upon Cahokia itself as the site of a temple or ceremonial activities. In the mounds round about are buried the few great personages in this culture. Rich and powerful these Cahokians must have been, in their day and time, to have raised such huge monuments and structures. When in their prime, the barbarian eyes of the Mississippi area must have been turned upon this, the metropolis of their era; but again the ultimate had been reached, and eventually came the end, so that before the white man came to this country the forest had overgrown these mounds and the contemporary Indian hunter had passed over them, ignorant of the culture once flourishing there.

What became of these people is still a puzzle. That they left descendants is probable, and it is thought that the peoples around Etowah, Georgia, were ancestors

of the Creeks met by the first European explorers. Now
and then a modern Indian thinks he remembers a tradition, but these are so vague they offer no help. As we have
said, they may well have reached the climax of the building urge and then suffered a social and economic decline.
Once they weakened, the less favored Indians could begin
to plunder them and thus hasten their collapse. However
this may be, we recognize a unique development in the
aboriginal history of the United States, marking another
era in the march of time. They did their best and, having
wrought in earth, left lasting monuments to their skill and
intelligence.

Aboriginal Apartment Houses

Long before the arrival of Coronado or Columbus, another
architectural pattern was taking form in the southwestern
United States. At Mesa Verde, in Colorado, the tourist
stands in fascination among the ruined rooms of apartment
dwellings built within crescent-shaped hollows in the faces
of cliffs. These are often called cliff houses, but the term
cliff dwellings is usually used to designate small habita-
tions perched here and there in barely accessible places.
Nearby on the top of Mesa Verde are the remains of
dwellings built partly underground, called pit houses, and
in these lived the Basketmakers, of whose corn-parching
abilities we have already spoken. Both the pit and the cliff-
house dwellers belong to what is called the Anasazi culture, from the Navaho name meaning "ancient ones." The
former, named for their fine work in basketry, used this
material not only for the watertight containers in which
they cooked their food, but for sandals, which were expertly woven. They lived on a diet of corn which they
grew, nuts and berries which they gathered, and small
animals which they snared or netted. Dogs were kept as
pets. Most clothing was woven from plant fibers, particularly yucca, and robes were often made by winding narrow
strips of rabbit fur around fiber cords, which were then

put side by side and held in place by twining. Many of the Basketmaker "mummies" (not embalmed in any way, but preserved through the centuries by dry southwestern climate) wore such robes.

Through the centuries these people gradually came to live in regular communities and at some time, probably around the seventh or eighth century (A.D.), they learned to make pottery. Some of their houses seemed to combine features of both pit-house and pueblo architecture. The later Basketmakers also learned to grow beans, and to use the bow and arrow. These people laid the foundation for the later Anasazi horizon, the Pueblo periods, named from the Spanish word for town or community.

Gradually, from about 700 A.D., the characteristics of the Pueblo culture developed. Features, especially of architecture, including the stone and adobe (mud-brick) pueblos and various details of their manufacture, and of pottery, which assumed many different shapes and characteristic decorations in different areas, became more and more distinctive as the Great Pueblo period was reached. Cliff Palace, Spruce Tree House and Square Tower House, three of the large and well-known pueblos at Mesa Verde, belong to this Great Pueblo period. So do Pueblo Bonito and Aztec Pueblo in New Mexico, which were built in the open and were among the largest of the apartment houses. Pueblo Bonito in Chaco Canyon, New Mexico, may be singled out as one of the greatest structures of its kind.

This building contained around eight hundred rooms and could easily have accommodated almost three hundred families, or well over a thousand persons. In ground plan it looked like the letter *D*; the first story varied in width from five rooms at the middle to three rooms at the tips of the crescent. The front was crossed by a straight row of rooms, one story high and two rooms wide. These formed a kind of wall reaching from one end of the irregular crescent to the other, and enclosing a large open court. Entrance was by ladder; thus Pueblo Bonito combined the qualities of residence and fortress. It is reminiscent of a walled town, but here there are neither streets nor alleys. Each story of this great house was at least one room less wide than the one below, thus affording a series of terraces—four in the middle of the *D*, fewer at the sides —one in front of each outer row of rooms. As the rooms were not well lighted, much of the necessary household work was done on the open terrace in front of the family room. The living rooms are about twelve by eight, with a seven-foot ceiling. The walls are expertly made, of stone and adobe. Here and there are circular rooms called kivas, like those seen in the modern pueblo villages in New Mexico and Arizona. These kivas served both as ceremonial rooms and as a sort of men's clubhouse, where women were allowed either not at all or only on special occasions—if they possessed the required ritual knowledge.

It is not necessary to describe the life at Pueblo Bonito and other places of its kind, for we know that the general pattern of this way of living survives at Zuni, Acoma, among the Hopi and other modern pueblos. They depended upon corn and game for food. They were good potters and raised cotton, from which they wove good cloth. The turkey was domesticated. They did not have pearls but were rich in turquoise, which they mined and fashioned into beads and pendants. Their implements were of stone and bone. They were good masons and invented an ingenious ventilating flue for their kivas.

Archaeologists have said that these buildings belong to the Great Pueblo period. Long before dating by radiocarbon was known, dates were assigned to these structures by a process called dendrochronology, or tree-ring dating. Studies of the annual growth rings of trees in the area showed such an unmistakable pattern of wide and narrow bands (corresponding to years of moisture and drought) that samples of progressively older trees were collected and the overlapping patterns produced a master calendar which now dates back as far as the first century A.D. By matching samples from the ceiling beams of ruins with the master pattern, specialists are able to date many of these ruins. Thus Pueblo Bonito is said to contain timber cut over a period beginning about 900 A.D. and ending about 1130. The ruin at Aztec, north of Pueblo Bonito, contains timbers ranging from 1110 to 1121 A.D. in cutting dates. The three ruins mentioned at Mesa Verde contain timbers cut within the years 1019 to 1274 A.D. How long these buildings were occupied after the last timber was cut no one knows, but from all indications not much more than a century, probably less. The same tree rings indicate that at Mesa Verde a severe drought starting in 1276 A.D. lasted until 1299, and it is believed that this may have contributed to the abandonment of the pueblos in that particular area. In the present Hopi village of Oraibi stands a room or house with timber cut in 1370 A.D. So the Hopi Indians seem to have lived at this place since that date. Yet the chances are that Pueblo Bonito and Aztec Pueblo were in ruins before that.

Thus we have been able to glimpse not only *what* was happening in the ancient Southwest, but by means of the tree rings, we can know *when* it happened. Let us see what was going on in Europe while Pueblo Bonito flourished. About the time building was started, England too was in a formative stage. King Alfred was fighting for his life with the Danes. A little later the Norsemen were sailing around Greenland and Labrador. In 1066 the Normans crossed over from France and seized England. Perhaps Pueblo Bonito was then in decline, for it seems to have been abandoned during the time of the Crusades in the Old World. Since our schoolbooks say these events belong to ancient history, we can say that the inhabitants of Pueblo Bonito were ancients, too. Then note that even a modern Hopi village seems to have been built at least 122 years before Columbus arrived in the West Indies and 244 years before the Dutch began to build New York City.

Within the last decades it has been possible to estimate the dates at which some of the great mounds were built, and as more material is uncovered, further dates are forthcoming. Radiocarbon dates obtained from plant samples in the Newt Kash Hollow shelter indicated that these people lived about 700 B.C. Radiocarbon dates at various Hopewell sites indicated that this culture flourished from

about 300 or 400 B.C. to about 400 A.D. It was earlier
supposed that the great mounds at Cahokia were roughly
contemporaneous with Pueblo Bonito, and radiocarbon
dates have confirmed this belief; materials from different
parts of the site have yielded dates ranging from 925 to
1565 A.D., most of them falling between 1045 and 1225.
Materials from various parts of the Etowah site in Georgia
yielded dates ranging from 1040 to as late as 1725 A.D.,
but most fall between the eleventh and the fifteenth centuries. It took more than two hundred years to complete
Pueblo Bonito, and it appears to have taken a long time
to complete the mounds at Cahokia and Etowah as well.

In the country surrounding the Mound Builders and the
Pueblos were many tribes, some of which did a little
farming, but they were primarily hunters. Building had
no great appeal for them, and they remained stone boilers
for the most part. The possible exception as builders were
the stone-boiling wood carvers of the Northwest, to whom
we have referred. Compared with what went on in Mexico,
Middle America and the Andes to the south, even the
efforts of the Pueblos and the Mound Builders seem of a
much lower order. Some scholars believe that the urge to
build filtered through from Mexico. History records similar influences in the Old World, so there may be some
basis to the idea. Agricultural influences came from the
south, so perhaps other customs did too. Yet here and
there original improvements are in evidence, life being a
flux of give and take.

Many people are not content with such information as
we have given; they want to know just how the ancient
builders set about making a mound. Archaeology can tell
us something. No bones of domestic animals, except the
dog, were found. We assume, therefore, that men, women
and children were the sole power to be mobilized. Skilled
archaeologists can dissect a section of earth so as to reveal
much that escapes the untrained eye. In certain Ohio
mounds the loads of dirt as dumped upon the rising surface of the mound have been revealed and found to
average around twenty to thirty pounds. These loads

could have been carried in baskets, skins or other vessels, but in two instances archaeologists found the tell-tale imprint of a basket, showing that the carrier had thrown down the basket without emptying it. The load in one case weighed about thirty pounds. The weaving of the basket was visible in outline. If the calculating reader takes about one third of a cubic foot as a standard load, he can estimate the labor involved in mound building. Some mounds in Ohio are known to contain more than twenty thousand cubic yards of earth. Possibly fifty laborers could do such a job in a thousand days—that is, at the rate of twenty cubic yards a day. After all, the job is not so impossible. An organized village might have a population of five thousand people, probably the maximum for the place and time. Half of these might be adults, with two or three hundred available most of the time for mound work. Work would be seasonal, but if everybody worked for a week, now and then, the job could be done within a year or two. Yet some mounds show bands or layers of earth, clearly indicating that they grew by accretions spread over a considerable period of time. Of course the few burials found in mounds do not account for the total population; they are exceptional heroes either because of social position or because they were chosen for the occasion. Religion and veneration must have played a part. As we have said, many earthworks seem to have been places of worship rather than burial. Perhaps like the cathedrals of our day they received the bodies of the great. While all details are lost to us, it is certain that the emotional value of building earthworks was great, and the chances are that the whole population participated in it with zeal.

If you ask why these people ceased to raise earthworks, the only answer is that they were human. History presents no case of a people without change and extinction either by war, famine or, more often, by absorption into another mode of life.

No doubt the greatest earthworks were built at the crest of a social evolution when the standards of size and perfection reached such a level that the cost was too great.

The building urge burned itself out; the survivors sought new interests, their old life disintegrated, possibly shattered by war. No longer used or venerated, the mounds became overgrown with vegetation and eventually covered by the forest. Estimates are that mound building in the Southeast continued long after it became extinct in the Ohio and middle Mississippi Valley areas, and that in the Southeast, mound building was at its peak from about 1300 to about 1500 A.D., after the great pueblos were built, and after the Crusades in the Old World. Some of these cultures were still extant, though apparently in decline, when the first Europeans came to America.

Chapter V

THE COMING OF THE GRAND PIPE

A FRENCH missionary stopping at an eastern Canadian Indian village was surprised to see a group of strangers approaching, the leader bearing a large beautiful pipe with a great stem decorated with duck heads and eagle feathers. His Indian friends were awed, as well they might be, at this beautiful symbol, but above all by the stately serious mien of the visitors and their attitude of reverence for it—all indicating that here was something new and important. The good father recognized its aesthetic appeal and sensed the enthusiasm with which his flock welcomed this new ceremony, but naturally he feared it as a pagan rival. The French called these grand pipes calumets; they were first observed among the Indians of the Upper Mississippi country. What the good father did not understand was that these strange Indians were missionaries also, believing in the power of the grand pipe and its ritual to make their world a better place to live in. No one but an Indian could have grasped the full meaning of the message the bearer of the calumet brought to the good father's village. Nor do we of this generation and time understand it either. Yet something seems definite: one of the underlying ideas seems to have been the bond of brotherhood. The bearers of such a pipe, representing their tribe, presented more than a pledge, approached in the true spirit of a friend, even as a brother, and expected that they be met in the same spirit. The belief in the purity and grandeur of this new relation among men gave them faith that the grand pipe would of itself soften the hearts of all who came into its presence and thus unite them in friendship. Even the most ignorant Indian could understand this more practical quality. In other words, the grand pipe was not only a symbol of peace and brotherly love but a charm to compel it, the symbol of a fine idea. Thus it came about naturally that in time the calumet was called a pipe of peace. Approaching strangers, a calumet would be displayed not merely as a sign of friendship, not simply as a flag of truce, but something which in itself had power to compel acceptance.

Perhaps the peace pipe is one of the first things that come into the popular mind when Indians are mentioned. Certain it is that the ordinary pipe and tobacco in any form have long been associated with the popular picture of an Indian. Not so many years ago every cigar store in the land was heralded by a wooden Indian holding some cigars in his left hand and threatening the passer-by with tomahawk upraised in his right. Too bad most of these large wooden carvings were discarded and split up into firewood. Even their history is obscure, except as revealed in a few private collections. It all began in England, as far back as 1600, when small wooden Indians began to appear as counter signs where tobacco was sold. Later, large carvings stood in front of tobacco shops and early in 1700 were seen in the colonies. We are told that once a tobacco shop in the nation's capital exhibited a life-sized carving so realistic and so threatening that good citizens were frightened. First the chagrined shopkeeper took the tomahawk out of the Indian's hand, but this did not help matters much, so he reluctantly sacrificed the whole figure. In wooden-Indian days there was no excuse for forgetting the source of tobacco and all that went with it, but now, in the days of machine-made cigarettes, we need to be reminded that all the world learned the use of tobacco from the Indian. The first time Columbus set foot upon the American shore Indians made him a good-will offering of tobacco leaves, and later he saw some of them smoking cigars. But, for the moment, we are interested in the coming of the pipe to the Indians of the United States. The picturesque calumet may have been a recent development in 1492, but the archaeologists can show us great pipe bowls of much earlier date, especially from the Ohio

Valley and some of our southern states. Doubtless, what the good father saw in Canada long before happened over and over—a group of strangers carrying a grand pipe of some kind as a symbol of some fine new idea. However, all has perished except these stone bowls. That the same ideas were associated with these ancient pipes as with the calumet is unlikely, but we can be reasonably certain that they were equally serious. The elbow pipe seems to appear in the eastern United States after the potters and the corn raisers flourished there. So, following corn, the pipe is the next most spectacular phase of Indian culture; again, it is the most unique and widespread contribution of the Indian to the world; everywhere, in every country, smokers are today paying silent and unconscious tribute to these ancient aboriginals.

There is a great deal in historical documents about the calumet, sacred pipes and the offerings of smoke to the gods above and below, which may be summarized by saying that tobacco was a sacred plant, the burning of which found favor in their eyes, and that even the offering of a few leaves or a filled pipe to a guest carried with it the idea of friendship sanctioned by more than human power. Here and there we find it recorded that even a member of an enemy tribe, entering a house and smoking with the host, was thereby guaranteed protection and safe conduct upon his return. This of itself testifies to the high place tobacco held among the Indians of eastern North America.

There is reason to believe that the pipe was invented in the eastern United States. No pipes were found in the strata of Kentucky caves belonging to the first gardeners, nor was there evidence of tobacco until well near the top layer. After maize appears, pipes and tobacco are common. Again, though tobacco in some form was used over most of aboriginal North and South America, elbow pipes were restricted to the eastern and central United States, with scattering examples in outlying areas. Apparently older than the elbow pipe, and far more widely spread, was the smoking tube. Such tubes, usually of stone, are

found in all parts of the United States, in Mexico and to
the south. Cane tubes were employed south of the United
States, and in Mexico cigarettes, or tobacco rolled in corn-
husk. As we have said, cigars were used in the West
Indies and in South America.

We have done nothing with tobacco that the Indian did
not do. There are good reasons for believing that the use
of tobacco originated in the West Indies or in South
America and spread thence into the United States. Many
species of wild tobacco grow here and in Canada, some
of which were used by the Indians of later times, but the
best tobaccos came from the West Indies and South
America. The presence of wild tobacco in the United
States means that the invention of smoking could have
occurred before agriculture was known. So we cannot be
sure as to the first smokers, but everything points to the
elbow pipe, or the true pipe, as originating in the time of
the corn farmers.

We are all interested in the origin of things. As children,
we were always asking "why?" and as grownups we have
merely changed the direction of the question. The "why?"
of tobacco would be answered if we knew how its use
began. So now, how? Here again we must guess, but
there are some suggestions as to where the answer lies.
By this time we should be sufficiently warned not to
expect so complicated a matter as the use of tobacco to
come into existence full blown. Like other customs of its
kind, it must have grown from very small beginnings. As
we look about over the customs of the several tribes, we
note how widespread is the burning of incense as a purifying medium or as an acceptable offering to the unseen. It
is natural to suspect that tobacco was once used in this
way. Some of our eastern Indian tribes did not smoke a
pipe in a sacred ceremony but burned the tobacco in a
little fire, the acceptable smoke offering ascending to the
powers to whom they prayed. Even as far west as the
Missouri, historic Indians sometimes offered tobacco in this
way. This really explains nothing; it merely suggests what
seems probable. We suppose somehow and sometime,

among a people making smoke offerings of tobacco, inhaling the smoke was looked upon with favor, but whether the simple rolling of a cigar or even a cigarette was the first step, we have no way of knowing. What does seem a good surmise is that the invention of the elbow pipe occurred long after the use of tobacco was widespread. There are geographical reasons for assuming that the tube preceded the invention of the true pipe.

The picture that unfolds, then, is that smoking took on new patterns or styles when the corn farmers adopted the elbow pipe. Smoking a pipe became more and more the symbol of hospitality. Offering a guest a smoke is thus an ancient custom, probably as old as the domestication of corn. Yet the social use of the pipe did not necessarily lessen the place of tobacco smoke and its aroma in serious ceremonies; if anything, it enhanced the symbolic quality of the pipe. And so evolved the ceremonial pipe and, eventually, the grand pipe or the calumet. Many of the old writers testified to the beauty and impressiveness of the calumet ceremony. At the opening of the present century, the writer saw some fine pipes and the accompanying ceremonies. They were impressive, perhaps more so than any of the other surviving ceremonies. Today, when some of our western Indians entertain a distinguished person or a President of the United States, they usually present him with a new pipe, large in size, with a bowl of red stone, a stem of wood and decorated with a wild duck's head, some dyed horsehair and wrapped with porcupine-quill braid. The newspapers call such a pipe "the pipe of peace," but it has no such significance. It is a modern gift pipe, a symbol of friendship and esteem.

Tobacco spread over the world so fast that a great deal of research was needed to prove that it was not known in the Old World before 1492. Within little more than a century it encircled the globe. Thus the historians of tobacco say it reached Portugal and Spain by 1558; France, 1559; Italy, 1561; England, 1565; Turkey, 1605; Russia, by 1634; Arabia, 1663. The Spaniards carried it to the Philippines, where it was soon grown and shipped to China; from China, tobacco smoking passed into Siberia; later into Alaska to the Eskimo, thus completing the circuit of the world, from southeastern America back again to northwestern America. Apparently then, as now, whatever his race, the person who used it once became an enthusiastic devotee. An old English writer comments upon how the passion became so strong that men and women were willing to trade their last morsel of food for tobacco; whether smoked, chewed or snuffed, the desire is the same. In a short time after its introduction into England there were said to be seven thousand tobacco shops in London, dispensing over three hundred thousand pounds a year. Sailors, being human, quickly acquired the habit and so spread it to all parts of the world; but the trader, also, found it easy to transport tobacco and sell it at a handsome profit. In a short time even the Australian blacks, the Hottentots and the Andaman Islanders were trading what little they could produce for pipes and smoking tobacco. Even in parts of Canada and the United States, where tobacco was rarely used, the fur traders offered the Indian large chunks of it in compressed form, which they recognized as superior to their own. Many tribes in the eastern United States continued to raise their own tobacco for ceremonial occasions, but for regular smoking tobacco they came to depend upon the traders. Of course such tobacco was expensive and often hard to get, which led to adulteration and to substitutes. Some of these seem to have been pre-Columbian. In the United States bearberry or sumac leaves were dried and mixed with tobacco, to which mixture the Algonkin name *kinni-kinnick*, meaning "that which is mixed," is usually given. This name is now generally used, covering all mixtures and substitutes, such as leaves of laurel, manzanita, squaw bush or maple bush, and the inner bark of red willow, dogwood, cherry, arrowwood, poplar or birch. A much longer list could be compiled, suggesting that when tobacco was not available or was too expensive, the Indians experimented with the plants available in their respective habitats. Perhaps tobacco was not the first plant smoked,

but we have no information concerning a time since
tobacco was discovered when some other substance was
preferred. Everything else smoked was regarded as a
substitute.

The French, English and Dutch seem to have been the
first to exploit the pipe and for good reason. They made
early contact with the Indians of eastern North America,
the pipe smokers. It was the returned colonists and traders,
already habituated to the pipe, who astonished their European friends by puffing smoke from their mouths and
noses. The Spaniards and Portuguese traded and settled
where the cigar, cigarette and snuff were the aboriginal
passions. They favored these methods rather than the
pipe. Fashionable Paris preferred snuff to the pipe, and
so in Queen Anne's time the aristocracy of England took
snuff too; those were the days when the snuffbox was the
sign of gentility. It looks as if each part of Europe first
adopted the tobacco method of the Indians with whom
they had been in contact, but later all the forms of using
tobacco spread rather evenly. Those interested in social
change can find good examples in the fluctuation of tobacco preferences.

In recent times in the United States, chewing tobacco
has come more and more into disfavor and the cigarette is
advancing. Many of our great-grandmothers smoked clay
pipes; later it became bad form for women to smoke, but
now it is quite the thing for them to smoke cigarettes. Yet
cigars and pipes are considered improper for women. Possibly in another generation the women will smoke pipes
and cigars and the men be limited to cigarettes. Snuff
may become popular again, and so on, but that tobacco
will be abandoned seems unlikely.

Even from the first there was opposition. The enthusiasts
for the new habit made extravagant claims for its virtues.
As a medicine, it was heralded as a cure-all. We suspect
there was a lot of wishful thinking here as in other similar
situations. When we want something very much we mar-
shal all the arguments we can raise for its defense, and
one of the strongest is the claim to medicinal, sanitary or

healthful values. Many forms of vice have been defended on such grounds. One of the first great antagonists to tobacco was King James of England, but the economic importance of the plant soon overcame all official opposition. One of the popes forbade its use in churches. After its appearance in Russia it was put under the ban.

Then there was that grim old sultan of Turkey who decreed the death penalty for its use. We are told how he went about the streets in disguise begging someone to sell him a little tobacco, and when his request was complied with he drew his sword and cut off the victim's head. Even if this tale be true, this was futile; the craze could not be stopped, and Turkey soon became famous as the producer of fine tobacco. In general, most of the efforts to stop the use of tobacco failed, and though occasionally religious organizations have forbidden its use, these restrictions have, for the most part, proved ineffective.

From the information we have, there were about as many successive changes in the way the Indians used tobacco as among the white people. Archaeologists think that straight tubular pipes preceded the elbow kind. We have seen that cigars and cigarettes each had their own regions of prevalence in 1492, as did chewing and the taking of snuff.

Because of the sacred background to the use of tobacco the question is often asked as to smoking for a pastime. Did the Indians do that originally? Along the Atlantic side of the United States, at least, it seems that they did. More tobacco seems to have been raised there than in the interior of the continent, so an ample supply was usually on hand. There is some reason to believe that in less favorable parts of the continent tobacco was saved for ceremonies and special occasions. Apparently women did not smoke then, but in trade days, and since, the older women were fond of smoking, using a smaller pipe than that preferred by the men.

We have dwelt at some length upon the history of tobacco because among the many things and their related customs that the Indians have passed on to the rest of the world, none is so unique and so original as the smoking of tobacco. The scientifically minded speak of the whole range of habits, customs and fancies associated with tobacco as a culture complex; indeed, we find ourselves in a maze of complexity when we try to state all the essential points about tobacco. It developed in Indian society and, step by step, became a great complex before the white man crossed the Atlantic Ocean. Scores of beautifully carved stone pipes have been found in Ohio mounds, revealing that certain cults of the pipe were in flower when mound building was the vogue. Much fine pottery is found in the Lower Mississippi Valley, and this also seems to have been the work of the tobacco users.

Inspiring as all this is, our interest turns back to the grand pipe, the calumet, which is no more. Its glory and romance belong to history. No one knows just where this interesting, intriguing notion of the calumet started. The Pawnee have traditions that they passed it on to the north, but some of the Siouan tribes think it was given them in a vision and so came directly from above. Such traditions and beliefs do not help us much, because we feel sure that the originator of the idea, to whom it must have come as an inspiration, possibly in a burst of emotion, explained it as something handed down to him; and when another tribe learned to venerate it, they, too, said it was handed down, soon forgetting that they had borrowed the idea. Nor have we reason to believe that the part of human nature which comes into the world with the nerves and brain of the infant was much different in the Stone Age from what it is now. So a tribesman who went to live and learn for a time among the originators of the calumet and returned a thorough convert might be expected to enhance his own prestige by claiming that he was the one to have the vision, to have met the gods and received from them directly this new idea and the ritual in which it is formulated. Even were he modest and unusually honest, his understudies might quite naturally attribute its origin to him. So we cannot take such traditions literally. Our own history tells us that when the French explorers

went into the Mississippi country they were received ceremonially, the most conspicuous feature being the so-called
"dance of the calumet" which involved the presentation of
such a pipe to them. When a calumet was formally thus
given to a Frenchman he became as one of its devotees,
between whom and himself there were bonds of friendship. All were thereby made brothers. When he met
strange Indians he needed only to show the calumet as
evidence that he was a devotee; if members of that tribe
also venerated the calumet they, too, were friends, bound
by ties and obligations of friendship. This, at least, is what
the writings of travelers convey to us.

Columbus was not met with a calumet, nor do any of
the Europeans landing and settling upon the Atlantic coast
mention it. For example, when Henry Hudson met Indians
around Manhattan Island, they came with fresh green
tobacco leaves in their hands. Something of the same
notion, but less formalized, must have been associated
with these tobacco leaves as with the calumet. Certainly
tobacco itself was the symbol of something other than
mere fear or hostility. The eastern Indians of Canada
seem not to have known of the calumet when they first
met the French, but we soon read that strange Indians
appeared from the west bearing calumets which, with
appropriate ceremonies, were presented to their hosts
who, in turn, began to venerate them. They seem to have
joined this fraternity, or whatever you choose to call it,
which is still something of a mystery to the white man.
What we really know about the inner cluster of ideas
behind it all is found in a ceremony which survived until
recent years among the Pawnee and a few of the Siouan
tribes. Here, at this late day, after the enthusiasm and
zeal of the converts to this new ceremony had run their
courses, it seems to function in a different way, though
still as a bond of friendship between individuals. A symbolic pipestem is now used, not perforated so it can be
used with a pipe bowl, decorated with feathers and tufts
of horsehair. Further, a pair of these stems are used, one
in each hand. There is nothing unusual in this use of a

symbol for what was once a real pipe, since we use many symbolic objects in similar ways, such as the key to a city, or a cross. Most large museums have on exhibition a pair of these symbolic pipestems.

Farther north, among some of the Cree and the Blackfoot, a more realistic ceremonial pipe is still venerated. The white people call it a medicine pipe. These pipestems are kept in bundles, formerly of nicely tanned skins but now of fine cloth, with a number of ceremonial objects to serve as accessories in the demonstration of the ritual associated with the pipe. Curiously enough, a pipe bowl is rarely found in the bundle, but when it is to be unwrapped a stone pipe bowl of suitable size is brought in for the occasion. This pipe is really smoked at the appropriate point in the ritual. Nevertheless, it is the stem that is symbolic and in that sense sacred. These stems are of wood, usually thirty or more inches long, decorated with a kind of fan of eagle feathers, heads of water birds, and sometimes a tuft of horsehair. These pipes are used neither in councils, feasts, nor in making peace; an ordinary large decorated pipe is considered sufficient for such occasions.

Again, the power symbolized in these medicine pipes is believed to guard the welfare of the people, particularly its keeper, his household and everyone who prays to it. In the few rituals concerning which we have information, the basic idea seems to be that the Thunder gave these pipes as a pledge that he would spare and otherwise protect those associated with them. In 1809 Alexander Henry obtained the following statement from a Blackfoot Indian:

"Thunder is a man who was very wicked and troublesome to the Indians, killing men and beasts in great numbers. But many years ago he made peace with the Blackfeet and gave them a pipestem in token of his friendship; since which period he has been harmless. This stem they still possess, and it is taken great care of by one of their chiefs, called Three Bulls. Lightning is produced by the same man that makes thunder when he visits the earth

*in person and is angry; but they know not what causes his
wrath.*"[1]

Another account recorded about a century later among
the Dakota Indians states that two symbolic pipestems are
used, often spoken of as "horsetails" because they bear
tufts of horsehair, but otherwise remind one of the calumet
stem. The related ceremony is called *Hunka* and seems to
mean a bond of friendship and brotherhood between two
persons. However, all who have entered into such bonds
have obligations to each other. In the course of the ritual
accompanying these decorated stems, the leader says:

*"My friends, this man has done as a Hunka should do.
He has given of all that he had. He took the food from his
mouth and divided it with me. He gave me his moccasins,
his shirt and his leggings, and now he is naked and has
nothing. I will put the red stripe on his face, for he is
Hunka. I put this stripe on his face so that the people may
see it and know that he has given all his possessions away,
and know that they should give to him. I will put the
stripe on his face and on the face of his Hunka so that
they will remember this day, and when they see one in
want they will give to that one."*[2]

Some neighboring tribes have an analogous ceremony
with similar decorated stems; for example, the Pawnee,
Omaha and Osage.

While the original calumet seems to have been used in
a slightly different way, we see that fundamentally the
calumet kind of decorated pipestem carried with it everywhere the idea of a bond of friendship as deep and lasting

[1] Alexander Henry and David Thompson, *New Light on the
Early History of the Greater Northwest*, New York, 1897, Vol.
2, p. 529.
[2] J. R. Walker, "The Sun Dance and Other Ceremonies of the
Oglala Division of the Teton Dakota," Anthropological Papers
of the American Museum of Natural History, 1917, Vol. 16,
Part 2, p. 138.

as that between true brothers. This much we can understand: that the grand pipe came to be regarded as the symbol of a sacred bond and that its entrance into a village indicated a new and better phase in human relations. When a stranger came, bearing such a grand pipe, everyone knew that he came in the spirit of peace and friendship.

PART II
THE GREAT INDIAN FAMILIES

Chapter VI

THE GREAT INDIAN FAMILIES

THE American Indian of 1492 had been long in the making, but we know little of the stirring events and the bloodshed that brought it all about. Ten thousand years of history command our respect even if most of the details are lost. But 1492 opens with a different outlook, for since then we are confronted with a mass of historical information about the modern Indians. There are many good books from which we can learn a great deal about them—the deeds of their great men, the futile sacrifices made to maintain their freedom, the tragedies they faced even to the bitter end.

The English and French, the chief colonizers of the United States and Canada, found the country occupied by many independent tribes, many at war with each other. The elders of neighboring tribes talked peace and at times sincerely sought it, but the marauding traditions were so carefully fostered that raiding for blood, captives and plunder was on the level of second nature. Among some tribes, the Indian who had not taken part in a raid was a curiosity. The honors and social esteem of the tribe went to him who had killed his man. The tribes were rarely large, operating in independent units of a few hundred persons, old and young. This often perplexed the European, accustomed to well-disciplined nations, and opened the way to constant friction. Yet what puzzled the European even more was the fact that there were almost as many forms of speech as tribes. To get some notion of what this means, suppose that every town along one of our highways had a different language. What a troublesome world that would be! But worse than that, each town would have some customs of its own, to violate which

Map of the Original Habitats of the Important Indian Tribes of the United States

HUDSON
BAY

Naskapi

D   A   Cree

Saulteaux   Muskekowig
Eastern Cree

Montagnais

Abittibi

Malecite

Ojibway   Nipissing   Algonkin   Abnaki   Micmac
Ottawa   Passamaquoddy
Penobscot

Eastern   Missisauga   Pennacook
Dakota   Menomini   Huron   Six   Massachuset
Winnebago   Nations   Poktumtuk   Wampanoag
Sauk-Fox   Wyandot   Iroquois   Mohican   Pequot
Neutrals   Munsee   Narraganset
Forest Potawatomi   Piankashaw   Erie   Delaware   Shinnecock
Peoria   Wappinger
Iowa   Prairie Potawatomi   Susquehanna
Miami   Nanticoke
T E S   Kickapoo
Illinois   Pamunkey
Missouri   Shawnee   Mattapony
Chickahominy
Osage   Powhatan
Tutelo
Quapaw   Tuscarora
Cherokee   Catawba   Croatan
Caddo   Upper
Chickasaw   Creek
Choctaw   Koasati   Yuchi
Kichai   Kusa
Tunica   Lower Creek
Taensa   Alibamu
Natchez   Biloxi
Atakapa   Apalachee   Seminole
Chitimacha

Timuquanan

was dangerous; to be the friend of one would automatically make one an enemy of another, etc. Such a confusion of tongues seemed at first unexplainable, but when scholars began to study them, some order displaced what had been chaos.

Speech is a practical matter and, to be serviceable, words and their meanings must be highly standardized; but when people live in small, self-contained groups, such uniformity need not go beyond the bounds of the group. Again, a vocabulary is never fixed in its details, even when supported by written standards, but when carried on merely by word of mouth can change rapidly. On the other hand, the form or grammar of a language is ultra-conservative, so much so that a scholar can soon convince himself that English, French, Dutch, Spanish and Italian must have been derived from a common parent tongue. In the same way students of Indian speech soon discerned that in spite of all the apparent confusion the tribes could be arranged in families, according to the parentage of their speech. We know, too, that this means descent from an ancestral tribe in which the elements of the language were crystallized. Specialists in this field of research have identified the leading families of Indian languages and listed the tribes belonging to them. Such lists are analogous to tribal genealogies—a number of tribal family trees, as it were.

The sorting out of these tribal family trees has been a long and arduous process which is not yet complete. In 1891 J. W. Powell grouped the languages of the American Indians into more than fifty families, most of which were named for the tribes which spoke them. Later, in 1929, the linguist Edward Sapir arranged Powell's language stocks into six major groups. Although Sapir intended his work as a guide for further study, research since 1929 has tended to substantiate most of his classification. Recent work by the linguist Morris Swadesh has revealed additional relationships among the American Indian languages. Using the method of glottochronology, he compared a list of basic words, such as man, woman, far, big, hand, heart, hot, good, walk and others of a similar sort. These words were chosen because most of them exist in every language, and they are likely to remain unchanged in a language for many centuries, even if technological innovation introduces or changes other parts of the vocabulary. Word lists from a number of languages can be compared, and the degree of relationship is calculated on the basis of the percentages of shared words or cognates. Linguists have also been able to estimate the time at which one language separated from another, and in many instances their estimates have been confirmed by archaeology.

There is still much to be done in this field, for as yet even the experts disagree on many of the finer points of classification. For the time being, we shall continue to use the Sapir grouping; but bear in mind that even this is not the last word in groupings, for there appear to be many relationships of which Sapir was unaware. His arrangement provides a convenient grouping of the great Indian families we are about to meet.

To form a comprehensive notion of the Indian in the United States, we must familiarize ourselves with the names and characteristics of some of these families and with their outstanding tribal members. The chief stocks are the Algonkin-Wakashan, Hokan-Siouan, Penutian, Nadene, Aztec-Tanoan and Eskimo-Aleut. Within these language groups are the families, or related groups of tribes, and the individuals of which we will speak. Many of these are well known, such as the Iroquois, the Caddo, the Sioux, the Athapascan, and the family to which we will turn first, the Algonkin.

New England
Abnaki
Penobscot
Massachuset
Poktumtuk
Wampanoag (Massasoit, King Philip)
Pequot
Narraganset (Canonchet)
Mahican
Mohegan

Labrador
Naskapi

Atlantic Coast
(New York–Virginia)
Wappinger Confederacy
Delaware
Nanticoke
Powhatan Confederacy

Central Area ("The Old Northwest")
Delaware
Shawnee (Blue Jacket, Tecumseh)
Illinois
Kickapoo
Miami (Little Turtle)
Potawatomi
Sauk and Fox (Keokuk, Black Hawk)
Menomini
Chippewa, or Ojibway, Saulteaux
Ottawa (Pontiac)
Cree

Plains Country
Cree
Blackfoot
Gros Ventre,
    or Atsina
Blood
Piegan
Arapaho
Cheyenne

Western Relatives
Kutenai (?)
Interior Salish (?)
    Flathead
    Coeur d'Alêne
    Kalispel
    Spokan
    Okinagan
    Pend d'Oreilles

West Coast
Ritwan
    Yurok
    Wiyot

Wakashan (?)
    Nootka
    Kwakiutl

Coast Salish (?)
    Chehalis
    Nisqualli
    Cowlitz
    Squamish
    Comox
    Tillamook
    Bella Coola

Chapter VII

THE GRAND OLD ALGONKIN FAMILY

THE Algonkin were the first Indians to welcome the Dutch, English and French and the first to shed blood in resisting the merciless advance of their settlements. They were a powerful family holding most of the country east of the Mississippi, from Tennessee and Virginia on the south to Hudson Bay on the north, a vast domain of forest lands, well watered by streams and lakes over which they glided in skillfully fashioned birchbark canoes. No other people possessed such a beautiful boat, so light it could be carried by a strong man from one stream to another, thus making it possible to go from the mouth of the Ohio to Lake Erie, thence to Quebec and beyond. Yet not all the Algonkin lived in the woods, for out on the plains of southern Canada, as far west as the Rocky Mountains, were the Blackfoot tribes, who made no use of canoes but hunted buffalo for food; in the plains of the United States were the Arapaho and the Cheyenne and, finally, two small tribes away out in northern California.

Before the white man came, the Algonkin were usually able to take care of themselves, but a southern family had crept up into their country along the Appalachian ranges in Pennsylvania, into the valley of the Mohawk in New York and across Lake Erie into Canada. This was a warlike family which we know as the Iroquois. Many Algonkin lost their lives resisting the invasion of these foreigners, and there was still war between them when the whites came. Our school histories tell us how that renowned French explorer Champlain, after settling at Quebec, joined a war party of friendly Algonkin which descended into the lake to be called Champlain, later meeting their enemies, the Iroquois, and defeating them, probably because Champlain and his few French companions used guns—implements that were strange and terrifying to the Iroquois. The Iroquois never forgave the French for this injury and made friends with the English and Dutch, joining the former in all their wars against the French and thus preventing the latter from occupying the Mohawk Valley.

The Algonkin were not merely at war with the Iroquois but often with each other. There were about a hundred Algonkin tribes, all independent like tiny nations, all sooner or later quarreling and starting feuds—little vicious circles impossible to break. In revenge for past injuries a few members of one tribe would stealthily approach the camp of a hostile tribe, take a scalp or two and escape if they could. Some sign or mark would be left to identify the tribe of the raider; that was important, to enrage the friends of the victim. The relatives of the victim accepted this challenge and sooner or later went out to revenge his death. Not infrequently a whole family would be destroyed. When a hostile tribe scored too often, a large party might go out, destroy a village or at least engage in a real battle. But such a victory never brought peace; the feud was still on. On the other hand, the various Algonkin tribes were not scattered over the country at random, as might be the case if there were no traditional bonds between them, or a feeling of relationship deeper than their petty feuds, enabling them to hold a large continuous territory against intruding alien tribes. History shows us, however, that while these weak family bonds were strong enough to unite a tribe or two against an alien tribe and thus successfully resist an intruder, they did not suffice when a body of closely federated tribes set out to penetrate their territory. This is how the Iroquois were able to force their way up along the Appalachians and, later, the reason why the Algonkin tribes fell an easy prey to the English, who when they found themselves at war with one tribe were usually able to bribe other Indians having scores to settle to join in the war. So these petty feuds between tribes, even in the same family, contributed to the downfall of all.

Yet there is more to these perpetual feuds, since the ideals of the tribe were such that the highest honors went to the man who was most daring and ruthless in such raids; the elders of the tribe continually exhorted the young to be brave, aggressive and ruthless. These same elders often counseled peace, often met with representatives of their traditional enemies to talk peace, but at home preached the glories of the warpath. Obviously, under such conditions, all promises to cease raiding and killing were futile, and it follows that since the greatest values in Indian life were of and in war, these pages will often deal with destruction, terror and death.

The most famous individual Indians in our early history were Algonkin; for example, Pocahontas, Chief Powhatan's daughter, who married John Rolfe, a leading Englishman in the Virginia colony which she often helped, and Massasoit, a Wampanoag sachem, or leader, and Squanto, who welcomed the Pilgrims at Plymouth and taught them how to raise corn. Among the important tribes in New England were the Penobscot, Narraganset, Pequot, Massachuset, Wampanoag and Mahican. Some of the first settlers quarreled with Indians, who in turn sought reprisals until open war was declared; the whites burning towns, killing women and children, selling captives into slavery; the Indians retaliating in kind. The settlers cut off the heads and hands of Indians they killed and set them up on poles in the towns to enrage the Indians, who in turn scalped and tortured such whites as fell in their way. In a short time all the colonies were offering bounties for Indian heads and scalps. An infant's scalp brought just as much as that of a man or woman. War followed war, producing great leaders on both sides, but the most conspicuous Indian leader was Massasoit's son, King Philip, feared by the English for his ability; the struggle between the settlers and the Indians is known as King Philip's War (1675–76). Philip fought valiantly to the last. Washington Irving has immortalized him in literature, portraying his strength of character under the stress of great sorrow and adversity. Another great leader, Canonchet, a Narraganset sachem and Philip's general in battles, showed equal nobility, as when captured and sentenced to death, he said "that he liked it well, for he should die before his heart was soft, or he had spoken anything unworthy of himself."

How the Algonkin Lived

The word wigwam is an Algonkin term for house, the type being an oval framework of poles, bent into dome shape and covered with slabs of elm bark or similar materials. Where available, birchbark was preferred, especially in summer. Sometimes the winter coverings were mats made of cattail stalks, these giving more warmth than bark. The fire was in the center, the floor was of tamped earth, and platforms around the sides served as sleeping and sitting places. This housing was simple and comfortable enough for Indians. Clothing was not elaborate; even in winter the men went about in moccasins, leggings, breechcloth and a robe. The characteristic woman's costume was a skirt formed by folding a rectangular skin around the waist. On occasion, a jacket was worn as an upper garment. Except in the Far North, the women tended small plots of ground in the forest; the chief crop being corn, though squashes and beans were added. Many foods typical of the eastern Algonkin were adopted by the colonists, as lye-hominy, succotash, wild rice, persimmon bread, popcorn and maple sugar. The economy of these Indians, however, was that of forest hunters, and deer was the chief food animal, furnishing fine skins for clothing as well.

Most household utensils were of bark and wood, though some baskets were made of wood splints; but what attracts the attention of the European is the wide use these woodland Indians made of certain bass fibers from the inner bark of such trees as linn and swamp ash. These fibers were shredded from the bark and twisted into thread and twine by rolling back and forth under the palm of the hand on the naked thigh or calf of the leg. Balls and skeins of this twine were used for many purposes. As we have said, their life was simple; for example, good thread is the basis for weaving, but the Algonkin attempted nothing more than narrow bands for burden straps and certain rectangular bags woven without a loom, using a process called twining. Menomini Indian women in Wisconsin still make these rectangular bags, but now they often use colored wool. Yet the Algonkin also made a black pottery for use rather than ornament. Curiously enough, they made clay pots with pointed bottoms, reminding one of certain ancient black European pottery. When Europeans first crossed the Atlantic, the Algonkin mode of life was that of a Stone Age; metal tools were unknown. Both chipped and polished stone techniques were used, and bone implements were common.

However, the soul of a people is reflected in what we call their mythology—a combination of allegorical fiction, philosophy, mysticism and ethics. As these Indians practiced no systematic writing, this body of lore was the only source of reference in their thinking and their solutions of social situations. The content of this mythology differs more or less from tribe to tribe, but still there is much in common which may be taken as old Algonkin. Their great supernatural hero, usually called Manibozho, Manabus, etc., remade the world after his supernatural enemies had destroyed it by a great flood. The underlying idea was that if he could get a little mud from the bottom of the submerged world, he could make it grow into the land. So assuming there was mud at the bottom, he sent down, one after the other, four diving animals, the last of which succeeded. The restoration of the world and the making of man follow, and as in our own sacred literature, Manabus gave directions for living, so that if anyone questioned the wisdom of a folk custom the Algonkin answer would be, "Manabus made it so." The thunder and the lightning were elevated to the level of a god, the idea being that this god took the form of a great bird, perhaps because the thunder belonged to the heavens, a region accessible to birds only. White people call this god the Thunderbird.

Incidentally, the whites were puzzled by some of these traditions. The idea of destroying the world by drowning the undesirable forms of life was strikingly familiar to them, but in this case there was neither a Noah nor a man-made ark. Some of the animals found refuge on a mountaintop with the god Manabus. His problem was to restore the land which he formed out of mud. This order of events was unexpected by the white man, his belief being that long before the flood man was made from earth. The Indian recognized the similarities in the two beliefs and was disposed to look upon the white man's belief as confirming his own. But the white man was horrified to note that the Algonkin god Manabus sometimes acted like Satan and so inclined to the theory that all Indian beliefs were the work of the devil.

Every Algonkin man of consequence was expected to have a supernatural guardian spirit. Every success in life depended upon the good will of this guardian, not necessarily unseen, because at times this spirit might reveal itself to its ward. It was a fine belief, since the Indian could go upon long lonely journeys, knowing that his invisible guardian was always present. Totem is the name given such a spirit, an Algonkin word and idea contributed to the white man's social philosophy. These guardian spirits were usually animal and bird gods, or beings standing behind the lives of these creatures and accounting for their existence. Thus, in general, Algonkin thought was biased in favor of a kind of brotherhood of men, animals and birds, all guarded by the same supernatural power. Perhaps no white man has ever quite understood the totemic philosophy of these Indians, but with them it was fundamental.

As with most peoples, magic and medicine were interwoven, but rather more use was made of vegetable medicines by the Algonkin. Their doctors were keen to find new medicines and so continually scoured the forest for strange plants. The whites held the Indian root doctors in great esteem, often calling upon them for aid, so that even now our folk medicine is rich in Indian recipes.

Ceremonies and ritualism were not carried to the same extreme as among other Indian families, but note should be taken of the Midé Society, a kind of ritualistic order found among many Algonkin in which there were a few ranks or degrees through which the initiate passed. The public was permitted to see a spectacular performance in which it was made to appear that a white shell was shot into a member, who thereupon passed into a trance. The Midé Society was thus partially secret and often intrigued Europeans into imagining its origin to have something in common with the Masonic order. The songs and evolutions in this ceremony were recorded in a kind of picture writing on birchbark, which reminds us that the Algonkin were unique among Indians of the United States and Canada in the use of this kind of picture writing. It is true that they made only limited use of it, yet this way of writing seems to have originated with them and is frequently cited as one of the simplest forms of all writing. This much, at least, must be credited to the Algonkin.

Dress and Fashions

Since it was Algonkin our forefathers knew best, we pause long enough to describe their appearance. We all hear that paint, feathers and skins were essential to a well-dressed Indian. Let us begin with the women. No one worried much about clothes during the first ten years of life. It saved a lot of trouble to let the children go naked, especially in summer. When they got really dirty, plunging them into the stream was sufficient. During the summer and in moderate weather young women bathed frequently. Though brought up as nudists, when they took to clothes they were prudish enough. A woman would not be seen without a skirt, but nothing else mattered—

except in cold weather, or when wishing to appear dressed up.

The Indian woman had a lot of work to do and saved her best clothes for rare occasions. Her skirt was simplicity itself—a rectangular piece of skin, long enough to go around the body and to reach from the belt to below the knees. A belt held it in place, and the slightly overlapping edges were on the right side, thus forming what is called the Algonkin slit skirt.

The younger women, at least, took good care of their hair. Since it was always glossy black and seldom became gray, dyes were rarely used. The principal dressing was bear fat. Long hair was prized, many young women allowing the hair to hang down behind, and often it reached the hips. A favorite coiffure was to gather the hair into a thick mass resembling a beaver tail hanging down the back of the head. This was frequently ornamented with wrappings.

To keep the skin smooth and sightly they used fish oil and eagle fat. Red pigment might be mixed with the fat, thus changing the color of the face. Again bright red was applied to the forehead, the temples and cheeks. Young women often used black pigment around the eyes and on the forehead.

The men, however, excelled in the use of paints, not only using background colors but adding ornamental figures of birds and animals. These figures were not uniform, each man feeling free to be original. Tattooing was known but not highly developed.

Paints were both mineral and vegetable in origin; the separate colors were kept in little bags, which with bags of fat, enclosed in a larger bag, formed a toilet kit, carried by both men and women.

The Indian man gave even more attention to his hair than did the woman. He dressed it daily with bear fat to make it glossy, sometimes mixing soot with it to add to the blackness of the hair. Most of the eastern Indians cut the hair close on the sides of the head, leaving a cockscomb from the forehead to the back of the neck. On the top of the head this ridge of hair was cut like a pompadour, while the remainder was of natural length, braided and trailing down the back of the head like a scalp lock. They were fond of tying bits of shell, metal, stone, etc. into the hair. To make the cockscomb more conspicuous they made artificial roaches of deer bristles dyed bright red. When these were tied upon the head the Indians looked like plumed knights.

The preferred headgear of eastern Indians, men and women alike, was a band of embroidered skin around the head, to which bangles were hung or into which a row of upright feathers was set. The necessary costume required of men, the minimum for decency, was a breechcloth. Moccasins were worn when on the march, with leggings and a robe. Shirts, trousers and jackets made of cloth were worn after the white people came among them.

The Powwow

Whenever a community of Indians in New England was confronted by a problem, they gathered around a large fire, prepared some food and deliberated. Yet they went somewhat further than a white community would, since they called upon the medicine men and women to do what they could to solve their difficulties. Somewhat after the fashion of a religious community of whites, prayers might be offered and certain sacred songs might be sung, accompanied by drumming and the shaking of rattles. Every now and then a pipe would be filled, lighted and smoked, with the idea that it was offered to the unseen powers who were thus invited to smoke with the older Indians who were the leaders of their people. Some of the Indians in New England called such a gathering a powwow. The word soon found a place in the English language, not only as a noun but as a verb; to powwow meant to participate in such a gathering. Such gatherings were common to Indians generally, and since songs were the important part of their rituals, some tribes called them "sings," others named them dances, and so on. But in colonial times powwow was used as synonymous with "making medicine," or the practice of magic.

A powwow, then, refers to an Indian community in action, trying to solve its current problems. During the periods of friction with the whites, the sound of drumming and singing in an Indian camp aroused fear lest the Indians were discussing war. Whenever a peace proposal was made to a village, a powwow was called. There would be speaking and discussion interspersed with praying, dancing and singing. These might be continued for days before a decision was reached.

A food shortage was a serious matter and would lead to a powwow. The details of the situation would be scrutinized and cold logic applied to them, but if that failed, the medicine men would be called upon, prayers offered to the gods, and so on. In the end, however, some course of action would be decided upon. If an epidemic broke out, there would be such a conference. Any crisis or any major difficulty would be met in the same way. Sometimes this procedure was called a council, but whatever its name, it was always basic in Indian government.

Fate of the Atlantic Tribes

In New England the densest Indian population was in Massachusetts, Rhode Island and Connecticut, probably for some of the same reasons that the greatest white population is there now. It is the part of New England with the least snowfall and the most favorable agricultural lands. So far as we can see, the Algonkin of Pilgrim days were not a seacoast people in the sense that they took their entire living from the sea. They made some use of sea food, to be sure, but in the main depended upon the game of the forest and the corn raised in their gardens. Archaeologists tell us that the many shell heaps along the seacoast suggest that it may have been otherwise at an earlier date, but we have no means of knowing whether the shellfish eaters of that time were Algonkin. Anyway, the Algonkin of historic time were not keen about living at the shore and so were willing to retire into the forests as the whites occupied the coast. All might have been peaceful if the white man had been content to stay near the sea, but soon he began to yearn for more farmlands, then to clear away the forest and to destroy the game. He urged the Algonkin to move back into the forest with each advance of his own, but there was a limit to the retreat of the New England Algonkin. His powerful enemies, the Iroquois, held the country west of the Hudson, so a fight to the finish was inevitable if he tried to cross that river. Of course the New England Algonkin were fighting each other also. For revenge, one or more tribes would join the colonists in seeking to exterminate the tribe with whom the colonists happened to be at war, and in such a land of feuds it was easy for the colonists to hire Indians to do some of the fighting for them.

However, the deadliest weapons of the white man were his diseases, his demoralizing vices, particularly prostitution and liquor. The first reduced the population to a fragment, the last tended to demoralize and incapacitate the survivors. Even had the Algonkin been more peaceful and the colonists less brutal, disease and vice would have achieved the same result in time.

At the outset there were many Indian tribes and villages in New England, all Algonkin. The large groups with which the colonists contended were the Mahican, Narraganset and Pequot in Connecticut and Rhode Island; Mohegan, Poktumtuk, Massachuset and Wampanoag in Massachusetts; the Abnaki in New Hampshire and Maine. The village was the unit. Often a number of villages were loosely federated under chiefs, and these in turn formed the tribal groups mentioned above. The strategy of the English, especially those of Plymouth colony, was to foment mischief among these tribal groups and thus get them to destroy each other. We should remember also that, notwithstanding the sterling character of the colonists, they tortured their own kind by fire and sword, chopped criminals to pieces and scattered them to the four winds; bloody and violent deaths were familiar to them. They even burned to death people suspected of witchcraft. In this respect the Indians and whites were about on the same level. Further, the colonists believed themselves the best of God's children, those He loved most and Who stood behind them expecting them to destroy the Indians to make way for His own children. True, they offered the Indians the choice of joining their church and living under harsh discipline or the sword. There is more good literature upon the so-called Indian wars in New England than for other parts of the United States because the writers of the time, like their fellows, gloried in the killing of Indians, in massacring their women and children, even in burning them alive in their own huts; for this no one thought apologies were called for, but on the contrary all went to church to thank their God for delivering these heathen into their hands.

Wars in New England

The chief Indian wars listed are with the Pequot, Mohegan, Wampanoag and Abnaki, but it would not be far wrong to say that war began with the first settlements and continued until about 1770. The Pilgrims were barely settled around Plymouth Rock before they were hiding behind trees, shooting at Indians. What are formally called Indian wars actually refer to retaliations by a few soldiers or a squad of enraged citizens who burned a village or two and killed all the Indians upon whom they could lay hands. The advancing frontier in New England was never quite free from turmoil. Even the constant intercourse between Indians and whites was marred by homicides, for killing an Indian was not considered murder; but when an Indian was too quick for his white antagonists, it was recorded as another outrage. Finally, to make the picture complete, we must not forget that between 1675 and 1763 the French were actively contesting the advancing English frontier by inciting the Indians to raid and harass the settlements and often leading them in person. The formal declared wars between the French and English were:

King William's War	1689–97
Queen Anne's War	1701–13
King George's War	1744–48
French and Indian War	1754–63

The first line of contact was in the strip of country extending through northern New England and southwestward across the Hudson into Pennsylvania. The Indians operated chiefly against the English in an unsettled zone between the French colonists in Nova Scotia and along the St. Lawrence on the one hand, and the Atlantic coast settlements of the English on the other. As the French advanced to the Great Lakes and down to the Ohio River, the line of war extended westward; but the New England frontier continued to be a bloody battleground until the end of the French and Indian War. As we visualize the situation we see that the Indians and the French were resisting the same enemy, the English frontier, the Indians living between the French and the English offering a shield to the French. So, whereas the English sought to instigate the Indians to fight one another, the French urged them to join hands in raiding the English, supplying them with arms, paying for white scalps, white captives, etc. Perhaps, after all, the Indians were not the villains New England history makes them appear, but rather the unfortunate victims of two rival invaders. The Indian fought for revenge and to protect his home; naturally, all peoples do that, but had there been no Frenchmen in the rear to incite them and supply them with powder and ball, the Algonkin might have gradually withdrawn into the forests with less tragic results. We say *might* because ultimately the result would have been the same.

The Indian methods of warfare infuriated the English colonists, who, though habituated to a certain amount of bloodletting, expected their antagonists to come out into the open and fight. Instead, the Indian sneaked along in the brush and behind fences to ambush the farmer at the plow, but if the farmer took refuge in his log house they set fire to his grain and his outbuildings and killed his livestock, with no apparent motive except to enrage and to mock him. Even we could not come through such experiences without an urge to burn every Indian's house and knock his family on the head. There should be little difficulty in understanding the state of the New England frontier if we keep these situations in mind, nor need we be told that scarcely a year passed without Indian and white clashes.

For about a century this continued. The number of recognized important Indian battles in the list of the American Geographical Society is eleven, ranging in time from 1637 to 1747, but this number does not include the far more numerous surprise raids upon laborers in the fields, upon isolated farmhouses and occasional attacks upon armed whites. Further, the Indians carried away as captives more women and children than they killed. No one has attempted to compile the number of colonists killed in these raids, but since the farms were widely scattered and frontier towns were small, many raids resulted in no deaths and many others in only one each. The number of farm buildings burned and livestock killed was impressive: we are, for example, informed that though all the farmers in one community escaped, twenty or more buildings were burned, and so on. We must bear in mind that the advance settlements of the whites were the chief objective of the Indians; it was vital to their cause that this advance be checked.

If the reader has any doubts as to the reality of Indian resistance in New England, he should read the pertinent literature. A brief summary may suffice, however, as during the years 1675 to 1677 the raiding Indians burned twenty-five towns, even such as Springfield, Providence, Deerfield and Sudbury. In a few of these not a house escaped the flames, and several were raided two or three times until the destruction was complete. The writings of the time give some estimates of fatalities, the most cir-

cumstantial documents placing white deaths at eight hundred and those of Indians at nine hundred. Relative to the
population of the time this was a heavy loss. The property
losses were relatively greater. The Indians engaged
showed more persistence, were less demoralized by a
single reverse and made more attacks upon armed men
than in most other Indian wars.

The Algonkin front between the Hudson River and
North Carolina was in a more fortunate position. The Ohio
Valley in the West was thinly populated, and though
some Iroquois-speaking tribes spread over Pennsylvania,
they were not as aggressive as those of New York State.
Large stretches of the Appalachians were mere hunting
lands. The Susquehanna Indians held the heart of Pennsylvania, and the powerful Delaware tribes of the Delaware
Valley dominated eastern Pennsylvania and most of New
Jersey. Of course these are group names, these Indians
living under subtribal groups in many villages; the Nanticoke held Delaware and the adjoining territory, where
some of their survivors still reside. In eastern Virginia was
the Powhatan Confederacy. Jamestown was settled in
1607, and by 1622 the colonists were fighting these Indians, losing over three hundred of their number but inflicting more damage on the Indians. In 1644 another
climax was reached, costing a large number of white lives,
but this time the Indians were reduced to helplessness
and eventual extermination.

The Pennsylvanians got on rather well with the Indians,
but the Dutch were soon fighting with the tribes around
Manhattan usually designated as the Wappinger Confederacy. Before New York was much of a town, a citizen
murdered an Indian bringing furs to market and possessed
himself of the goods. The town government winked at
the crime; after all, what did one Indian more or less
matter? There were other similar offenses. Finally, a party
of Dutch went to Staten Island to kill all the Indians they
could find. Soon the struggle was on, for Indians were
always quick to retaliate in kind. In 1655 a citizen shot an
Indian woman pulling some peaches from his favorite tree.

Soon after, about two thousand armed Indians walked into the city, demanding satisfaction. After terrifying the city, they knocked at the door of the murderer and when it was opened shot him dead. They then left the city, destroyed outlying houses and killed a number of people. At the end of the war more than a hundred women and children were held as captives in the Indian villages. Soon the English came into possession of New York, and by 1688 the remnants of the local tribes agreed to give up their homes and move on. What they did was to scatter as refugees among the Delaware and other Algonkin groups, and so ends history for the Indians of Manhattan.

Retreat of the Delaware

On the Middle Atlantic front were the Delaware, occupying the valley of the river of that name and claiming lands almost to the Hudson and Manhattan. In William Penn's day their capital, or the home of the head chief, was near what is now Germantown; in other words, Penn started a rival capital almost at the same place. The great chief of the time was Tamenend, or Tammany. The Indians held him in such great esteem that the whites often spoke of him as Saint Tammany, and as such he became the ideal of Indian virtue. Even as early as the French and Indian War it became fashionable to form societies with rituals and slogans drawn from Indian culture, so in 1772 a society came to notice under the name "Sons of King Tammany." About 1786 a Tammany Society was set up by veterans of the Revolution, for much the same purpose as the present American Legion. This society was destined to survive as a political organization in New York City, and the name for its building, Tammany Hall, will be recognized by our readers as a popular symbol for a political organization long dominant in the state and even in the nation. The ritual of the society contains such terms as chief, sachem, wigwam, wampum, etc. Originally there were thirteen state organizations, with such tribe names as Otter, Eagle and Tiger. The latter was assigned to the organization in Delaware but later became a symbol for the surviving organization in New York, hence the familiar cartoons of the Tammany Tiger. While much of the glory and virtue associated with the old chief, Tammany, originated within the minds of white men, the historical data available suggest an Indian of the highest rank and worthy of a prominent place in history.

The Delaware called themselves the Lenni Lenape, which meant "true men" or "real men" in the sense that we would use the term "we, the people." Most of the names we use for Indian tribes were given them by others; among themselves something like "we, the people" not only sufficed but asserted the superiority of the group. The Lenape are famous in literature because of a document in picture writing, called the Walam Olum. This may or may not be a genuine Indian document, but its contents are in the style of Indian legends and some of the incidents referred to are found in the recorded myths of the Algonkin. If the reader is interested, he should examine the Walam Olum in any large library. Further, the reader of Cooper's novels will recall many references to the Delaware by the famous Natty Bumpo, who stoutly extolled their virtues in contrast to the iniquity of the Mingo, or Iroquois.

We have noted that the Delaware seem to have recognized a head chief, immortalized in Tammany. The several divisions of this tribe had chiefs and counselors, as did most Algonkin. The people lived in small villages of rectangular bark-covered houses instead of the usual dome-shaped wigwams of other Algonkins. They were hunters but raised corn and other vegetables. In keeping with their greatness, they cherished a systematic philosophy and mythology, according to which there was one great power over the universe, but subject to it were four gods—the four directions, from which came the four winds—and other great powers. A series of spirits and powers, in descending order, made up the rank and file of the supernatural host.

Enough of the Delaware history is known to write a

kind of epic, if a genius cared to try it. We find them at the height of their power and glory under the great Tammany; but the disturbances due to white contact on the east and south, and especially the unceasing hostility of the Iroquois on the north and west, wore down their resistance, until about 1720 when they became subjects to that arrogant Indian family and were held up to scorn by them, and called such names as "old woman," or "wearers of skirts." Their humiliation was greater because of their former proud status. The whites wished them out of their traditional homeland and, still fearing the Iroquois, they began to drift toward the setting sun. About 1724 they camped in western Pennsylvania. Later, a few families found a home on the Muskingum in Ohio, and as the white pressure increased, the main body moved to Ohio about 1751.

Yet even here they were insecure; the land was not theirs originally, and the whites did not respect their claims, regarding them as wanderers, people without a country. Some of the Delaware drifted into Indiana, where about 1770 the Miami tribes agreed to tolerate them. The Muncie band settled near the present city of that name, now famous in sociological literature as Middletown. During the French and Indian War they fought on the side of the French and in the Revolution sympathized with the English. They were among the tribes defeated by Wayne, but even as early as 1789 some of them secured permission from the Spanish authorities to live in Missouri, to which place more than half of them migrated, the remainder moving into Ontario to escape punishment by the United States. Reservations were given them in Ontario where their descendants still live.

The Missouri contingent continued to be wanderers, for we find them in Texas in 1820. Here they were far from welcome and so turned back toward the northeast, reservations being provided for them in Kansas about 1835. Their existence there was anything but happy, so in 1867 they went to Oklahoma, where some of them joined the Cherokee Confederacy, the remainder moving in with the

Caddo. That is the story of their great retreat from the advancing frontier. There is nothing quite like it in Indian history, except the story of the Algonkin Shawnee who accompanied them from Ohio. Once the Delaware left their lands in the East, they could establish no valid claim anywhere. In a way they were shielded by their aggressive friends the Shawnee, otherwise their end might have been speedy. In New Jersey and eastern Pennsylvania they numbered about ten thousand, but their troubles with the whites and the Iroquois greatly weakened them, and each westward shift to a new home took heavy toll in disease and discouragement. The border wars along the Ohio also kept them down, so that when finally settled in Oklahoma and Ontario, they numbered less than a sixth of their former strength. Their retreat covered a period of about one hundred and fifty years; seven times they sought homes in the wilderness, each time in a different environment, ranging from New Jersey, through the deciduous forests of Ohio, to the wooded Ozarks, and at last into the grassy plains of the buffalo country. On the average they were allowed but twenty years at a place, two moves within the life of an average person. Defeatism must have had some place in their psychology. We note their leaders were present at many treaties with other tribes, and though they doubtless stood up for their needs, it is difficult to see how they could have been other than gloomily cynical over the solemn promises made at such times. Between 1778 and 1861, almost a century, the Delaware participated in some forty-five treaties, an average of one every two years. In each case they saw their claims rejected, were frequently accused of treachery and lack of gratitude and were charged with preferring to loaf rather than to work, with immorality and paganism. We dwell upon this record because though an extreme case, it is typical—a hundred and fifty years of retreat, finding no land they could call their own.

Chapter VIII

THE OLD NORTHWEST

WE had a look at the frontier in New England and southward from New Jersey. The powerful Iroquois held the heart of New York State from Albany to Buffalo. For a long time they withstood the advance of the white frontier, or rather they formed a wedge past which the frontier moved to the west. They aided in smashing the Algonkin of New England by preventing their retreat across the Hudson River. In the Middle Atlantic area the Iroquois crushed the Delaware Confederacy, relieving the colonists of that task. In Virginia and the Carolinas the colonists bribed the traditionally hostile tribes to kill each other off and, on occasion, themselves destroyed villages. Few tribes east of the Appalachians escaped extinction, which testifies to the intensity of conflict between the eastern Algonkin and the colonists. The tribes surviving retreated into the forests of Kentucky, Ohio, Indiana and Michigan. Curiously enough, this area, once the home of mound-building tribes, was thinly populated at the time; for, in 1600, Ohio and parts of Kentucky were visited by hunting parties only. Into this open space the Delaware, Shawnee and other Algonkin remnants retreated after their initial defeats in the Atlantic area.

By 1700 the French crystallized a policy the object of which was to hold the country west of the Appalachians from New Orleans to Quebec. Toward this long thin line the English frontier was advancing steadily. The French were at home in the network of lakes and streams which made it easy to pass by canoe from one series of watercourses to another and thus keep communications open from Quebec to New Orleans. They did not attempt to colonize the country between Louisiana and Detroit but tried to induce the Indians to live in peace with each other. They were moderately successful, because in suggesting resistance to the advance of the English frontier they provided an outlet to the Indians' raiding and scalping ambitions. The success of the French with these Indians is often cited as due to a more enlightened policy than that pursued by the English colonies, but this overlooks the troubles of the French in Louisiana and eastern Canada, where extensive settlements were made. In Louisiana they entered into wars of extermination, as we shall note later. In eastern Canada, also, they fought it out with the nearby Indians. In short, their success in the Upper Mississippi and Ohio country was chiefly because they did not form colonies and because they had a common enemy in the advancing English frontier, strong and menacing enough to keep the adventurous Indians busy. Vivid word pictures of these French and Indian relations are found in the writings of Parkman, the historian, but it serves our purpose merely to note that the French line was thinnest in the middle, or along the Ohio River, the very place where the British frontier was to strike the hardest.

The first conspicuous advance of the British colonial frontier was into Kentucky, an Indian name said to mean "the dark and bloody ground." Trappers and Indian traders were the first, as always, but soon came men with their families to build cabins, clear the land, and to farm.

Around 1750 the surviving Algonkin of the East joined their family relations in the Ohio country. There were now concentrated in this area under French influence such Algonkin tribes as the Shawnee, Miami, Kickapoo, Potawatomi, Sauk and Fox; Chippewa, Ottawa, Illinois and Delaware. These began to draw together, under the influence of the French, to resist the advances of the English frontier. The powerful Iroquois were loyal to the English and still feared by the Algonkin. The most important French forts controlling the situation were at Detroit, Niagara, Pittsburgh, Vincennes and Mackinac Island, the main links in a chain of lesser forts stretching from New

Orleans to Quebec, a kind of bristling crescent into the
hollow of which the English frontier was advancing. The
French relied upon the Algonkin to hold the English back
in Ohio and Kentucky. To this end they armed the Indians
and encouraged their depredations. While England and
France were at war in Europe, the French led small
bodies of troops, supported by larger groups of Indians,
against the colonists of the East. Not infrequently, certain
Algonkin chiefs received uniforms similar to those of officers of high rank in the French Army. All this training and
experience was turning the Algonkin of the Northwest
into a hard fighter, a good marksman and a genius in
ambuscades and surprise attacks.

The final stand of the French was the so-called French
and Indian War, 1754–63. In reality, the fighting reached
a war level some years earlier, and the name for the war
itself indicates the large share the Algonkin had in the
conflict. In July 1755, Braddock led an English and colonial army against the French Fort Duquesne, the site of
Pittsburgh. The reader knows that sorrowful tale, how a
relatively small body of Algonkin and a few from other
families, under French leadership, defeated the English
and the colonials. However, the main campaign of the
French and Indian War was around Lake Champlain and
Quebec. The French brought in large bodies of Indian
warriors from the Ohio country to assist Montcalm in defending Ticonderoga and other strategic points. Yet in the
end the English took Quebec and with it acquired all the
French territory east of the Mississippi.

The Algonkin leaders now faced a dilemma. They had
enjoyed the war; it gave them a new outlook on life and
educated them in European ways of fighting; they had
been praised by the French; their easy victories over the
English destroyed what little respect they still had for
them; their raids upon English settlements had enriched
them in scalps, captives and other booty; their own villages were secure, so their outlook upon life was most
promising. Naturally, their grasp of European affairs was
next to zero; the significance of what happened at Quebec

was outside their ken. The English were not in their country, but just when the future seemed brightest their French friends told them all their country was now in the hands of the English, that a handful of English soldiers would soon arrive to take possession of Detroit and all the other forts, that English traders would come to take their furs. This they could not understand. They began to look upon their French friends as cowards and traitors. They saw themselves not only deserted but handed over to the enemy.

Pontiac's War

The fall of Quebec gave a new impetus to the advance of the English frontier. Settlers swarmed the Appalachians, alarming the Algonkin who saw plainly what the future held in store for them. Pontiac, an Ottawa leader, rallied the Indians to continue the war against the English, planning an attack along the whole frontier. He was successful in taking every important fort but Detroit and Pittsburgh. This was in 1763. Pontiac, in person, laid siege to Detroit. In the meantime settlements were raided, families massacred and buildings destroyed. An Indian and white war was on in a large way. The Algonkin tribes participating were the Delaware, Miami, Shawnee, Ottawa, Potawatomi and Ojibway.

Pontiac maintained a vigorous siege of both the forts at Detroit and Pittsburgh for many months but, having no artillery, he was unable to carry them by assault. Nevertheless, he planned his efforts with skill; the experience of fighting with the French was put to good account. Eventually the garrisons at both forts were relieved, Pontiac's allies withdrew their support one by one until he gave up the war and went to St. Louis, where he was murdered. Pontiac has been immortalized by Parkman and, in any case, makes a strong claim for first place in Indian history. That he was a great Indian is beyond doubt. What stirs our emotions is the picture of Pontiac, standing alone, deserted by the French, but attempting single-handed to bring the French and Indian War to a success-ful issue in the West, to prevent England from taking possession of the country. The might of England was against him, yet what a fight he put up!

During Pontiac's War, an English army under Henry Bouquet moved into eastern Ohio, forced the Shawnee and Delaware to make peace and surrender their white captives. So comparative peace prevailed for a while, but still the Indians raided the settlements for about a decade, when a new situation arose. The thirteen original colonies began a war for independence with England. The English at Detroit and the other western posts were not in rebellion, neither was Canada. So the English neighbors of the Algonkin, who up until this time did everything they could to suppress raids upon the settlements, now urged them to make vigorous raids upon the frontier of the colonies. The Indians were supplied with arms and bounties were offered for white scalps. The Iroquois, some of whom had supported Pontiac, were in the main loyal to the English. Thus, even such hereditary enemies as the Delaware and the Iroquois found themselves fighting for the same cause. As in the French and Indian War, Algonkin were transported to Canada to fight with Burgoyne. This new line-up did not bother the Algonkin much, for they were again fighting against the menace of the frontier, and the war aided in the transfer of their confidence from the French to the English of Detroit and Canada.

The Last Stand

When the colonies won their independence and secured title to all the land east of the Mississippi, the Algonkin were again handed over to their enemies. Washington's government now claimed their lands, demanded that they become loyal and keep the peace. On the other hand, the

English in Canada, wishing to keep as much of the Indian trade as possible and recognizing the possibility of eventually recovering the Northwest, encouraged the Indians to resist the Americans, guaranteeing them arms and ammunition. So as far as the Algonkin were concerned, the war with the Americans was still on. In 1790 Washington found it necessary to send a military force to curb them. General Harmar, in command, gathered his forces at a point near Cincinnati, marched northward toward the heart of the Indian country, met the Indians in force and was disastrously defeated.

In 1791 another army under General St. Clair marched into the same country, to return in rout. This was the high point in the power of the Algonkin. They even called upon their enemies, the Iroquois, to make common cause against the whites and drive them back into the Allegheny Mountains. But the Americans were now aroused. General Anthony Wayne was ordered to prepare a new army and carry the war to a finish. He spent a year or more in drilling his troops until they were hardened, dependable regulars. From time to time delegations of Algonkin came to Wayne's outposts, saw his preparations and made vague overtures for peace, but Wayne insisted upon full surrender. The Indians tried several attacks upon his outposts but failed every time.

Finally, in 1794, Wayne's army approached the heart of the Indian country near what is now Maumee, Ohio. Some time before, a tornado had passed through that locality, plowing a path through the forest and twisting the fallen trees together into an ideal obstruction to advancing troops. The Algonkin called the place "Fallen Timbers," and here on a two-mile front they awaited Wayne. The general planned his attack carefully, then his center advanced and with leveled bayonets charged into the fallen timbers. In former wars the English had learned that Indians could not stand up against a bayonet charge, so the battle was little more than a skirmish. No other stand was made against Wayne, who burned the deserted towns of the Indians and destroyed their corn and all other property he could lay hands on. Winter was coming on, so the Indians sued for peace.

No great leader like Pontiac came to notice in these wars, but there were men of no mean ability among the Algonkin. Little Turtle, a Miami, was perhaps the most outstanding, for he was a leader in the earlier defeat of Harmar and took a leading role in driving St. Clair from the field. However, he seemed to sense the futility of resisting Wayne's army, and after making an unsuccessful attack upon Fort Recovery, one of the American outposts, counseled peace. However, the other leaders were confident of success because they were encouraged by the English. It is recorded that a number of Canadian English were with the Indians at Fallen Timbers. The Algonkin engaged were Delaware, Shawnee, Ottawa, Miami and scattering members of other tribes. The Iroquoian Wyandot were also present. It is believed that at least two thousand Indians were in line. Blue Jacket, the Shawnee, seems to have been the commander in chief, while among the younger chiefs, destined to be famous, was Tecumseh. We saw how the French left Pontiac to the mercy of the English. The Indians opposing Wayne were not only encouraged by the English but, in part, led by them, yet the warriors fleeing from Wayne's cavalry found the gates of the English fort closed against them. Again they were deserted in time of need.

At what is now Greenville, Ohio, Wayne arranged a truce with the Algonkin in accordance with which they gave up most of Ohio and part of Indiana. The older chiefs recommended submission to the inevitable. The reality of the situation was apparent to them—their star was setting. But the English still encouraged the younger Indians in the belief that with English help they could drive the Americans back into the Appalachians, the Indians failing to realize that nothing short of a huge English army could do that; it was the same siren song leading the Algonkin to destruction.

The War of 1812

A young Shawnee Indian, surviving the campaign of General Wayne, was not discouraged. In history he is known as Tecumseh, born near what is now Springfield, Ohio. He was a man of brain and ideas who visualized a great Indian state in the Ohio Valley and the Lake region, which should live in peace and harmony with its white neighbors to the east and English Canada on the north. It was an idea often entertained by white men, who should have known better. Had Tecumseh lived as a European, experienced the education of a Jefferson or an Adams, he would have realized the fallacy of the arguments in support of his vision; but he was conditioned by his Indian outlook, knew nothing of European history, could not understand the power and drive of white nationalism, which not even the good intentions of its devotees could stay, let alone induce to tolerate an Indian state in its wake. To all of this he was necessarily blind. He knew that before Wayne, the Indians had triumphed, that they had fought well with the English in the Revolution and before that with the French. He believed that the English of Canada would not only support such an Indian state but would respect its borders. He did not see that the English friendliness in Canada was little more than intrigue; that local English interests were stirring up the Indians to check the advance of the United States, in order to leave the way open for their own expansion. Tecumseh believed the Indians powerful enough to win against the United States, if they would unite under one leadership. Knowing what we do of Indian backgrounds, we realize that such a union would have been impossible. Discipline in the military and political sense was unthinkable to the Indian, even as a means of self-preservation. But Tecumseh was of the caliber to do his best.

So after the battle at Fallen Timbers, Tecumseh traveled from tribe to tribe, talking and speaking in councils, up into Wisconsin and Minnesota, down into Tennessee and to the Gulf. Everywhere, as was the Indian custom, he was treated with dignity and respect, but his great ideas were received with indifference. Yet Tecumseh was not discouraged. He shuttled back and forth, gradually winning over the tribes along the Wabash River. At the same time he kept in touch with both English and United States leaders. He appeared before the latter as an able advocate of the rights of his people, always commanding the admiration and respect of the whites because of his impressive personality. The most important white man in his day was William Henry Harrison, governor of the Northwest Territory, stationed at Vincennes. Harrison was also a fighting man with a powerful personality, which may account for his frequent conferences with Tecumseh.

By 1810 Tecumseh thought his plans were maturing. He now traveled continuously back and forth, planning a general uprising. One of his brothers was a medicine man, blind in one eye, an emotional fanatic rather than a powerful intellect. True to his profession, he read the future and so went by the name of the Prophet, his Indian name being Tenskwatawa. He was less practical than Tecumseh and put his faith in magic, promising that when the time came to fight he would invoke the powers to make all white bullets harmless. General Harrison, through his efficient intelligence service, learned that Indians were concentrating on the upper Wabash near Tippecanoe River. Accordingly, in the autumn of 1811, he set out with a well-trained army of about eight hundred men, reaching the Tippecanoe unmolested, where he camped in a strong position. Tecumseh, visiting in the South, had warned the Prophet to keep the peace with Harrison until he returned, but whatever the reason, the Indians ventured to make a surprise attack. But the general expected something of this kind and was ready.

The attack was well planned and vigorous. Some historians consider it the greatest of all Indian battles. Whereas Wayne's troops routed the Indians in a quick charge, Harrison was kept busy holding his lines of defense for two hours. However, the Indians failed to break through and finally gave way before charges of cavalry and infantry. The battlefield is now a park where bullet-scarred trees may be seen, and in the distance is a large boulder upon which, well out of range, the one-eyed Prophet sat making medicine.

Tecumseh was furious at first and then despondent. He knew the cause was lost. Some of the tribes lending friendly ears to his pleas would now refuse to take up arms. Gloomily he withdrew into Canada. When war between the United States and England broke out the next year, he joined the English and was commissioned a brigadier general in command of Indian volunteers.

The victory of Wayne at Fallen Timbers and the later victory of Harrison at Tippecanoe were fortunate preparations for the War of 1812. The Indians had been cowed, forts had been constructed and a considerable number of men trained for war in this environment. Detroit became the center of activity; battles were fought upon both sides of Lake Erie with varying success, but the English failed to secure a permanent footing in United States territory. Tecumseh was in most of these battles, but observing that the English were losing, became despondent. He, with his Indian brigade, accompanied the English general Proctor in his retreat before the Americans under Harrison. Tecumseh regarded Proctor as incompetent and when at last the English came to bay, took off his uniform and returned to Indian costume. Harrison's cavalry broke the English ranks at the first charge. Some authors say that Tecumseh, seeing an American officer on the ground wounded, rushed out, tomahawk in hand, to get his scalp, but was shot dead by the wounded soldier. Anyway, Tecumseh did not survive the battle.

We dwell upon these events because here was a man. He was a great orator, and had high ideals of honor and justice. Both he and Pontiac surely deserve a place on the honor roll of the Algonkin Family. And there are others.

Keokuk and Black Hawk

The reader may recall an Indian portrait upon a former
issue of paper money, a serious, harsh countenance and a
necklace of bear claws. That was Keokuk, one of the most
popular Indians of his day, a skillful leader and a distinguished orator. The name Black Hawk also should be
familiar, since a war is named after him, one in which
Lincoln served as a soldier. Both Keokuk and Black Hawk
were contemporary members of the Sauk tribe, often
called Sacs. In museums and special publications on Indians, the name of this tribe is coupled with that of the
Fox Indians because they were almost identical in language and usually operated as a single tribe. They first
came to notice in Michigan and Wisconsin but soon drifted
westward to the Mississippi; one division now living near
Tama, Iowa, the other in Oklahoma. To digress a moment,
the most distinguished civilized member of their tribe was
William Jones, who was graduated from Harvard University, received the degree of Doctor of Philosophy in
anthropology at Columbia University and was killed by
natives in the Philippines in 1907.

Black Hawk was born in 1767 and Keokuk in 1780.
Black Hawk was inclined to war, going out with raiding
parties at an early age to burn settlers' cabins and take
their scalps. Keokuk had other ambitions; he longed to
become a great peace leader and an orator. The Sauk
tribe aided Pontiac in his great struggle in 1772–76, and
doubtless the tales of this war fired the imagination of
the boy Black Hawk. As his sympathies were with the
English, he took part in the War of 1812. Keokuk, on the
other hand, was friendly to the United States, though he
did not take up arms in their support. He was a liberal in
that he favored changing old customs and adopting some
features of white civilization when such innovations
seemed advantageous.

After the War of 1812, with the consequent weakening

of the tribes on the Wabash, white settlements spread rapidly westward. From time to time the Sauk and Fox sold some of their lands, Keokuk favoring the treaties but Black Hawk always opposing such agreements. He led what may be called the radical and militant wing of the tribe. At last, in 1832, Black Hawk repudiated the sale of their lands east of the Mississippi and prepared for war, crossing the Mississippi to the lands the tribe had sold to the whites and making his last stand on the Wisconsin River. Keokuk remained neutral. At first Black Hawk seemed to win, but finally he was defeated, taken prisoner and sent to Fort Monroe, Virginia. For several years before the war Black Hawk, following in the footsteps of King Philip, Pontiac, Tecumseh and others, sought to federate the Indians to resist the whites. A number of mighty Algonkin warriors had tried this before, without success. Keokuk was too logical to support such a hopeless undertaking. After the tribe settled down on their reservation Black Hawk was allowed to return to his people in Iowa.

Keokuk was now dominant and made head chief. It is said that Black Hawk so resented this that he removed his breechcloth and with it struck Keokuk in the face. A few years later, in 1838, Black Hawk died. Lorado Taft, one of our most distinguished sculptors, executed a heroic statue of this celebrated chief, which was erected on the banks of Rock River near Oregon, northern Illinois. Keokuk's greatest achievement was his appearance in Washington, as an advocate for his people, to contest the claim of the Sioux Indians to lands occupied by the Sauk and Fox. Here his great oratorical powers were shown at their best. His logic and command of the facts were also above adverse criticism. In short, he won his case. He toured the important cities of the nation, where great honors were showered upon him. He died in 1848. In 1883 his bones were moved to Keokuk, Iowa, a city named in his honor, interred with great solemnity, and a large monument was set up to perpetuate his memory. There is also a bronze bust of him in the Capitol at Washington. Most of the great Algonkin have been honored by America because they were fighting men, but in Keokuk we have an exception, one who was truly great in wisdom, who had the gift of speech, who understood the futility of resisting the relentless advance of the frontier, yet demanded justice from the whites and the right to live in peace among them.

Chapter IX

THE WESTERN BUFFALO HUNTERS

So far, all the Algonkin tribes we have considered lived in the forests, but there were a few stragglers living in the grasslands of the West. The forests around the western end of Lake Superior fade out into the prairies and they, in turn, pass into the dry plains before the Rocky Mountains are reached. These open lands were the home of the buffalo, where they were found in great herds, but scattered buffalo were met with in Indiana, Kentucky, Ohio and even western Pennsylvania. Thus the Algonkin originally living in the country west of the Appalachians were not entirely ignorant of this animal.

Out in the buffalo country lived such Algonkin as the Blackfoot, Piegan, Blood, North Blackfoot, the Atsina (Gros Ventre), Arapaho and the Cheyenne. The Blackfoot, Arapaho, Atsina and possibly the Cheyenne were in the Plains a long time before the discovery of America, so here is a mystery which scholars have not yet cleared up: Did these early Algonkin in the Plains move out of the forest, or are they survivors of the original Algonkin, a Plains people, who expanded eastward, thereby becoming forest dwellers? Most scholars favor the former view, because most of the old archaeological materials in the East seem to belong to a people living like Algonkin, and since nearly all of the Algonkin tribes do live in the forest, it seems more sensible to think of the forest as the place where they became numerous and strong. What may be more to the point is that the Cheyenne seem to have lived upon the edge of the forest next to the grasslands, out in Minnesota and Dakota, but moved out into the Plains for good after the horse was available, became habitual buffalo hunters, lived in skin tents rather than in bark houses, and forgot how to make pottery and tend gardens. The Blackfoot and Arapaho groups seem to have been in the Plains much longer than the Cheyenne, and if they, too, came out of the woods, it was to hunt the buffalo on foot, carrying their baggage on their backs or packed by dogs. Anyway, they do not recall having kept gardens, nor are they certain that their ancestors made pottery. In all matters they were, when first discovered, typical Plains Indians. Perhaps the best guess is that all the Algonkin came either from the forests around the Great Lakes or out of the Canadian forests north of the Saskatchewan River. In historic time some of the Ojibway and Cree of that area left the forests to become horse Indians, chiefly because of white pressure from behind, the same old story of retreat in face of the relentless advance of the frontier.

The Blackfoot Group

Far out in the very northwest corner of the Plains, next to the Rocky Mountains in Montana and in adjacent parts of Alberta, Canada, were the powerful Blackfoot tribes: the South Piegan, North Piegan, Blood and North Blackfoot. Under their protection were the Gros Ventre (Atsina), a division of Arapaho, and a small tribe of foreigners, the Sarsi of the Athapascan Family. The Blackfoot first came to notice about 1750, when contact was made with them by white fur traders. Even at that time they were well supplied with horses, and one of the first white men to write about them from firsthand information says that the chief of one tribe rode a white mule. When first observed, they were without guns and other European goods, but within twenty years they were well armed, had begun to expand in power, to raid the surrounding Indians and otherwise to terrorize all on their borders. They were a grassland people, ranging just east of the foothills of the Rocky Mountains in a region well supplied with buffalo and favorable to raising horses. Visitors to Glacier Park have a chance to look out upon the South

Piegan reservation, a part of their ancient home. Like other buffalo-hunting Indians they lived in skin-covered tipis (tepees), dressed in buffalo and deer skins, made no attempt to cultivate food plants and owned many horses. Several books have been written about them, and Arthur Nevins composed an opera based upon their mythology.

The Blackfoot tribes held a large body of land. Turning to a map of Canada and the United States showing the Rocky Mountains, and taking them as the western boundary to the Blackfoot country, draw a line east through Edmonton to Battleford, thence due south to the Missouri in Montana, thence westward through Great Falls, Montana, and back to the Rocky Mountains, south of Glacier Park. This block of territory is about four hundred miles long and averages about three hundred and fifty miles in width, an area large enough to make three states like Pennsylvania. Here they stood with their backs to the mountains, facing eastward. They had little to fear from behind, because that bold, rugged, almost impassable mountain wall held off aggressors from the west. The Chinese had to build a wall to keep out their enemies, but the Blackfoot found a far more effective barrier, built by nature, before they arrived in their "fatherland." Streams helped to mark the northern and southern boundaries, but these were no barriers to Indians. On the east all was open grassland. Against this front and its flanks, a line a thousand miles long, pressed advancing frontiers, not, as yet, white frontiers but frontiers of predatory Indians eager for new lands, scalps and plunder. On the eastern front were their hostile Algonkin relations, the Cree, Arapaho, Atsina and Ojibway. Interspersed among them were certain members of the Siouan Family, and on the south, bold and aggressive were the Snake, Crow and other tribes of whom we shall hear later. With this picture in mind we can better appreciate the problems confronting the Blackfoot. They were in a pocket, and all depended upon their ability to hold both the front line of defense and their flanks. If adversity and hard knocks are necessary to make a people great, the Blackfoot tribes had no excuse for mediocrity.

The South Piegan held the southern and southeastern front. Here were buffalo hunters, Indians recently equipped with horses, trying to press in to scalp the Piegan hunters and to plunder their camps. It was on this front that the Piegan made their first acquaintance with horses, suffering defeat because of this new and unexpected way of fighting. They were now at a disadvantage, but not for long, because the need was great. The Piegan soon raided enemy camps, capturing enough horses to start herds of their own and to mount their fighting men. Soon they were superior not only in the number of horses but in horse tactics.

About this time Cree and Assiniboin Indians began to raid their northeastern front, armed with guns received from traders on Hudson Bay and the Great Lakes. Here was more trouble. Fortunately these gunmen from the east raided and fought on foot. So, though the Blackfoot were still using bows, arrows, lances and clubs, they made up for this deficiency in horsemanship. Anyway, they held their own, though at an increased cost in man power. Then to make matters more serious the Cree and the Assiniboin began turning their flank on the north. Now the whole line of defense was in danger, but gradually this handicap was overcome by capturing guns, trading with the enemy on occasion, just as civilized nations do, even in time of war, and, finally, inducing the strongest trading companies to build trading posts in their own country.

The first white people to visit them, little more than two hundred years ago, were impressed by their cleanliness, the businesslike way in which their large camps were handled, the discipline under which they operated and the dignity and personality of their leaders. These white travelers knew the Algonkin and other Indians directly east of the Blackfoot, so, obviously, they found a contrast here in favor of the Blackfoot. The fur traders who first did business with the Blackfoot tell us that a little later the South Piegan were the most powerful and the most interesting tribe, because they were holding the south and southwestern front, where the pressure from other Indians was continuous and most aggressive. We are not surprised that one veteran trader writes that they were the best behaved, the most honorable and, therefore, his preferred customers.

Once the Blackfoot were equipped with guns, they began to smash through the enemies' lines and to take the offensive. The Piegan even raided through the pass south of Glacier Park, to the west of the mountains, where the Indians were still poorly supplied with guns.

Two English trading corporations were permitted to set up posts in their country, and on the Missouri, in Montana, were some United States posts to which they could go, provided they went in force, because some of their most powerful enemies also traded there. But, beyond this, there was no evidence of a white menace to the Blackfoot until about 1820, when white trappers looking for beaver began to come in from the southeast. We should not forget that all but a fraction of Blackfoot territory is in Canada, where the advance of the white frontier was slower than in the United States. Since the invading trappers were from the United States and their chief Indian enemies came from the same direction, the Blackfoot attacked them at sight. They were encouraged to do this by the Canadian traders on the ground that these foreigners had no right there anyway. But the raids upon the trappers were carried far down into Montana, partly because the Blackfoot claimed that country and partly because by killing the trappers their furs could be seized, carried to Canadian posts and there exchanged for trade goods. This was a more exciting way to get furs than to spend the winter in trapping. In time this looting of trappers became a business rather than a matter of defense, but so powerful were these Indians that they succeeded in keeping white men out of their country for a long time. As just noted, the impenetrable mountains were behind them, and the advancing white frontier in the United States flowed past them on the south; they were not in its line of march.

The Blackfoot seem to have been at the height of their power about 1830, travelers and fur traders estimating their population at ten to eighteen thousand souls. They still defied their Indian enemies and kept the white trappers from breaking in. But though the white frontiers were not pressing upon them, they were soon to feel the power of this new enemy. In 1836 smallpox, the dreaded white man's disease, swept through the tribes on their eastern border; the reports state that many camps lost more than three fourths of their number. Within a few months raiding parties of Blackfoot had carried the scourge home with them; about half their population died.

Again, in 1845, and once more, in 1857, the same disease swept through their camps, and now, reduced to about one third of their former strength, they were less able to resist white pressure, but as their Indian enemies suffered even more, they still carried on boldly. We hear a great deal these days about conquering populations by spreading diseases. Of course, in those days, the whites did not do it intentionally, but the Algonkin could tell how it worked if they chose, for in New England, and again in the West, smallpox made the advance of the frontier easy. It was the white man's most deadly weapon.

Discipline and wise leadership characterized the Blackfoot, and though weakened by losses from smallpox, they were about to suffer a body blow from another white man's weapon. The Canadian trading companies restricted the sale of liquor to Indians, which was a wise policy, but it encouraged illicit trade from the United States. Soon the "whisky traders," as they were called, came among the Blackfoot Indians, encouraging them to steal horses and cattle from white ranchers to trade for liquor. The chiefs opposed the procedure, knowing that in the end it would bring on war, but the younger Indians wanted liquor above all things. The traders told them not to listen to their chiefs, and in this way the whole tribal government was pulled down, prostitution and excesses of all kinds encouraged. A reservation had been set aside in northern Montana for the South Piegan and an agent appointed, but he was powerless to stop these evils. Conditions grew steadily worse until 1868, when the settlers of Montana began to enforce law and order. The difficulty lay in the proximity of the Canadian border: the "whisky traders" could operate from Canada, and Indians from that side could cross the border to steal cattle and horses and, once back across the line with their loot, were safe. As may be expected, the Piegan in Montana were blamed for everything, and, being the only Indians within reach, they suffered most. In 1869 a few soldiers fell upon a peaceful camp of South Piegan, killing men, women and children; the same sad story all over again. However, this is the only real engagement between the Piegan and United States troops. The next year smallpox came again.

The South Piegan were now completely broken, few in number, morally debased, with little social control. They surrendered completely to the United States, agreed to live under an agent and not to cross the border into Canada. The remainder of the Blackfoot became Canadian Indians, and that government now took steps to see that they stayed at home, but it was not until fifteen years later that their raids into Montana became negligible. Buffalo were still numerous in Montana, and the Piegan lived by hunting. In 1875 a new agent was appointed for the South Piegan, under whose wise guidance the power of the chiefs was restored and the tribe saved from utter ruin; but there were troubles ahead still. By 1883 the buffalo were gone and the hunters returned without meat. There was hunger everywhere, children crying for food, women wailing and men praying. In desperation they boiled old bones and the bark of trees. Death stalked through the camps, but the power of their leaders held. Eventually food reached them and conditions became normal. Those wonderful leaders pulled them through. In the years that followed, under the strain of reservation life their number declined until 1900; since which time they have been increasing, becoming more and more adapted to white ways.

The North Piegan, Blood and North Blackfoot in Canada suffered somewhat less from starvation and smallpox and are now living on reservations and gradually adjusting themselves to the ways of a white world.

Unlike the other Algonkin, the Blackfoot did not engage in formal war with the white man and so did not suffer defeat in that sense, but disease and vice came instead to carry away their population and to destroy their power. The end was the same. Unlike the Algonkin of the Delaware and the Shawnee, they could not retreat before the advancing frontier but, like their relatives in New England, were forced to stand and take the consequences, in this case not to meet with extermination but to fall victims to a train of tragic circumstances almost as deadly.

The Arapaho and the Cheyenne

The Arapaho now live on reservations in Oklahoma and Wyoming. Their nearest relatives are the Atsina in Montana. The Atsina were called "big bellies" in frontier days, not necessarily because they developed prominent abdomens but because they lived upon Big Belly River, now known as the South Saskatchewan. Early in the eighteenth century they seem to have been numerous and to have held the plains country along the river from which they took their name, but sometime before 1800 smallpox carried away about three fourths of them, whence the Assiniboin and other non-Algonkin tribes raided them until they took refuge with the powerful Blackfoot. According to tradition, the Atsina were one of a number of closely related tribes of which they and the Arapaho alone survive. These tribes once held the buffalo country southward from the Saskatchewan. When white men came into the country, they found the Arapaho around the Black Hills in South Dakota, the Atsina with the Blackfoot in Canada.

Historians believe the Cheyenne moved from Minnesota

to the Sheyenne River, which one may find upon a map of North Dakota, a stream which flows east into the Red River of the North. From here they moved southwest to the Missouri River; according to their belief, about 1675. For a time they planted corn, beans and squashes, as they had done in their old home; but buffalo were plenty, and then came horses, making it still easier to hunt, with the result that soon after 1800 they became true Plains Indians. They made friends of the Arapaho, with whom they were intermittently allied.

These two Algonkin tribes performed the famous Sun Dance in what seems to be its most complete form, so if they did not originate the ceremony they are, at least, the people who gave it the most conspicuous stage setting. In many other respects they are the elite of the horse Indians, especially in all that has to do with ceremonies. The Cheyenne treasured a sacred bundle in which were, among other things, a kind of hat, made of skin and hair from the head of a buffalo cow, and four arrows, two for hunting and two for war. These objects and the rituals connected with them were their holiest relics, and in times of danger the tribe went forth to battle bearing them. Once, so we are told, they marched against the Pawnee but were defeated and the arrows captured. However, the keeper of the bundle made new arrows to replace them. There is nothing strange about this, because the ritual required that every now and then the arrows be newly feathered and the stone points reset. The details of these arrows and their significance can be found in books dealing with the history of the Cheyenne.

The Arapaho possessed something of the same import though less spectacular, probably because not directly connected with war. The chief object venerated was a large pipe, kept in a bundle, never opened except with elaborate ceremonies and looked upon as little less than a god, or better, the object which assured the presence of the powers that hold the fates of human beings in their hands. It is a curious pipe, reminding one of a gigantic cigarette holder. The tobacco is loaded in the end, just as if one should fill the end of a cigarette holder and smoke it like a pipe. Such tubular pipes were sometimes used by the Cheyenne for ordinary smoking but were much smaller than the Arapaho sacred pipe, which with its stem was almost as long as a man's arm. Another object kept in a bundle and held in almost equal reverence was a hoop or wheel. The attitude of the Arapaho toward all important matters impresses observers as even more devout than that of most Indians. They extended symbolic thinking to many everyday acts; for example, when a woman did some beadwork or painted a skin bag to beautify it, the designs she used were given names suggesting hidden meanings and sometimes ideas of deep religious import. Cheyenne women were even more artistic than the Arapaho but did not take the designs they used so seriously. Their beadwork is less known among white people than that of the Arapaho, probably because the mystery of design meanings fascinates students of contemporary art. Moreover, the designs used by many Indian tribes, aside from their artistic merit, appeal to us because of their originality and boldness in the choice of colors. We are always moved to wonder how these Indians came by such unusual designs, and when we find a tribe reading meanings into them, welcome the information as probably explaining the origin of this unique art. Yet there is no reason to believe that the Arapaho originated this art, and since other Indians use many of the same designs without such "hidden meanings," we suspect that when the Arapaho went out of the forest into the grass country they copied their designs from their non-Algonkin neighbors, but being a highly mystical and religious people, took it for granted that these intriguing designs meant something and so read their own feelings and beliefs into them. Nevertheless, they deserve credit for enriching this borrowed art and making something more than an idle pastime of it. Perhaps, if we could see the world as an Arapaho saw it, we would pronounce their beadwork and painting upon skins one of the great fine arts.

The history of the Arapaho and the Cheyenne repeats

in part the old formula. The advancing white frontier did
not press upon them until after 1840, when they were
ranging in southeastern Wyoming and eastern Colorado.
The gold rush to California in 1849 brought fleets of ox
wagons across their country, their first great alarm, a
warning of what was to follow. Like most Indians the
Arapaho were still raiding their aboriginal neighbors, but
were rather peacefully inclined toward the whites, though
some individual tribe members for the love of adventure
joined other tribes in conflicts with the whites.

The Cheyenne seem to have been more aggressive, not
only against other tribes but in opposing the advance of
the frontier. Historians tell us that they were active in
raiding white settlements, joined in most of the Indian
wars of the plains country and lost more warriors in these
enterprises than any other tribe.

The first serious break came in 1864 when, after individual Southern Cheyenne had made petty raids upon
travelers and settlements, a detachment of the United
States Army surprised their camp near Chivington on
Sand Creek, a branch of the Arkansas River. The soldiers
were given instructions to take no prisoners of any age or
sex; so we need not be surprised that, of the one hundred
and fifty killed, about two thirds were women and children. Over a hundred were scalped and mutilated by the
soldiers and the scalps exhibited in a theater in Denver.
However, the nation at large disapproved of this brutality,
and Congress authorized an investigation. Naturally the
Cheyenne were aroused and, supported by some Arapaho
and others, began to raid and kill on a wide front. We pass
over the minor engagements, merely noting that in 1868
came the crushing defeat usual in Indian wars, when
General Custer attacked a large camp on the Washita in
Oklahoma, the Indians losing about a hundred men and a
large number of women and children, though there were
few atrocities this time. Some skirmishes followed, but at
last the Southern Cheyenne yielded to the inevitable and
settled down on a reservation. They had lost most of their
horses, many tents and much personal property, not to

mention many lives. They were fairly peaceful until 1874, when all the Indians in the southern part of the Plains began to feel the pinch of encroaching settlements and observed increasing violations of their treaties with the government. A Comanche leader, a new prophet as it were, began to preach an uprising. The Southern Cheyenne were easily drawn into this conspiracy.

The chief concern of the Indians at this time was the depletion of the buffalo, because professional white hunters were killing them for their skins. The Indians were intelligent enough to see that the end was in sight, and no people of fighting traditions will take a threat of starvation lying down. However, by this time the military strength of the United States was far superior to that of earlier days. Breech-loading rifles, Gatling guns and light artillery were on hand. The Indians began with an attack on a trading camp in northern Texas at a place known as Adobe Walls, but were beaten off. This brought out the military; shortly thereafter the main camps of the Southern Cheyenne, together with those of the Kiowa and Comanche, were attacked by Colonel Mackenzie. Most of the Cheyenne escaped, but they lost their horses and personal property.

We shall not follow further events of this war, since its story falls more appropriately under the head of the Siouan Family. All we need say is that the Cheyenne shared the fate of all and now live on two reservations, one in Montana, the other in Oklahoma.

1. RECONSTRUCTION OF PUEBLO BONITO, NEW MEXICO — A building of the prehistoric period in which the highest level in such architecture was reached. *Morgan, 1881.*

2. EASTERN ALGONKIN INDIANS—
These Indians lived in shelters
of bark, usually dome-shaped;
their canoes were either dugouts or were made of birchbark; though primarily hunters,
they raised corn and beans;
they had not learned to weave
cloth but wove bags, mats, and
baskets; they made some black
pottery. Though they had summer and winter villages and
often changed the locations of
these, they could hardly be
called nomadic.
Painted by A. A. Jansson.

3. DRIVING BUFFALO INTO A POUND – Drawn from observation among the Cree Indians of Saskatchewan about 1860. *Hind Expedition.*

4. THE SALMON FISHERS —The subject is a reconstruction to show the old method of salmon fishing among the Indians of the Alaskan coast. They built a dam of logs to form a pool in which the migrating salmon were entrapped and speared. *Painted by Will S. Taylor.*

Chapter X

THE NORTHERN AND WESTERN ALGONKIN

If the reader turns once more to a map of eastern Canada, he will note an unsettled stretch of country extending from northern Manitoba on the west to Newfoundland on the east, and up into Labrador. Most of this is still a forest and was and is the home of the northernmost Algonkin, the Cree in the west, the Naskapi in the east. Near Ottawa, the French met the original Algonkin, or those from whom the name was derived. The name was soon extended to include some eighteen to twenty-two divisions ranging eastward toward Nova Scotia. Included in these were the Ottawa, who later settled in Michigan, where they participated in the wars of the frontier. When Champlain came, these Algonkin were harassed by the Iroquois, then pushing northeastward and down the St. Lawrence. In their distress the Algonkin turned to the French, who gave them some help, just enough to save them from annihilation. We suppose that most Indians were ruthless, but it is certain that the Iroquois were; they would have exterminated all these Algonkin if they could. The coming of the French probably saved them from complete extinction and immortalized them by giving their name to one of America's greatest Indian families.

The Naskapi

Far up in Labrador live the Naskapi. No white man seems to want to live in their country, so they cannot claim to be martyrs to white expansion. They have taken from the white man many of the conveniences of civilization, as guns, kettles, steel tools, traps, cloth—and liquor, when they can get it; but, for the most part, they have been free to work out their own social problems. In museum exhibits they are distinguished by long skin coats upon which are painted original designs in red. The effect is pleasing and impresses the artistic as of more than usual merit. Yet, in spite of it all, if the reader asks what these Naskapi achieved with all their freedom, we fear the answer is, not much.

Occasionally they guide a few white hunters through their country, otherwise, their life is hard; many of them die young, but the tribe has survived by solving the problem of existing in a harsh environment. Possibly they are as happy as most of us. Formerly their enemies were the Eskimo on the north and the much more formidable Iroquois on the south who raided them merely for the sake of killing. Even now some of them look toward the south with apprehension, lest the Iroquois of tradition return to murder their women and children and take away their scalps.

The Tribes of the Great Lakes

A group of Algonkin tribes clustered around the Great Lakes, especially Lakes Huron, Michigan and Superior. Lake Superior almost connects with a series of small lakes and rivers culminating in Lake Winnipeg, which drains into Hudson Bay. With a large map before one, the intricacies of these waterways become impressive; with their light birchbark canoes the Algonkin of the lakes could, by means of a portage or two, paddle from Detroit into Hudson Bay. Near where Chicago now is, a short carry would enable them to launch their canoes in the headwaters of the Illinois and descend to the mouth of the Mississippi. It is not strange, then, that the Algonkin held most of the lands around the lakes and, in recent times, showed a tendency to expand westward. The important peoples of the lakes are the Ojibway, or Chippewa (the same people, but the Indian pronunciation falls somewhere between the two English words), the Potawatomi, the Menomini, Sauk and Fox, and Cree. The Chippewa north of the lakes, near Sault Sainte Marie, are usually called the Saulteaux, and they with the Cree occupied the country on that side, while the Chippewa, Potawatomi, the Menomini, Sauk and Fox ranged on the south. Henry Wadsworth Longfellow's legends of Hiawatha are tales of the Chippewa, not the Iroquois, as he supposed; Longfellow followed the ethnologist Schoolcraft, who mistakenly equated the Chippewa and Iroquois heroes of somewhat similar names.

Turning to the map again, the reader may note how the lakes form two pockets or dead ends in the land. Thus Michigan proper is hemmed in by Lakes Huron and Michigan. Here the Potawatomi and the Chippewa, by holding off the Indians to the south, were safe enough, except for quarrels among themselves. On the west, a triangle between Lakes Superior and Michigan is suitable for a similar stand. Further, Green Bay offers smaller secondary triangles easy to defend. Here several powerful tribes made their home. The Menomini held the Green Bay country for ages and still reside nearby on a reservation. The Sauk and Fox and later the Potawatomi formed the outer defense, for facing them on the west were formidable antagonists belonging to the Siouan Family, as much dreaded in the West as were the Iroquois in the East.

The lake country was heavily forested with birch and coniferous trees, whereas the Ohio Valley, Pennsylvania, New York and New England were covered with deciduous beech, oak, elm, chestnut, etc. Associated with these distinctions in trees were many other environmental differences which, in turn, were responsible for culture differences between the several tribes residing therein. For one thing the coniferous country was not favorable to the raising of corn, so the Algonkin of the lakes depended upon wild plant foods. However, nature compensated for this by furnishing wild rice, a semiaquatic plant growing in the margins of lakes and in the backwaters of rivers. The colonists called it wild oats, or wild wheat, because at that time Europe was ignorant of rice. Wild rice prepared in the Indian way is now one of our luxury foods, increasing in popularity from year to year. Among the Indians of the lakes it was a satisfactory substitute for corn. Though growing wild, the guarding of the crop, gathering it in canoes and the subsequent hulling, drying and smoking rendered its production about as arduous as in the case of corn. The women did most of the work. Incidentally we note that to prevent the rice heads from being carried away by birds, the stalks were tied in bunches with the ever-ready basswood fiber twine which we cited as characteristic of the Algonkin Family. So, in the cabins of the wild-rice-using Algonkin, women and girls spent their time twisting string and twine and the young males took practical note of the industry and skill of the girls, appraising their relative values as future wives.

The use of birchbark is another striking specialty of these Indians, particularly those north of the lakes, for aside from canoes it is used for covering houses, for containers or for substitutes for baskets and earthenware and occasionally for paper upon which to inscribe messages in picture writing. Some pottery was made by the tribes south of the lakes, but in the north boiling was done in birchbark vessels, often hung over the fire but not touching it. Fish and waterfowl formed a considerable part of the diet but were secondary to deer and moose. Maple sugar was manufactured in season. The winters were long and the snow often deep, so naturally snowshoes were in use.

A famous secret society known as the Midéwin flourished south of the lakes, especially among the Ojibway, Menomini and Potawatomi, who are often spoken of as the typical Algonkin. We do not know whether they are the direct descendants of the original Algonkin, but it is certain that on the south side of the lakes the culture of the Algonkin seems to offer a richer emotional life, such as the rituals of the Midéwin and various sacred bundles. Another unique innovation was the so-called "juggler's lodge," a framework of sticks large enough to conceal a man, covered with bark or skins. Numerous objects were placed inside. Then the magician, usually called a shaman by anthropologists, was securely bound by a cord and placed in the lodge, out of sight. After a time, strange noises were heard, the objects within flew out at the top, the magician was heard conversing with the spirits. The listeners might now ask questions, which the magician repeated to his guardian spirits and to which answers might be given. When the lodge was lifted away, the magician was usually found tied up again. Such procedures are familiar to those of our readers who may attend spiritualistic cabinet demonstrations. Among the Algonkin this procedure seems to be prehistoric; perhaps our own magicians learned it from them.

The Cree and the Ojibway rarely fought the whites, not because they were less warlike than other tribes but chiefly because there were no extensive settlements in their country; even now a great deal of it is forest and unfrequented watercourses. The Ojibway sometimes joined the French against the English, but after the French and Indian War enjoyed a peaceful career, except when at war with the Siouan Family. Late in 1600 the fur traders at Hudson Bay and on the St. Lawrence began fitting out the Cree and Ojibway with guns and ammunition, whence some of them began to raid westward to Lake Winnipeg; before many years their advance parties harassed the plains country through southern Canada and along the United States boundary, even out into the Rocky Mountains. About this time horses reached the northern plains, so some of the most adventurous Cree and Ojibway took to horses and hunted buffalo in the open plains, eventually giving up many of their old customs for those of the foreigners of the plains. These adventurous Algonkin are known as the Plains Cree and the Plains Ojibway.

The West Coast Peoples

Two small tribes on the Pacific coast in northern California claim our attention. These are the Yurok and the Wiyot, sometimes linguistically grouped as the Ritwan. How they reached their West Coast home no one knows; but it must have been a long time ago, since their speech is very divergent and they live like Californians rather than like any other Algonkin tribe known to history. Their villages front the ocean or rivers; they use dugout canoes and do a moderate amount of fishing. Their houses are of split planks and though not so large or handsome as those further north, are on the same general plan. In general they live like other northern California tribes. The values which guide their lives—especially the Yurok—reflect our own to a degree which may surprise the student of other cultures. Although differently enforced, legal principles and ethics include much that is familiar to every American. The Yurok family and pattern of relationships among relatives is similar to that of many Americans, unlike other Indian families, which may include a larger number of relatives, or which may be organized into larger groups, such as clans.

The history of these peoples is both intriguing and mystifying. Their traditions give no hint of relatives in the East; that relationship was discovered by scholars interested in their speech. Like all peoples living in a self-contained group, they think of themselves as the most important and superior tribe; nor do the two tribes recognize any relationship between themselves, except that they are neighbors. Probably they will always remain a mystery. For all we know, they may be the stay-at-homes, living near the cradleland of the Algonkin Family; but a more reasonable guess is that they wandered into a far country and forsook the ways of their Algonkin forefathers.

Possible Relatives

Finally, some students of language look upon the Kutenai, Wakashan (Nootka and Kwakiutl tribes) and Salish as once belonging on the Algonkin Family tree but now going it alone, as it were. Of these the Kutenai language was long thought to be unrelated to any other and the people were noted for their strange tongue. Reference to a map will show how these neighboring groups of tribes form a block in southern British Columbia and northern Washington, articulating with the Algonkin Blackfoot on the east and reaching westward to the Pacific Ocean. Thus the Algonkin and their relatives hold a broad band of territory from Nova Scotia on the east to Puget Sound on the west.

The Nootka, one of the Wakashan tribes, live on the west coast of Vancouver Island and nearby parts of Washington. They were visited often in the eighteenth and nineteenth centuries by explorers and traders to the Northwest Coast, Captain Cook being notable among them. The Nootka were whale hunters, who set out after their quarry in long, fire-hollowed boats. These people frequently raided neighboring tribes, not only for plunder, but for slaves, and the slave trade in this area was very active.

Their neighbors, among them the Kwakiutl, shared many characteristics. Their houses of split planks were large and elaborate; before them stood tall, elaborately carved totem poles. These, representing the clans from which a family was descended, can still be seen in parts of Washington and British Columbia. Perhaps the most famous custom is the *potlatch*, from a Nootka word meaning "giving." This ceremonial feast was given on any important occasion—when a son or daughter came of age, or as a memorial to a deceased family member, or to save face from a social blunder. Gifts of blankets, furs, copper plates, shells and the like were distributed—as many as the host could afford. Much of this wealth was destroyed, and sometimes a slave was killed, in part to show the utter contempt of the host for worldly goods and human life, and in large part to indicate the greatness of the clan chief who could afford such devastation. The potlatch was in effect an expensive competition. It is an extreme form, perhaps, of "conspicuous consumption," or "keeping up with the Joneses," practices common in the United States today.

The older books on Indians speak of the Salish as a separate family; the newer ones admit this but insist that they are an offshoot from the Algonkin stem. They are usually divided into two groups, the Coast Salish and the Interior Salish. Each group includes a number of different tribes, speaking related dialects or languages. Coast Salish tribes which are well known include the Chehalis, Nisqualli, Cowlitz, Squamish, Comox, Tillamook and Bella Coola, among others. Their home was along the coast and rivers of northwestern Washington and adjacent British Columbia. How long these peoples have held this country no one knows. Archaeologists think they have been here for ages, judging by the extensive shell heaps around Puget Sound and along some of the inland rivers, which when dug into show a long, continuous occupation by the same people. The Salish were once numerous, and were classified under more than seventy dialectic groups. At the time of discovery there were several hundred villages. This has been considered by some the most densely populated area of aboriginal North America. It was fine country for Indians, and many clustered around Puget Sound, which has proved a favorable locality for white people too. Inland, the country was cut up by mountain ranges interspersed with beautiful valleys; for the most part, a well-watered forest area, except for open country around the upper Columbia River.

The Interior Salish occupied this country, as well as British Columbia and Washington, and the adjacent parts of Idaho and Montana. Well-known tribes include the

Flathead (sometimes simply called Salish), Coeur d'Alêne, Kalispel, Spokan, Okinagan and Pend d'Oreilles.

The Flathead were the farthest east, occupying the Bitterroot country of western Montana, but they made annual excursions eastward through the main range of the Rocky Mountains to kill bison. At such times they lived in tepees in an organized camp, like the other Plains tribes. The Blackfoot and the Crow were their chief enemies, for it was into their country that the Flathead went to kill bison. Obviously they were brave and warlike to venture out into the plains and to hold their own when there. They claim to have surprised a Blackfoot war party early in 1800, killing every one of them. For a time this gave them reasonable security while in the bison country.

The Salish tribes in Washington enjoyed many advantages. Deer were plentiful, edible roots were at hand, and salmon ran up the rivers frequently. So fish and roots may be taken as the economic base to Salish culture. The salmon live in the sea but, at intervals, crowd into the rivers, ascending even the small creeks, to lay eggs, the young returning to the sea to complete the life cycle. The best time for fishing is when the mature salmon ascend the rivers, for then they can be scooped out with nets, speared or trapped. When a run is on, the whole tribe is busy. Naturally so many fish cannot be consumed at once, so they are cleaned and hung upon poles to dry. Such stores of dried fish guaranteed a dependable food reserve, so the Salish enjoyed a high degree of economic security.

Algonkin Characteristics

So we take leave of the First Great Indian Family in our history, a wide-flung people, in the main, dwellers in the forests and upon the shores of rivers and lakes. They were the first to welcome the European traders, to encourage settlement and, naturally, the first to fall before the deadly firearms of the white man. In the southern half of their domain the frontier advanced steadily, but they gathered

strength as they retreated, often reddening the night sky
with burning cabins, startling their victims with war
whoops and carrying away their scalps to be danced over
by their women at home. Here and there they made valiant
stands, occasionally defeating armies sent against them but
more often suffering defeat themselves; continually pushed
back, their few surviving remnants to be rounded up ultimately in Oklahoma. They number but a fraction of
their former population, yet still hold onto their old traditions and derive what satisfaction they can from their past
glories. The names of their great men will live in history
even after their tribes become but a name. Monuments
have been erected for many of them. Now marking the
sites of their great military struggles are parks and memorial columns which, more often than otherwise, com-
memorate the victories of the whites, yet inadvertently
honor the Algonkin warriors who fought there. Uniformed
guides explain to the visitors who the Indian participants
were, the names of their leaders and the course of the
battle, as the case may require. Their passing was inevitable, but they deserve these monuments in recognition
of the truth that, within their limitations, they put up a
good fight.

The Algonkin of the lakes and the northern woods were
not forced to the wall, and so there are many survivors;
some even now live much as did their forefathers. Their
struggles were with Nature rather than with the white
man, so they rarely get even a footnote in the pages of
history, and their great men and women passed unheralded to the grave. This is the price they pay for survival.

Since the Algonkin east of the Mississippi are the Indians of American history, we should fix their peculiarities
in our minds. They were a woodland people. In the ag-
gregate their type of life can be comprehended under such
key words as tomahawk, warpath, scalp, maize, maple
sugar, hoe, birchbark canoe, snowshoe, tumpline, toboggan, wampum, moccasion, wigwam, squaw, sachem, sagamore, bury the hatchet, pipe of peace, powwow, totem.
If you understand something of what these words mean

you begin to comprehend what the life of an Algonkin was like.

These Indians believed in a great all-pervading power which we know under the name Manitou. They believed that this power made over the world as we see it today and that it ordered all the events and tragedies as have happened and will happen. They were masters of the art of tanning deerskins, taught the white man woodcraft, yet made indifferent pottery, knew nothing of iron and almost as little of copper, their textile arts were simple, but they could spin good strong cord from the fibers of the nettle and other common weeds, not to overlook the cord they made from the bark of the linn tree. Yet, they wove nothing but bags and belts, soft tanned skins being made into clothing. Hunting was the economic base of their existence and power, just as industry and trade are for our own civilization. They raised some maize and vegetables, but this was woman's work, such as she could do when free from her housekeeping duties; at no time did they depend upon agriculture as their main support.

Quite different was it with the Algonkin of the western plains. They were buffalo hunters, used tepees, dressed like other Plains Indians, used horses after 1700, acquired firearms before the end of that century, abandoned all agriculture and most traits of the Woodland Algonkin, if they ever had them, and have little ground for a claim to a place on the family tree, except in the vague resemblance of their speech to Algonkin standards—and it takes an expert to detect these resemblances. None of them have traditions of living east of the Mississippi, nor think of themselves as other than Plains Indians.

The Arapaho had a reputation for ceremonialism and so remind one of the Pawnee, but their ceremonialism was of a different kind, not grandiose and poetic but meticulously detailed in routine. They specialized in the Sun Dance, with a torture feature like the Dakota. On the other hand they took delight in symbolic interpretations for common objects, even for the designs executed in beadwork.

The Cheyenne were taller than the Arapaho, resembled the Dakota and were equally warlike. They, too, were Plains people, living in tepees and using dog travois. They were horsemen and put up a strong fight for their liberties. They were less ritualistic than the Arapaho and more realistically minded. Their sacred arrow bundle, carried to battle like the Ark of the Covenant, was the most distinctive characteristic in the minds of the other Indians.

The Blackfoot were the strongest in man power and most aggressive on their own frontiers. Their distinction lay in an elaborate organization of the privileged into a series of graded societies and an unusual development of the bundle-ceremonial-ritual idea, to the end that almost every man owned some kind of a bundle. A system of transfer had been evolved according to which bundles and rituals could be passed on to another person in return for gifts of property in horses, clothing, etc. There were a few large bundles which, when transferred, called for several thousand dollars' worth of property.

We have also glimpsed the life on the Northwest Coast, home of still other Algonkin relatives. Here the livelihood depended upon the produce of the sea, which was plentiful. The ease of seacoast subsistence left time for other pursuits, such as the elaborate carvings and extensive preparations for potlatch feasts.

As a fit closing to this summary we remind the reader that the Algonkin were a religious people, though all Indians were religious. The Algonkin looked upon the landscape as a stage where the gods walked in person, though usually unseen by man. He felt their presence when he walked abroad; at home he heard them in the wind and the distant rumble of the thunder. He made frequent prayers. Smoking a pipe was in the nature of a religious ritual, and even when given a glass of liquor he frequently offered a drop to the heavens, the four winds and the earth, in reality a prayer to all the important gods. There were prayers when he set out to hunt, and again when the game was killed. If his way of life called for the planting of corn, there were numerous prayers and offerings at every stage of the cultivation cycle. The woman seeking clay for pottery usually prayed to Mother Earth for permission to remove the precious clay. Even the colored earths for paint could not be taken up lightly; one must always approach the digging place in a humble and reverent manner. Frivolity and trifling must have no place in such functions. The dignity and sincerity with which an old Indian could approach what for us are the most ordinary situations in daily life can scarcely be exaggerated.

As we have said, pipes of tobacco were smoked in most ceremonies. Incense of various kinds was frequently burned near the fireplace, and objects and persons bathed in the smoke to purify them for ceremonial use. The sweat bath was another common way of purifying the body and preceded every important ritual. Food, ornaments and clothing were frequently sacrificed as offerings to the gods. After trade goods were obtainable, a piece of fine cloth might be tied to the branch of a tree as a prayer offering. Where trees were scarce, prayer offerings were placed on rocks, at springs or the foot of cliffs. Occasionally vows were made to inflict self-torture, bits of skin might be offered to the gods, and now and then a finger was chopped off. It is not far from the truth to say that religious observances accompanied the Indian even in his sleep, for dreams were interpreted as communications with the unseen.

Northern Tribes

Six Nations
  Seneca
    (Cornplanter, Red Jacket)
  Cayuga
  Onondaga
  Oneida
  Mohawk (Joseph Brant)
  Tuscarora (after 1715)

Southern Tribes

Cherokee
Tuscarora (before 1715)

Independents

Huron, or Wyandot
Erie
Susquehanna, or Conestoga
Neutrals

Chapter XI

THE IROQUOIS FAMILY

A PAWNEE Indian, now long dead, told the writer that in the remote past the Iroquois and the Pawnee were neighbors and friends. Further, there was a tradition that once, in a great council with the whites, an Iroquois orator urged that all the rights and privileges reserved by the Iroquois should be shared by their brothers, the Pawnee. We do not know how true this may be, but anthropologists now say that the Iroquois and the Pawnee once lived as neighbors near the Lower Mississippi, and those who find joy in the study of Indian languages say that the speech of these two peoples has something in common, though the languages appear to belong to separate families.

The name Iroquois usually applies to the six tribes in New York State: the Seneca, Cayuga, Onondaga, Oneida, Mohawk and Tuscarora. Yet their neighbors, the Huron, Erie, Neutrals and Susquehanna, not to mention some five or six other less-known tribes, spoke languages of the Iroquoian Family. But that is not all, for down in the lower Appalachians were the powerful Cherokee, consisting of three or more divisions. All these together made up the Iroquoian Family. Their territory was far less in extent than that of the Algonkin, and possibly they came upon the scene much later, but they commanded respect, especially the Six Nations in New York and the Cherokee in the South. Even a few years ago the Algonkin of the Far North were still praying to their supernaturals to spare them from the fury of the terrible Iroquois. Apparently, a long time ago, the original nucleus of the family crossed the Mississippi and seized the lower Appalachians. They must have begun to expand in number so that new tribes were formed, pushing northward along the highlands, through

Pennsylvania and into Canada. This was Algonkin country, but the Iroquois were ruthless invaders, spreading death and destruction wherever they went. They were farmers as well as hunters—that is, their women tended truck patches in which corn, beans and squashes were grown. All this and more they brought with them from the southland. Probably from the Algonkin whom they hated, they learned to make sugar from the sap of the maple tree. Some of the first French visitors to the Iroquois were served popcorn over which hot maple syrup was poured. One of the party wrote letters to friends in France, praising this new food and advocating its introduction into the home country—"snow-food," he called it; we now call it crackerjack, which is a better term because it means superfine and democratic.

The most adventurous Iroquois moved into New York State—the advance guard, as it were. Settled in the Mohawk Valley, they began to increase and to prosper. They fortified their villages with stockades; some of the first white visitors called these castles. Though of the same family, they were habitual fighters and so fell upon each other as soon as the Algonkin were cleared from the region. According to tradition, the valley of the Mohawk and the country of the Finger Lakes in New York was then a scene of murder and arson instead of peace.

The League of the Six Nations

Conditions were sufficiently deplorable to call forth a reformer, known to history as Hiawatha. He probably lived late in 1400 or early in 1500. According to tradition, he went up and down the Mohawk Valley, preaching a new order of brotherly feeling between the tribes, not necessarily peace for all men, but rather a union of relatives for defense and offense. He must have been something of a fanatic to keep so everlastingly at it. At first everyone was hostile. The traditions of Indian life had always been for absolute freedom of action, and each community was jealous of this right. Aboriginal United States was a land of ultrademocracy, every small group functioning for itself. The Indian was a lover of freedom, but he used that freedom to plunder and kill his neighbor if he could. So each Iroquois tribe hesitated to bind itself to a majority vote; the idea of a confederacy did not appeal to them.

Apparently, Hiawatha was so persistent that his own tribe banished him, so he went to live with another. They were more tolerant, finally agreeing to come into the proposed federation if others would. Eventually five tribes agreed—Mohawk, Seneca, Cayuga, Onondaga and Oneida. The scheme Hiawatha devised was admirable; it was an unwritten constitution authorizing the election of a representative body and formulating rules for calling it into session. The vote was by tribes. If war was to be declared, the vote must be unanimous. Disputes between tribes were to be arbitrated and not settled by violence. This unwritten constitution was admired by colonial statesmen because it gave each tribe almost complete independence but at the same time bound it to respect the wishes of others. This is why the white people spoke of these tribes as the Five Nations, recognizing that they were independent, but nevertheless were in a league for defense and offense. Later, as we shall see, the Tuscarora entered into the confederacy upon the same terms, thus changing the designation to the Six Nations.

The change from the designation Five Nations to Six Nations, about the year 1715, is confusing to readers of Iroquoian history, because before that time we should speak of them as the Five Nations, and afterward as the Six Nations. When the original five tribes formed the league their geographical position was in a line from west to east, as Seneca, Cayuga, Onondaga, Oneida, Mohawk. The Mohawk were between Utica and Albany, the Seneca were west of Seneca Lake. The league symbolized them as living in one long house with a door at each end, and so they spoke of the Seneca as the guardians of the western door and of the Mohawk as the guardians of the eastern door and also as the receivers of tribute. The Onondaga in the middle were spoken of as the keepers of the council fire, also as keepers of the wampum because they kept the wampum belts which recorded treaties. The main Onondaga village was the capital or seat of government where all official meetings of the league were held. When the Tuscarora moved up from the South they were given a nominal place in the council, but did not vote, being represented by the Oneida. The number of official delegates varied for the different tribes, but the votes were cast by tribes, one vote for each.

Hiawatha is considered the author and initiator of this now-famous league. After his death, as the power of the Five Nations grew, his fame grew with it, until he was believed a supernatural rather than a natural man. Later the white people were disposed to look upon him as little short of an Indian god and, in turn, Longfellow chose the name for the chief character in his beautiful poem, intended by him as a work of fiction, a kind of historical novel in verse. This masterpiece of literary art immortalized Hiawatha, although as we have seen, the tales were Chippewa.

In reality the famous league was a peaceful union for the Six Nations only; for their neighbors it meant war, and war characterized by frightfulness, the object of which was power and glory and, to a less degree, profit. Nevertheless, students of politics and government have found much to admire in the working of the league. There is some historical evidence that knowledge of the league influenced the colonies in their first efforts to form a confederacy and later to write a constitution.

Anyway, it appears that about 1744 Connecticut and Pennsylvania negotiated with certain Indians to adjust land claims, during which proceedings an Oneida chief suggested to the colonial delegates that since the league had worked so well with the Iroquois, something similar be set up to govern the relations of the colonies. There is some evidence to indicate that at another conference in Albany, in 1775, an Iroquois speaker made a similar suggestion.

The Huron

Lake Huron derives its name from another once powerful group of Iroquois-speaking tribes. They seem to have had some kind of a league of their own. When the celebrated Frenchman Cartier explored (1534–41) the St. Lawrence River, he found these Huron strung along that river to its mouth, but their homeland was in Ontario between Lakes Huron and Erie. During the next century, as the French began to settle along the river, they found the Huron had withdrawn to their homeland and were at war with the Five Nations. In 1615 they were reported as a powerful people composed of at least eighteen towns, all fortified. They were great agriculturalists, according to Indian standards, and especially famous for their tobacco. In fact, they were often called "the Tobacco Nation."

So the scene opens in 1615, with French observers upon the ground to record the trend of events. The Five Nations in New York had become arrogant and proud. They brooked no rivalry, not even among their relatives, but, for a time, the Huron were able to hold their territory and to strike back. The Five Nations were subjugating Algonkin tribes, requiring them to furnish fighting men, thus steadily increasing their man power. Their leaders could now afford to sacrifice men to gain a victory. Then Dutch traders came up the Hudson with firearms and ammunition. By 1643 the Five Nations were well equipped, one observer of the time writing that they could muster over four hundred musketeers. The Huron were too far away from the French traders to get many guns, so they were forced to fight with bows and arrows. The Five Nations now planned to destroy the Huron. It was not to be a war of subjugation; they hated the Huron intensely, like brother against brother. After taking the first town, they massacred its entire population, and so one town after the other had the same fate. If they took captives, it was to torture them to death. The French observers were horrified, but could do nothing to stop the hostilities. By 1649 the deed was done. It is believed that more than ten thousand Huron were killed. Those who fled into Michigan and elsewhere were ruthlessly hunted down for almost a century. To hear of a Huron was to thirst for his blood. Some of them escaped to the headwaters of Lake Michigan but were soon forced to hide in what is now Wisconsin. Eventually they found protection among the Algonkin of Indiana and Michigan, who, now well armed with guns, were successfully defying the power of the Five Nations. In the meantime the French were growing strong enough to aid and encourage the Algonkin enemies of the Five Nations. Then the English seized Dutch New York and armed the Five Nations as allies against the French, but it was too late, for the Algonkin in the West, under French leadership, were able to hold them back. So on every hand there were signs that the sun of the Five Nations was setting.

The Erie

Another large group of villages belonging to the Iroquois Family lived on the south side of Lake Erie. Numerically they were about as strong as the Huron but had fared better because they refused to aid any of their relatives in their struggles with the Five Nations. They did not join the league, nor did they become subjects. The French spoke of them as the Neutral Nation. But when the Five Nations began their ruthless extermination of the Huron, the Erie were too humane to approve. Huron refugees fled to the Erie villages, in what is now Ohio, where they were given food and shelter. The universal law of Indian hospitality made any other course unthinkable. So when the Five Nations demanded that these unfortunates be given up for torture and slaughter, the Erie refused. Then the Five Nations turned upon the Erie with even greater fury and by 1656 killed or captured all but a few who secretly hid among the Algonkin or joined the fugitive Huron in the West. The job was so thoroughly done that today Erie is but a name. One wonders about this terrible hatred of the Five Nations and their desire to destroy their relatives, in contrast to their more lenient policy in subjugating Algonkin and their friendly regard for the Pawnee. But such is the record of history, supported by Indian traditions.

The country north of Lake Erie, around Detroit, in northern Ohio and western Pennsylvania was now a wilderness. Over the ashes of once populous villages the forests spread and thickets obliterated the fields where once grew maize, squashes, beans and tobacco. And so it remained until settled by whites. The Five Nations did not want the land, but their reputation was probably sufficient to keep other Indians away from it. The remnants of the Huron and possibly a few Erie who found a temporary home among the Wisconsin Algonkin came to be known as the Wyandot. The Algonkin Ottawa were in the West also, having previously, in fear of the Iroquois, left their homes on the river which bears their name. Both these fugitive tribes sought lands further west, but the Siouan tribes barred the way, people as numerous, powerful and almost as dangerous as the Five Nations. So the fugitives drifted back to Michigan and Indiana, where later the Ottawa chief, Pontiac, became their great leader. The Wyandot had been wanderers for almost a century, but at last they found a home in northern Ohio, on land then claimed by the Algonkin Delaware, Shawnee and Miami. As allies of the Algonkin, they joined the French in their wars against the English, participated in Braddock's defeat, Pontiac's wars, joined the English in the Revolution, were at Fallen Timbers, Tippecanoe, and, finally, served under Tecumseh in the War of 1812. In the border warfare with the settlers, along the Ohio and in Kentucky, the Wyandot seem to have been the most ruthless. What was left of them, after the War of 1812, lived on assigned lands in northern Ohio and nearby Michigan until 1842, when they sold their lands and moved to Kansas and later to Oklahoma, where they now number but a hundred or two. To complete the tragic story, we note that when the Huron were destroyed a few took refuge with the French at Quebec, where their descendants live in the town of Lorette.

The Susquehanna and the Tuscarora

Most readers should be familiar with the Delaware River, which separates Pennsylvania and New Jersey. Not far west is the Susquehanna, which crosses Pennsylvania to the head of Chesapeake Bay. The former is associated with the Algonkin of the same name, unwilling subjects of the Five Nations. The valley of the Susquehanna was held by members of the Iroquois Family, relatives of the Five Nations. The Susquehanna Indians were a powerful people when the whites began to occupy the Atlantic coast. Captain John Smith, of Pocahontas fame, met some of them when he explored Chesapeake Bay, and wrote enthusiastically of their stature and efficient appearance. The historians of the time tell us that by 1663 their villages were well fortified, a few of them equipped with small cannon. A few years later the Five Nations destroyed the last of the Erie and then, with the same savagery, turned upon the Susquehanna. Their first attempt on one of these forts failed, because here they faced not only firearms but artillery. The policy then pursued was that of minor raids by which the Susquehanna were slowly worn down. In consequence, their numbers were greatly reduced by the time the Quakers settled near the mouth of the river, and finally what were left of them, known as the Conestoga, became Christians, and later they were massacred by a mob of white men, their fellow Christians. Their end was no less tragic than that of the Erie.

In the Carolinas were once many villages of Iroquois speech, known to history as the Tuscarora and at one time boasting twenty-four towns. Their wars with the whites began about 1711, but after a series of defeats they found their position so precarious that they appealed to the Five

Nations for aid. This was refused at first, but eventually they were invited to join the league and reside in northern Pennsylvania and adjacent New York. Thus they left the South to become the Sixth Nation, and from this time forward history speaks of the Six Nations instead of the Five Nations.

A Quarrel with the Pawnee

The Pawnee lived west of the Mississippi River in Nebraska. They, like their "brothers" of New York State, became powerful and, though not as destructive, raided far and wide. Ultimately they extended their forays eastward to the Mississippi and beyond. When the Five Nations were near the apex of their power, they forced the Algonkin of Indiana and Michigan to pay tribute in fighting men. They even reached out into the edges of the prairie country. On the Illinois River, near the Mississippi, were villages of Algonkin, who hunted buffalo, wore painted robes like Plains Indians but were agriculturists like their neighbors on the east. These Indians, in turn, were to feel the might of the Five Nations and eventually were reduced to the level of subject tribes. The terms of the agreement specified that the Illinois were not to attack other tribes except under the direction of the Five Nations, but that if they were attacked their conquerors would give them protection. Not long after, a raiding party of Pawnee, out for plunder and scalps, left their village in Nebraska, crossed into Iowa, continued eastward across the Mississippi and fell upon one of these subject villages, scalped all they could lay hands upon and left the place a smoking ruin. The other Illinois villages were alarmed and sent a messenger to the Mohawk Valley to call for the protection they had been promised.

A large force of Iroquois was assembled quickly, marched to the Pawnee country—a distance of almost a thousand miles—destroyed a village, killed all they could lay hands upon, then called the chiefs of the other Pawnee villages together, demanding that in the future they remain west of the Mississippi; the Five Nations, on their part, would keep to the east bank.

After 1700 the power of the Five Nations began to wane, except within their own borders. Here, for the most part, there was peace. Their women extended their gardens to the size of farms, produced large crops of corn, planted orchards and prospered generally, but during the Revolution most of them fought with the British and finally raided white settlements in Pennsylvania. This was too much for Washington, who sent a small army into their country, burned their villages, destroyed their corn, cut down their orchards, then withdrew, leaving them to face the winter without food and shelter. Broken in power and spirit, they eventually became reservation Indians.

Among their great men were Joseph Brant, a fiery warrior pictured with an ever-ready tomahawk in his hand, and Red Jacket, whose fierce countenance used to stare at us from a page in our school history. Because he fought against the British in the War of 1812, we reluctantly forgave him for what he did in the Revolution. Last, but not least, was Logan, whose tragic fate moves us all and who in the depth of despair made a speech which can justly be compared with some of the world's greatest. It thrilled us when we first read it in a little red brick schoolhouse; we still admire it.

How the Six Nations Lived

The ordinary techniques of living were about the same as among the surrounding Algonkin. The women raised some maize, beans and squashes, made maple sugar in season and gathered some wild food, such as acorns, nuts and strawberries. They took over apples from the whites and so kept a few orchards. Originally they kept no domestic animals except the dog, nor did they make much use of horses, cattle, pigs and fowl after contact with the colonists. The able-bodied men hunted, the chief game being

deer. If a goodly supply of venison and small game was not
on hand, these Indians were on the verge of starvation.
However, the store of corn, beans, etc., was usually large
enough to prevent much suffering during a temporary
shortage of game. Since clothing was of skin, hunting was
the important source of supply.

Social life was characterized by a series of feasts, as the
Strawberry Festival in the spring, the Bean Festival and
the Corn Festival. Certain ceremonial procedures gave
these gatherings a religious cast, but there was much in the
way of entertainment. A number of ceremonial societies
existed which performed their rituals now and then, as the
False Face Society (members of which wore grotesque
wooden masks), the Bear Society, Buffalo Society, Eagle
Society and Medicine Society.

The family organization of the Iroquois is maternal.
This means that one inherits through the mother. The
women usually continue to live in the long house where
they were born; thus they form a kind of block in each enlarged family. Their husbands do not really belong there,
and the brothers and uncles of the women come home
when anything is to be decided. In such a long-house
family of related women some individual becomes the
matron or head, thus exercising a great deal of power and
influence. In this family organization the groups, or clans,
have such names as Turtle, Bear, Wolf, Beaver, Deer,
Hawk, Great Snipe, Little Snipe. One must always marry
out of his or her clan.

The Mingo and Chief Logan

In literature, especially in Cooper's novels, the name
Mingo is encountered. It was used by the Delaware Indians to designate the Six Nations, or Iroquois proper.
The colonial whites adopted the name, but later applied
it to an independent band of Iroquois-speaking Indians
residing in western Pennsylvania. As early as 1750 this
band lived around the headwaters of the Ohio, where they

soon became friendly with the Shawnee and other members of the Algonkin Family. Thus their history becomes a part of that for the Algonkin, just as did the fugitive Huron under the name Wyandot. The Mingo drifted down the Ohio, and after moving from one place to another joined with the Wyandot and other scattered Iroquois-speaking bands, moving to Kansas and thence to Indian Territory.

In 1774, in West Virginia and adjacent Pennsylvania, the Mingo were at war with the white settlers crowding into their country, a struggle which continued intermittently until the end of the War of 1812; but their place in history is due to their famous chief, known to the whites as John Logan. Logan was born about 1725 and was murdered by a nephew in 1780. A monument has been erected at Auburn, New York, to honor his memory. His father was a chief, but he was believed to be of full French ancestry and was said to have been captured as a child and brought up as an Indian. This would make Logan a half-breed, but he was thoroughly conditioned as an Indian. His life was uneventful until 1744, when a mob of white men murdered a group of Mingo, including members of Logan's family. Naturally, the Mingo went to war and burned and scalped in retaliation, Logan among them. When the colonial governor, Dunmore, opened negotiations to adjust this matter, Logan is said to have made the following speech:

"I appeal to any white man to say, if ever he entered Logan's cabin hungry, and he gave him not meat; if ever he came cold and naked, and he clothed him not. During the course of the last long and bloody war, Logan remained idle in his cabin, an advocate for peace. Such was my love for the whites that my countrymen pointed as they passed, and said, 'Logan is the friend of the white man.' I had even thought to have lived with you, but for the injuries of one man, Colonel Cressap, who last spring, in cold blood and unprovoked, murdered all the relations of Logan, not even sparing my women and children. There

runs not a drop of my blood in the veins of any living creature. This called on me for revenge. I have sought it; I have killed many; I have fully glutted my vengeance. For my countrymen I rejoice at the beams of peace. But do not harbor a thought that mine is the joy of fear. Logan never felt fear! He will not turn on his heel to save his life. Who is there to mourn for Logan? Not one."

Ten years later Jefferson wrote concerning this speech: "I may challenge the whole orations of Demosthenes and Cicero to pronounce a single passage superior to the speech of Logan, a Mingo (Iroquois) Chief, to Lord Dunmore."

One thing we can say for Logan is that he was an Indian, he thought as an Indian, he fought, raided and scalped as did his kind. He met a violent death, though probably he would have preferred to die in battle. Yet, Indian though he was, he did what he could to save white prisoners from torture. In Ohio, near Circleville, stands an elm tree now carefully protected, and near by is a monument, because under that tree, in a conference with the whites, Logan's famous speech was delivered.

Cornplanter

This is a famous name among the Six Nations, especially among the Seneca. It is probably an old name, but the first to fix it in history was a mixed-blood, sometimes called John O'Bail. His father is said to have been a Dutch trader, later living in Albany. His mother was a Seneca. All the boy knew of his father was hearsay, but according to his own statements, after he grew up and married, he visited Albany to see his father. He says:

I still ate my victuals out of a bark dish. I grew up to be a young man and married me a wife, and I had no kettle or gun. I then knew where my father lived and went to see him and found he was a white man and spoke the

English language. He gave me victuals, while I was at his house, but when I started to return home, he gave me no provisions to eat on the way. He gave me neither kettle nor gun.[1]

We suppose that O'Bail was heartily glad to see him go. Some years later (1780) Cornplanter led a raiding party of Seneca into the Schoharie Valley, which took captive, among others, this same Mr. O'Bail. Cornplanter knew him at sight, but his father showed no signs of recognition. Finally, as the prisoners were marched toward home, Cornplanter stepped before O'Bail, saying:

"My name is John O'Bail, commonly called Cornplanter. I am your son. You are my father. You are now my prisoner, and subject to the customs of Indian warfare; but you shall not be harmed. You need not fear. I am a warrior. Many are the scalps I have taken. Many the prisoners I have tortured to death. I am your son. I was anxious to see you, and greet you in friendship. I went to your cabin, and took you by force. But your life shall be spared. Indians love their friends and their kindred, and treat them with kindness. If you now choose to follow the fortunes of your yellow son, and to live with our people, I will cherish your old age with plenty of venison, and you shall live easy. But if it is your choice to return to your fields and live with your white children, I will send a party of my trusty young men to conduct you back in safety. I respect you, my father. You have been friendly to Indians, and they are your friends."[2]

O'Bail chose to return to his family, and so he passes out of history. One has a feeling that it would have been better had he not crossed the pages of history at all, but remained the unknown father of a great man.

Cornplanter was born probably between 1732 and 1740 and died in 1836. There is no uncertainty as to the date

---

[1] J. Niles Hubbard, *An Account of Sa-Go-Ye-Wat-Ha, or Red Jacket and his People*, Albany, 1886, p. 216.
[2] *Ibid.*, pp. 218–19.

of death; the monument erected for him by the state of Pennsylvania gives his age as about a hundred years. During his life he claimed to have been present at Braddock's defeat, and he may well have been, since boys were occasionally allowed to go out with war parties. Going to war was the ambition of every male, and the younger they began the better. When the colonies revolted against the English, Cornplanter led his people to war upon the settlements, but when the war was over he accepted the result and from then on was a powerful advocate for peace with the United States. Most of the treaties after 1784 bear his name. He was honored in life by the nation and by the state of Pennsylvania. He had audiences with President Washington, General Wayne and other distinguished men of that time. He offered to lead a body of Seneca against the British in the War of 1812, but was not permitted because of his advanced age. One need but read the many testimonials of his white contemporaries to realize that Cornplanter was an uncommon personality, one of the great Indians of the time. An interesting insight into his character is conveyed by his request that his grave be not marked, so that it should be like those of his ancestors. Yet that was not to be, for neither Seneca nor white would respect so modest a request. He belongs to history.

Cornplanter had a favorite son in whom his hopes for the future rested, Henry O'Bail, whom he sent to school that he might be educated. The record shows that Henry served creditably in the War of 1812, leaving the service with the rank of major. So far so good, but soon he became a drunkard and passed into oblivion. Cornplanter had many sore trials in life, so it seems that he should have been spared this one.

Red Jacket

A different personality was the fiery, temperamental Red Jacket, also a Seneca, born about 1756. He was not inclined to war, but joined his people against the colonists in their rebellion against England. Cornplanter had contempt for him as a warrior, frequently denouncing him as a coward. It seems that Red Jacket always advocated peace, even when General Sullivan burned the Iroquois villages in 1779. His power of persuasion was great. He had a wonderful memory, acquired information at every opportunity, so that when he rose to speak no one could down him. He was not a deep thinker, not a good politician, not a real leader, but a great personality and a powerful pleader. He had convictions, ably defending his people in hearings and driving as hard a bargain as he could. After the Revolution, when the Algonkin were encouraged by the Canadians to resist the United States and try to recover the Ohio Valley as British territory, Red Jacket appeared at Detroit with others to represent his people. He was for peace with the United States and supported his delegation in their refusal to be a party to the contemplated war with the United States. Cornplanter also was there to throw his weight on the side of peace. Brant, whose life we shall sketch presently, was thoroughly pro-British, but he could not prevail against the oratory of Red Jacket and the personality of Cornplanter.

In the War of 1812 most of the Six Nations were loyal to the United States. There is no doubt about Cornplanter and Red Jacket, who after the Revolution stood consistently with the United States against all foes, Indian or white. Red Jacket joined the Army in 1812 and participated in several important battles upon the Niagara frontier. The close of this war marked the end of Indian bloodshed in the Ohio and Michigan country, so that the problems confronting the Six Nations were those of peace. At first Red Jacket seemed to favor civilization for the Indians, but gradually he became conservative, opposed schools, churches and many white innovations against which his powerful oratory was directed. He was a master of humor and sarcasm, when it served his purpose. He appeared at his best on one occasion in court, defending one of his tribe charged with murder. According to the ancient laws of his tribe a witch was executed by beating on the head with a club or a hammer. The defendant had executed a woman in this way because she was believed to be a witch. In his address Red Jacket pictured the horrors of Salem witchcraft in favorable contrast to that of the Indian, but declared that each race was sincere and firm in the faith that such cruel steps were necessary.

Unlike Cornplanter, Red Jacket was a great egotist. He demanded everywhere the respect he thought due him. Cornplanter hoped his grave would remain unmarked, but Red Jacket, on his deathbed, reminded his family of his greatness, saying: "When I am dead it will be noised abroad throughout the world, they will hear of it across the great waters and say, 'Red Jacket the great orator is dead.'"

Joseph Brant

Another name to be remembered is Brant, this time that of a Mohawk, not a Seneca. He seems to have been born in 1742 and died in 1807. An Englishman known to history as Sir William Johnson made his home with the Six Nations and strongly influenced them to oppose the French in the wars with England. He married an older sister of Brant and possibly for this reason took an interest in the boy, taking him to war against the French around Lake George and vicinity. Later, Brant was sent to school, was well educated and able to speak and write in English. He also joined the Episcopal Church. When the colonies revolted, he joined the British Army with the rank of colonel. His military record is one of efficiency, but his part in border raids and the Cherry Valley massacre earned him the title of Monster Brant. After the war he settled in Ontario. There he dreamed of a great Indian state in the Ohio country with himself at its head, a result to be achieved by war, supported by the English, with the United States. We have seen how the Algonkin entertained this idea and fought for it in the only way they knew, by raiding, burning and killing. Between 1783 and 1790 the

Indians of the Ohio country had killed more than fifteen hundred settlers and destroyed thousands and thousands of dollars' worth of property. The Six Nations had taken no official part in this. Cornplanter and Red Jacket, in opposition to Brant, did their best to maintain peace with the United States. In 1785 Brant toured the Ohio country, conferring with the Algonkin, urging them to unite against the United States and promising them the support of the British. Then Brant went to England to seek an official promise of military aid for his scheme when the Indians went to war with the United States. Naturally he was refused, though doubtless privately encouraged in the hope that all the Ohio country could be recovered and added to Canada. Upon his return Brant again sought to draw the Six Nations into the scheme, but Red Jacket and Cornplanter led the opposition as before. Nor was he more successful in attempting to organize the Ohio Algonkin, probably because those tribes had never submitted to a league or confederation like the Six Nations, and possibly because among them were the refugee Wyandot and others who still remembered how the Six Nations had destroyed their people and hunted them down, even in the Far West. Anyway, Brant seems to have taken no actual part in the Algonkin wars in the United States and died before the War of 1812.

With this we take leave of the Six Nations. They were once a powerful people and carried with them in their decline a proud spirit. Their standard of living was not much higher than that for other eastern Indians. They lived in long bark-covered houses, each family in a single compartment; the women cultivated the fields, the men hunted. The more able-bodied were usually out at war. During their most militant period their losses were heavy but were replaced in part by captives and levies from subject tribes. One of their curious customs was the ceremonial wearing of false faces made of wood, which now leer at us from cases in museums. They also made wampum belts famous, giving and receiving them as pledges,

Sa Ga Yeath Qua Pieth Tow King of the Maquas

5. A MOHAWK CHIEF — The wolf signifies his family totem or emblem. *From an engraving in the New York Historical Society Collection.*

6. AN ASSINIBOIN INDIAN – *Drawn by Bodmer, 1834.*

7. A MANDAN CHIEF IN FULL DRESS   *Drawn by Bodmer, 1834.*

8. AN HIDATSA VILLAGE IN 1879—The original form of house was oval, dome-shaped, and covered with earth. A few of these can be seen in the background. The log cabins came in after white contact.

or bonds, for keeping treaties and peace agreements. Their women made few attempts at weaving, preferring to make clothing of deerskins. They made moderately good black pottery and when occasion arose used elmbark canoes. One peculiarity of their history cannot be overlooked. As a people they pushed northward into the Algonkin country following the Appalachian highlands. Then they expanded rapidly, forming great divisions like the Huron, Erie, Susquehanna and the Six Nations. In the southland tarried the powerful Cherokee and the Tuscarora. Yet, when the northern divisions became great, one of them, the Six Nations, destroyed the others, only at last to waste away itself in an effort to control the Algonkin. It was not the white man who destroyed the Iroquois Family, though he dealt harshly with a few surviving remnants, but a case of brother against brother. Probably this is a sample of what was going on in America before the white man came and would have continued indefinitely had he stayed away. We sometimes feel sorry and sometimes ashamed for what the white man did to the Indians, but here we see what the Indians sometimes did to one another, something equally cruel and terrible.

The Cherokee

We have reserved for the finale a word about the Cherokee, a fine people whom the whites respect and to whom honor is due. Like their brothers of the North, they were a superior people, strong, but less destructive. True they also went on the warpath, took scalps, boasted of their killings, tortured prisoners and did most of the things other Indians did, but they were an intelligent, likable people. Their first real contact with white people was when De Soto marched through their country on his way to discover the Mississippi, but the behavior of the Spaniards did not impress the Cherokee as pertaining to a superior people. In fact, they wanted nothing further to do with them. Living far inland, they did not come into contact with the English settlers for a long time. So their first experiences with the English were happy ones; their dealings were with traders and officials anxious to make them allies. So, like the Six Nations, they became pro-British and were consistently hostile to the French and the Spaniards. Some time after the French settled on the Lower Mississippi, a small raiding party of Cherokee demonstrated their loyalty to the British by killing a prominent Frenchman. The Cherokee were too far away from the French and too powerful to be brought to account, but the victim's brother, living in Canada, bribed a few roughnecks belonging to the Six Nations to raid a Cherokee town. However, nothing much came of it; at least, neither the Six Nations nor the Cherokee were interested in fighting each other.

During the successive wars the British waged against the French, Spaniards and certain Indian tribes, the Cherokee were ready to lend a hand, and on several occasions rendered signal services. Yet at last the frontier overtook the Cherokee, and to the expanding British colonists in the South they were just another handful of Indians and were treated accordingly. The Cherokee were patient, but in 1756 they were so grossly mistreated that they retaliated in true Indian fashion. However, after some losses on both sides, a reconciliation was brought about. White aggression still continued, but the Cherokee were sensible and kept the peace, as they had always tried to do and did, except in the one instance when they were so brutally treated that they had to fight.

The revolt of the colonies against the mother country puzzled the Cherokee even more than it did the Six Nations. They had many friends among the colonials, and the white men of good standing, married to their women, were divided in their allegiance. On the other hand the Cherokee had been better treated by the Crown officials than by the rank and file of colonials, so they regarded themselves as allies of the Crown and venerated the British flag as something sacred to Englishmen, yet here it was flouted. British sympathizers were not slow to take advantage of this situation and turn the Cherokee against the colonials. This went so far that a war party was organized to destroy the frontier settlements. However, some mixed-blood Cherokee warned the settlers in time, so that nothing much came of it. All during the Revolution there was friction with the colonists, but no real war; the Cherokee were too sensible for that.

From the start the better whites saw in the Cherokee a superior people, and they in turn appreciated the values in European civilization. So, early in their white contact, the Cherokee welcomed good white men into their midst, especially the Quakers. Churches were built, schools established, and many young white men married into the tribe. Soon many Indians owned farms, with livestock and serviceable farm buildings. Under these favorable conditions they increased in population, expanding westward into the country beyond the Mississippi. Thus they had a frontier of their own and were geographically separated into two divisions, the Eastern and Western Cherokee.

That the Cherokee had not suffered deterioration through white contact is clear when we note that the census of 1825 revealed 13,563 in the Eastern division alone. One hundred and forty-seven white men and seventy-three white women were found to have married Cherokee mates. One thousand two hundred seventy-seven Negro slaves were owned. The Cherokee Nation was out of debt, managed its own affairs, produced cotton and wool and manufactured blankets. The Cherokee west of the Mississippi were not counted at the time, but Mooney estimated them at about seven thousand. It would be well if our narrative could end here; but now the state of Georgia began to claim the lands of the Cherokee, defied the United States Supreme Court, while lawless whites drove the Indians from their farms and seized their livestock, though some of these Indians were better educated than many members of the mobs despoiling them. The Cherokee resisted legally in every possible way, but the courts were deaf to all appeals. At last, in 1838–39, the United States Army rounded up the entire population and marched them to the West. We spare the reader's sensibilities by not recording the inhumanity and brutality of this whole affair, but every loyal American should read the record to stiffen his resolve to maintain an ever higher level of national worth.

Once in the West the fugitive Cherokee amalgamated with the western division, forming one of the Civilized Nations of Indian Territory and continuing their laudable advance in prosperity and civilization. In 1907 their self-governing functions were absorbed by the state of Oklahoma.

The Cherokee Who Stayed Behind

When the Eastern Cherokee were forcibly moved to the West, a small group refused to go. They hid in the mountains of North Carolina and Tennessee. Since the state of Georgia was the chief evictor and the other states were disposed to sympathize with their resistance, no effort was made to round them up. The United States government threatened to deny them any part of the compensation promised the others, but after a time Congress relented and assisted these Cherokee to secure land. This sounds as if their troubles were over, but they were just beginning, for the titles to their lands were juggled, to the end that the Cherokee were defrauded of most of their funds. The Civil War brought even greater confusion, leaving their future more doubtful than ever. Long litigation has been necessary to recover these lands, and some of their claims are still before the courts. In 1889 a corporation was formed to hold titles to and administer their lands; recently this corporation, which is the tribe itself, placed all its lands under the jurisdiction of the United States, to be held in trust. Their home is in the Smoky Mountains, North Carolina. Numbering over three thousand, with considerable intermixture of white blood, they now live much like the surrounding mountain whites.

These narratives of sorrow and defeat are becoming

monotonous. Whether the tribe fought with the whites or
not, there was an economic and social struggle in which a
mere handful of Indians was set upon by overwhelming
numbers. That they were not annihilated is due to the
belated justice of the whites, whose conscience usually
intervened just short of extermination. Having taken
everything from the Indians, they could afford to give the
few survivors a chance to live. In the old days, when the
Indians took white prisoners they forced them to run the
gauntlet. About all the white man now offers the Indian
is a chance to run an economic gauntlet to which there is
no time limit.

Sequoya

It is a truism that the history of a people is reflected in
the lives of its great men. The best-known Cherokee and
the one who contributed most to Cherokee civilization was
Sequoya, a name immortalized in the giant trees of
California. Sequoya was his Indian name, but his father
was a white man, George Gist, sometimes written Guest
or Guess. Little is known of Sequoya's early life, except
that he was born about 1760, was brought up as an
Indian and, due to an accident, was a cripple. His name
appears as a signer to treaties and other documents in
1816, suggesting that he was then a leader among his
people. He died while traveling in Mexico in 1843.

About 1809 he began to reflect upon the advantage
white men enjoyed because they could write their own
language. Convinced that a literate Cherokee nation
would be superior to an illiterate one, he set himself the
task of creating an alphabet. He persisted in the face of
great opposition and ridicule, until he achieved a work-
able alphabet and formulated rules for writing the language. In 1821 the leading men of the Cherokee agreed
to submit his alphabet to a public test. Not only was the
demonstration a success but the whole nation entered so

enthusiastically into its use that within a few months the greater part of the population could read and write. As yet there was no printing, but handwritten copies of documents were passed around and letters written. In 1827 the necessary characters were cast in Boston and the publication of a newspaper begun.

Sequoya knew no other language than Cherokee and took no active part in the production of newspapers and books, but the year following the adoption of his alphabet he crossed the Mississippi to introduce writing among the Western Cherokee. He seemed to like the country and shortly after his first visit made that his residence. Soon he began to dream of a universal alphabet for Indian languages; he traveled about a great deal, but naturally failed to achieve this impossible goal. His was an inquiring mind; he was a man of vision and with an urge to solve problems. Intrigued by a legend that a small band of Cherokee once wandered into Mexico and were thus lost to their people, he set out in his old age to recover their lost history, a journey from which he never returned.

He is justly famous. The impetus given his people regenerated them. How could it have been otherwise! Indians went from house to house with scraps of paper, pieces of bark and even boards upon which were messages in their own language in such perfect phonetic symbols that anyone with average intelligence could soon read and begin to write. Local observers tell us that within a year the Cherokee were a literate nation. Their rapid advance in civilization may be attributed to this achievement.

No one can read the history of the Six Nations and the Cherokee without feeling that strength, vitality and moral fiber were theirs. They were superior. In aboriginal days they were unrelenting exterminators of their own brethren. Their family might have swept the Algonkin into oblivion had not the Six Nations destroyed their own brothers, but, even so, they spread terror from the Mississippi to the Atlantic.

Arikara, or Ree

Pawnee

    Skidi, or Wolf Pawnee (Petalasharo I)
    Chaui, or Grand Pawnee (Petalasharo II)
    Kitkehahkis, or Republican Pawnee
    Pitahuerat, or Tapage Pawnee

Wichita

    Tawakoni
    Waco

Caddo

    Hasinai Confederacy
    Kadohadacho Confederacy
    Natchitoches Confederacy

Chapter XII

THE FAMILY OF THE CADDO

WE now turn to the lands west of the Mississippi, where lives a distinguished family which linguists believe was founded by a full-brother to the ancestor of the Iroquois Family. Both families seem to have grown strong in the fertile lands of Louisiana and Mississippi and then expanded toward the north—the Iroquois on the east side of the great river, the Caddo on the west. The most northerly member of the Caddo Family was the Pawnee, consisting of a group of powerful villages occupying the heart of Nebraska in the seventeenth century. The French were the first to give them a place in history under the name Pawnee Republics. At some earlier date a part of the Pawnee moved still farther north, settling along the Missouri River. This group is known to history as the Arikara or Ree.

The Pawnee claim they named the Ohio River; the Iroquois claim they did it. Perhaps both are right, since their languages seem to have a common origin.

The Pawnee took a deep interest in the heavens, especially in the stars, for they believed that some of the stars were gods; for example, the Morning Star, the Evening Star, etc. Long, poetic rituals were recited each year to invoke the presence of these gods. The Pawnee sages were also practical astronomers, making observations to determine the time for planting corn, the time for religious observances and other periods in their calendar. More than the Algonkin and the Iroquois, they marveled at the mystery of corn; they believed that corn came to the world as a maiden and that the germination of a grain of corn symbolized human and all other life. They spoke of this corn woman as Mother Corn and often expressed the belief that she was, in reality, the mother of men. They also believed in a male being who was supreme and hidden from human eyes, but who caused the world to be. They thought of him as expressed in the sky or the arch of the heavens, a being so remote that he never revealed himself to men but transmitted his power through lesser gods. Yet the Pawnee sometimes prayed to him and addressed him in song. Somewhat complementary to him was Mother Earth, from whose bosom all life sprang. It would be tedious to outline the Pawnee philosophy of the universe, but in dignity and beauty it compares favorably with that of Greek, Egyptian and other ancient civilizations. Among Indians it stands high. No wonder the Indians of New Mexico told Coronado, the first Spanish explorer to enter that country, that the greatest of men lived to the northeast. But when Coronado saw nothing but half-naked Indians whose speech he could not understand, he regarded his native guide as an impostor and killed him. To Coronado greatness meant gold. To his Indian guide it meant grandeur of conception and beauty in symbolism. The French, coming into the Mississippi country later, understood the situation better; they gave them the name Grand Pawnee.

The Pawnee boast that they never fought against the United States, and history seems to confirm their claim. Time after time they joined the whites to fight against other Indians, until, in recognition of their loyalty and ability, an army division of scouts was authorized into which qualified Pawnee men were enlisted. These scouts wore military uniforms when on parade and were especially honored. They rendered signal service in the Indian wars of the period from 1865 to 1885. Yet, ironically enough, the Pawnee were eventually dispossessed of their lands in Nebraska and forced to settle in Oklahoma, where half of them died from disease and exposure. Once boasting a strength of ten thousand, they now number just over one thousand, a remnant of a once powerful nation. Their northern relatives, the Arikara, or Ree, of the Upper Missouri were also once numerous, but as of 1950 they numbered about 550.

Other Caddoan speakers are the Wichita, known first from a visit by Coronado in 1541, and the Caddo. The latter have long confused both the experts and interested readers alike. The term Caddo may be applied to any of the groups speaking the Caddoan language, but usually it refers to a group of confederated tribes once located in eastern Texas and adjacent parts of Oklahoma, Arkansas and Louisiana. These tribes lived in beehive-shaped thatched houses, as did the Wichita. Houses of this type may be seen at "Indian City," Anadarko, Oklahoma. Like most of their neighbors, these Indians wore deerskin or buffalo clothing—the latter mainly in cold weather. Those in the eastern areas were also familiar with the bark clothing worn by their Southeastern neighbors. Men's work included hunting, warfare, ceremonial rituals and house building, while the women planted the fields (corn was the staple), gathered thatch, wood and the meat their husbands provided. These Indians believed in a "chief above," and temples were maintained to honor this deity. Beliefs of the Caddoan tribes also included traces of the star cult, known among the Pawnee and Wichita.

Dr. John Swanton published detailed descriptions from the early explorers among the Caddoan peoples. Recently, Dr. Stephen Williams has studied and outlined the locations of the various tribes in the different Caddo groups, and has traced their movements not only through the accounts of the Spanish and French explorers and later American Indian agents, but through historic archaeology. The story of these tribes, like so many others, is one of migration and wandering; it became more intense with each of the changes in administration—Spanish, French and American—of the territory in which they were living. At present, the remnants of the various Caddoan tribes are living in Oklahoma, as are the Wichita and Pawnee.

Petalasharo the Reformer

The most noted hero of the Skidi Pawnee was Petalasharo,
born about 1797. He was a wise leader, with vision and
grandeur of character. For many generations this tribe
had kept a large bundle of sacred objects with a ritual
devoted to the Morning Star, the greatest of the heavenly
heroes. This ritual was held in awe because it compelled
its followers to perform a gruesome and exacting task, one
that wrung the heart, and one in which failure at any
point meant misfortune and death. This was nothing less
than to sacrifice a virgin to the Morning Star. When the
ritual required, a war party was organized, purified and
sanctioned by serious ceremonies. If the signs were pronounced auspicious, this party set out for the enemy's
country. The object was to surprise a camp, kill and scalp,
but to spare an adolescent girl. The captive was carried
home, where she was treated with great respect, attended
by women, all in charge of a priest of the ritual. Nothing
was too good for her; she was luxuriously dressed and
treated like a queen. As far as possible every wish of the
captive was anticipated. The object of all this seemed to
be so to win her confidence that she would do anything
suggested. The ritual for this sacrifice has been recorded,
and from a knowledge of its contents we are not surprised
that even hard-boiled Indians found it a trial. We pass
over the details, but a kind of scaffold was erected, upon
which the girl was induced to climb, her hands and feet
were bound, then a priest rushed upon her, cut out her
heart and offered it to the gods. Afterward her body was
laid upon the prairie as a further offering.

When Petalasharo was mature and recognized as the
future successor to the ruling chief, a young Comanche
girl was captured, but when they were about to lead her
to the scaffold Petalasharo caught her up in his arms,
mounted his horse and rode away. This was so unexpected
that everyone stood still with astonishment. They doubtless

expected him to be struck dead, but he passed out of sight. He placed the girl upon a horse previously hidden away and started for her country. When within a short distance of her people, he sent her on, but he turned back. It was an unheard-of thing he had done, but since nothing happened to him and some of the head men approved of it, it was decided to discontinue the sacrifice in the future. It was the heroic deed of a reformer leading his people toward greater humanity.

Petalasharo died about 1841, and another strong man succeeded him. Since he took the same name they are sometimes confused in history. Petalasharo II was a member of the Grand Pawnee, and was born in 1823. He, even more than his predecessor, believed in keeping peace with the whites, saw to it that his people kept faith with their treaties, and that when the United States recruited the famous Pawnee scouts, only men of sterling character were chosen. In 1874 he was shot down by one of his own tribe because he opposed the moving of his people to Oklahoma. Judging by subsequent events after the Pawnee did move to Oklahoma, Petalasharo II was right.

Petalasharo I had led the opposition to human sacrifice, but occasionally a few of the Morning Star bundle priests went out and practiced it in secret. They still believed in the ritual. Petalasharo II discovered their secret and broke up one attempt at the risk of his life. It was his unrelenting opposition that finally abolished the practice.

Life in Pawnee Villages

The Pawnee were always mystery men. The other Indians round about saw in them a poise like that of gods or supermen. They were large in body, with big round faces. Their genius lay in ritualism and poetic interpretations of the heavens and the earth. In the material order of life they were just ordinary Plains Indians.

When white men came to what is now Nebraska, the Pawnee lived in some twenty villages scattered along the

Platte River. In 1700 their numbers were estimated as two thousand families and, a little later, as ten thousand persons, which would amount to about the same thing. When first observed, they had acquired some horses, but still lived in more or less permanent villages. Their houses were large, circular in ground plan, dome-shaped, the turf roof supported by a framework of logs. The ground diameter ranged from thirty to fifty feet and the height at the center from ten to fourteen feet. The floor was of earth, and in the center was a large fireplace, and a hole in the roof allowed the smoke to escape. Around the circular wall inside were tiny rooms for sleeping and resting. These were for the married couples, children, single persons, etc. No accurate data are available as to the number of persons living in such a house, but, judging from information about other Indians using similar houses, the average might be twenty to thirty. One would expect such a house to be the home of a middle-aged man and his wife, or wives, as the case might be, several married sons with their families, his unmarried relatives and his parents, if living. In addition there might be a poor relation or two and a few guests.

All food was cooked around the fire in the center of the house. There was plenty of room between the fire and the tiny living rooms for the storage of wood, food, etc. After horses became numerous it was not uncommon for the favorite riding horses to be stabled in the house at night. In fine weather the old men would climb to the roof and bask in the sun. Between the houses were stages or high platforms made of poles, upon which food could be stored and dried, skins aired, etc., out of reach of the hungry, thieving dogs loafing around. The women gathered the driftwood along the river and packed it home. They cultivated small patches of corn, beans and squashes in the lowlands near the river, but their main food was buffalo, herds of which grazed on the open plains near the villages.

The Pawnee social unit was the village. Men were expected to take wives from their own village unless too closely related and to reside in the village of their birth.

The villages were grouped to form four or more tribes. It seems that each village owned a sacred bundle in which were kept the objects needed to demonstrate the accompanying rituals. This bundle was in the keeping of the village chief during his term of office; his house thus became the village capital. Next there was a bundle for the chief of each tribe. When an important council was held, the chiefs of the villages assembled at the house of the tribal chief with their bundles. Finally there was a federation of the tribes with a Grand Chief, as the French called this official.

Medicine men, or magicians, were numerous and belonged to a society, their chief function being to treat the sick, to take preventive measures against sickness, drought, shortage of food and enemy raids. They had great faith in the power of charms, prayers and rituals. Every now and then the medicine men's society held a meeting, at which time tricks in magic were demonstrated. According to tradition, corn or other plants were grown from the seed in a few minutes, snow or hail produced at will, men killed and restored to life, etc., all of which reminds us of the performances of modern magicians.

The many bundles associated with the Pawnee scheme of village and tribal government called for a number of men skilled in their rituals. These were rarely medicine men, but formed a class of their own who might best be called priests, the learned class, or the wise men of the villages. They had to learn the rituals and songs by rote as well as the required prayers and sacrifices and were responsible for all procedures.

Like other buffalo-hunting Indians, the Pawnee were warlike. A number of men's societies were maintained, the ambitions of whose members were for adventures on the warpath. These societies, by their public parades and dances, as well as by direct instruction, fired the youth with enthusiasm for adventure and the ideals of bravery. But the greatness of the Pawnee lay in their mythological philosophy, their imaginative rituals and the seriousness of their attitude toward life.

Chapter XIII

THE SOUTHEASTERN TRIBES

THE Cherokee and the Caddo introduced us to the Indians of the southland, where lived a number of tribes speaking languages (Natchez, Tunican and Muskhogean) which were distantly related to those spoken by tribes we have already met. Roughly, their territory comprised what is now Georgia, Alabama, Mississippi and parts of Louisiana and Tennessee—the heart of the South. In De Soto's day they may have had a population of fifty thousand; today they exceed thirty thousand. The Natchez and Tunican tribes, and a number of less-known divisions, spoke languages related to the Muskhogean tongues; the best-known tribes of the latter family are the Creek, Choctaw, Chickasaw and Seminole. When first discovered they lived in villages of a few hundred persons each, the sites of more than two hundred of which have been accurately located.

De Soto's party, on its memorable march from Florida to the Mississippi, seems to have passed through the heart of the Muskhogean country; from the records of that expedition historians have gleaned much information as to their modes of life. Other explorers and missionaries followed and, finally, the French made settlements on the coast, especially in the country around New Orleans. It is chiefly from French historians and narratives of adventure that our best early information comes.

The Natchez

It is the opinion of our leading scholars that the Natchez and the Taensa, whose many villages lined the Lower Mississippi, were the most typical members of the family,

THE HOKAN-SIOUAN STOCK: SOUTHEASTERN TRIBES

Muskhogean Family
    Members of the Five Civilized Tribes
        Choctaw
        Chickasaw
        Creek (Upper Creek, Lower Creek)
        Seminole (Osceola)
    Alibamu
    Koasati

Natchez Tribes
    Natchez
    Taensa

Tunica

which probably means that they had a wide influence and exercised a kind of culture leadership. Possibly visitors from other tribes came to see, to learn and to carry away inspirations just as travelers have done ever since man was man.

One thing impressing the first white visitors was a temple, simple in architecture, but still relatively grand, in which were many sacred objects. Du Pratz, a French writer of the time, has this to say:

This temple, the front of which looks toward the rising sun, is placed on a mound of earth brought thither which rises about eight feet above the natural level of the ground on the bank of a little river. This mound loses itself in an insensible slope on the side toward the square. On the other sides the slope is more marked, and on the side toward the river it is very steep. This temple measures about thirty feet each way. The four angle or corner posts are of the inner part of the cypress, which is incorruptible. These trees in their actual condition appear to have a diameter of a foot and a half. They rise ten feet out of the earth and extend to the beginning of the roof. The Natchez state that they are as much in the earth as above it, a fact which must make it secure against the winds. The other posts are a foot in diameter and are of the same wood, having the same length in the earth as above it. The wall is a rough mud wall entirely smooth outside and a little sunken between every (two) posts inside in such a way that it is not more than nine inches thick in the middle.

The interior of this temple is divided into two unequal parts by a little wall which cuts it from the rising to the setting sun. The part into which one enters may be twenty feet wide and the other may be ten, but in this second part it is extremely gloomy, because there is only one opening, which is the door of the temple itself, which is to the north, and because the little communicating door is not capable of lighting the second part.

There is nothing remarkable in the inside of the temple except a table or altar about four feet high and six feet long by two broad. On this table is a coffer made of cane splints very well worked, in which are the bones of the last great Sun. The eternal fire is in this first part of the temple. In the other and more secluded part nothing can be distinguished except two planks worked by hand on which are many minute carvings (plusieurs minuties) which one is unable to make out, owing to the insufficient light.

The roof of this temple is a long vault, the ridge pole of which is not more than six feet long, on which are placed representations of three great birds (carved) on flat pieces of wood. They are twice as large as a goose. They have no feet. The neck is not as long as that of a goose, and the head does not resemble it. The wing feathers are large and very distinct. The ground color is white mingled with feathers of a beautiful red color. These birds look toward the east. The roof is very neat outside and in. In fact, the structure and roof appear of a perfect solidity. . . .

It is in this temple that two men tend the perpetual fire during each quarter of the moon. There are eight guardians for the four quarters, and a superior who is called chief of the guardians of the fire to command them and to see that they do their duty, and to have the wood brought for this fire. This wood must be clear wood. They employ for it only clear white walnut (or hickory) without bark. The logs are seven to eight inches in diameter by eight feet long. They are placed near the temple about the trunk of a tree with a rather short stem. This tree is covered with thorns from the earth to the top. I have given a description of it in the natural history under the name of passion thorn. I have never been able to find out why they have respect for this tree wherever they find it, unless it be on account of the employment to which it is destined. These guardians are interested in preserving the fire, for it costs their lives to let it go out. There is besides, for the service of the temple, a master of ceremonies, who is also the master of the mysteries, since, according to them, he speaks very familiarly to the spirit. In the great ceremonies he wears a crown which has feathers only in front and is thus a half crown. He also has in his hand a red baton ornamented with red or white feathers according to the requirements of the feast.[1]

Charlevoix, a famous French explorer of the time, has this to say of these Indians:

Every morning as soon as the Sun appears, the great chief comes to the door of his cabin, turns himself to the east, and howls three times, bowing down to the earth. Then they bring him a calumet, which serves only for this purpose. He smokes, and blows the smoke of his tobacco toward the Sun; then he does the same thing toward the other three parts of the world. He acknowledges no superior but the Sun, from which he pretends to derive his origin. He exercises an unlimited power over his subjects, can dispose of their goods and lives, and for whatever

[1] Quoted in John R. Swanton's *Indian Tribes of the Lower Mississippi Valley and Adjacent Coast of the Gulf of Mexico.* Bureau of American Ethnology, Bulletin 43. Washington, 1911, pp. 162–63.

labors he requires of them they cannot demand any recompense.[2]

Again, Le Petit, the Jesuit priest, tells us that:

The sun is the principal object of veneration to these people; as they can not conceive of anything which can be above this heavenly body, nothing else appears to them more worthy of their homage. It is for the same reason that the great chief of this nation, who knows nothing on the earth more dignified than himself, takes the title of brother of the Sun, and the credulity of the people maintains him in the despotic authority which he claims. To enable them better to converse together they raise a mound of artificial soil on which they build his cabin, which is of the same construction as the temple. The door fronts the east, and every morning the great chief honors by his presence the rising of his elder brother, and salutes him with many howlings as soon as he appears above the horizon. Then he gives orders that they shall light his calumet; he makes him an offering of the first three puffs which he draws; afterwards raising his hand above his head and turning from the east to the west, he shows him the direction which he must take in his course.[3]

None of the Indians we have so far discussed engaged in such elaborate sun worship as this. The social order of the Natchez and the Taensa was not really democratic, like many Indian societies, for here there were two ranks, nobles and common people. The French writers of the time speak of the commoners as "Stinkards," certainly suggestive enough. The nobility were of at least three ranks: at the head of the tribe was the Great Sun, next came the Suns, then the Nobles and, finally, Honored People. The latter, it may be guessed, were the rank and file of the aristocracy.

For example, we are told that to be a Sun one must

[2] *Ibid.*, p. 174.
[3] *Ibid.*, p. 174.

have a Sun mother, but a Stinkard father, which may mean that it was only the mother who counted. Again, a Noble was the child of either a Sun father and a Stinkard mother, or of a Noble mother and a Stinkard father. In other words, children kept the rank of their aristocratic mothers, while children of aristocratic fathers lost one place in the ranking. Thus, Honored People were children of either Honored women or Noble fathers, the other parent a Stinkard.

Well, it seems that the procedure is simple in one way, since the members of the aristocracy must always marry commoners, or Stinkards. The rub comes at the last, for Stinkards who do not succeed in marrying aristocrats must be content with Stinkards, and beget children who are Stinkards. Again, the children of Honored men were out of luck, for they were all Stinkards.

Forgetting this bewildering system, we may fix it in our minds that the Suns were the great personages. They were almost gods; in fact, they represented the Sun God. The Great Sun had supreme power of life and death over all subjects. When he died, all his wives were executed; note that his wives were commoners. The French were surprised to see that when the Great Sun went abroad he was carried in a kind of sedan chair. The other Muskhogean peoples also showed great honor to their chiefs and, according to some reports, a woman sometimes filled that office and was also carried in a kind of sedan chair. Most of the Creeks had aristocracies and commoners, and later on, most of the Muskhogean learned the advantages in Negro slavery, eventually owning a goodly number of such slaves, which implies still another social stratum.

Before going on with the story of these interesting people, let us have a look at their mode of life. Their houses were rather better than those of their neighbors; for the most part, they were rectangular with curved roofs, produced by bending saplings to form the rafters, somewhat like the bows on a prairie schooner. It is easier to make a roof like this than to follow our own method with straight rafters. Thatch or bark covered the roofs. The side walls were unusual: first, posts like the ribs of a basket were set up in the ground, then flexible sticks or reeds were woven through them horizontally. Finally, the whole was plastered with mud. When a whitewash was added, the appearance was pleasing. There were no windows and often no hole in the roof, leaving the smoke from the fire to find its way out as best it could. Many villages were fortified with palisades, indicating anything but a peaceful regime.

Farming was the major occupation. Maize, a kind of millet, sunflower, pumpkins, melons and tobacco were raised in quantity. For fat they used an oil made from the kernels of hickory nuts and in addition bear's oil when they could get it. They knew how to make lye-hominy and corn bread, which, in due time, made southern Negro cooks famous. One of their unique dishes, much praised by the whites, was persimmon bread. They had no domestic animal save the dog, which they sometimes ate; but there was usually enough game to supply the meat needed. As proof of the progressive spirit of this family, we observe that they quickly took over from the whites chickens and other poultry, horses, cattle and even pigs. Orchards of peaches, figs, etc., were planted around their villages.

They wore little clothing, from choice, but were famed for their fine soft deerskins and mantles of turkey feathers. Yet they were weavers of no mean order, using fine bark and nettle fiber. However, the cheap, highly colored textiles offered by the traders soon discouraged native weaving. The Natchez and their immediate neighbors seem to have been the best potters.

Almost everyone asks if Indians were always at war. Of course not; but there was always fighting somewhere on the continent. The French writers tell us that captives were tortured by the Natchez, in what we regard as fiendish ways. As with most Indians, adult men were called warriors, and their social standing was determined by the number of enemies slain or captured. Whenever a people maintain such ideals there is only one way for a youth to be respectable: take to the warpath.

Though the French settled near the Natchez, for a time there was little friction; the murder of four Canadians by the Natchez precipitated a "war" which was quickly stopped. A stockaded fort was built in 1716, and the next few years were relatively peaceful. When a new commandant was sent to the fort, however, and demanded the site of one of the Natchez villages for his own plantation, the Indians rebelled. They took the fort by surprise and killed the garrison. In the next few years similar uprisings took place. The French hired other Indians who had scores to settle with the Natchez to assist in exterminating them. A number were captured and sold into slavery in the West Indies; to have knocked them on their heads instead would have been more humane. The survivors fled to other Muskhogean villages, where their identity was concealed, but the fires in their sacred temples were extinguished forever. The Taensa met a similar fate. Just north of the Taensa lived the Tunica, a small tribe with a language once believed unrelated to any other form of speech, but now believed to belong to the same stock as the Natchez and Muskhogean. The Tunica lived much like the Natchez; they supported the French against the Natchez, but they too fell before the incoming European peoples, and by 1930 there was only one who could speak the old language.

The Creek (a loose confederation of some fifty towns) were too numerous to endure a similar fate. From the first they took a liking to the English. They sold their rights to land near the Atlantic Coast to Oglethorpe for the colony of Georgia. Taking the side of the English, they were naturally hostile to the Spaniards who held Florida, and were rather cold to the French in Louisiana. They helped the English settlements by protecting them against hostile Indians. Yet eventually the whites crowded them too closely, resulting in the Creek War of 1813–14, real Indian fighting equal to anything in frontier history.

When the Algonkin of Indiana and Ohio made their final effort against President Washington, Tecumseh pleaded with the Creek and their neighbors to join them in a united resistance along the entire western front, but the Creek hung back. Nevertheless, they were now feeling the pinch of encroaching settlements, and many of the tribe members were in favor of resisting further white advance. During the War of 1812 British agents seem to have fomented as much trouble as possible. Anyway, hostilities began in 1813, and, as usual, the first unsuspected attack of the Indians was successful. As many parts of the South were now thickly settled by whites, a small army was raised which, under Andrew Jackson, defeated the Indians by storming their fortified camp, killing the men, taking the women and children captive. The whites were relentless, everywhere the Creek were set upon, the peaceful villages suffering as much as the others.

In the end they were badly beaten, but not exterminated; there were too many of them. We have told you something of what befell the Cherokee, of the hopes of Pontiac and Tecumseh for an Indian state between the Appalachians and the Mississippi. But such hopes were not to be realized, for on every hand the white people demanded that every Indian cross the mighty river and forever leave the forests, which in turn were to give way to farms and cities. True, some white men talked about how the Indians once out in that far country could have a land to themselves, to live in peace and feast upon buffalo forever. One thing always palls upon us when we read the texts of Indian treaties and the speeches made in their defense by the white negotiators, and that is the naïve faith that each treaty was to stand forever. We are kind enough to believe that these white speakers were sincere. That is why we are depressed. No known Indian treaty lasted very long, many less than twenty years. The most intelligent Indians suspected that they were little more than scraps of paper, for nothing had as yet been able to check the westward flood of white men. So one wonders if we, in this generation, are not just as blind and stupid —not about Indians with whom we make no more vain bargains, but about our own ways of life, in thinking they are to go on forever.

Finally, came the turn of the Creek, the Choctaw and the Chickasaw. They were told about the grand opportunities awaiting them in the West—the same old siren song about an Indian state, where the white man would never intrude, the promised land west of the Mississippi.

The Choctaw and the Chickasaw

The country of the southeastern tribes was roughly halved by the Alabama and the Tombigbee rivers, though for practical purposes we can say by the boundary between Mississippi and Alabama. The Creek and Seminole were east of this line; the Choctaw and Chickasaw west of it. These two western tribes of the Muskhogean family were close relatives, somewhat like brothers, but when white men came they were not on friendly terms, often raiding and killing each other. The Choctaw lived in lower Mississippi; the Chickasaw to the north of them, extending into Georgia. We noted how the Cherokee and the Creek were friendly to the British and hostile to the French. Naturally, if the Chickasaw and Choctaw were implacable enemies, they would take different sides in the international struggle. Anyway, the Choctaw, who were in the south, joined the French; the Chickasaw, in the north, supported the British. Before white contact, both were powerful tribes, the Choctaw with a population of about fifteen thousand, the Chickasaw, eight thousand.

Again we find that our best early information is from the De Soto expedition, 1540. In aboriginal mode of life these tribes were somewhat more like the Natchez than the Creek. They were intelligent and progressive, beginning early to adopt certain aspects of white civilization. The Choctaw aided General Jackson in the war with the Creek and, in the main, were successful in keeping peace with the whites. By 1820 both the Choctaw and the Chickasaw were erecting schoolhouses and farm buildings and acquiring livestock. Nevertheless, they felt the menace of the frontier and lent an attentive ear to the government plea that they seek a utopia in the West. Finally, around 1830, they gave reluctant consent, the United States agreeing to compensate them for the buildings and improvements made and set them up handsomely in the new land. Like most such promises, these were never fulfilled. The moving of the tribe was so mishandled that it became a tragedy. Hundreds died on the way to their new home. However, once settled there, the two tribes began all over again. They organized republics, made laws, built schools and churches, maintained courts and militia. Reducing their language to writing, they soon became, like the Cherokee, literate nations.

In 1859 a kind of federation of five independent tribes was formed, the Cherokee, Choctaw, Chickasaw, Creek and Seminole, all in territory west of the Mississippi. From that time on, these people were known as the Five Civilized Tribes. Note that all except the Cherokee are Muskhogean.

All of them had trouble, of course; their lands were sought by ruthless whites, the United States government disregarded its most solemn treaty obligations, always siding with the local whites. Yet, in spite of all these injustices, the progress of these people was as commendable as their difficulties were great. After 1890 it was apparent that, sooner or later, they would be absorbed into a state and thus become citizens, though largely at the mercy of the whites. Oklahoma was admitted into the Union as a state in 1907. This automatically ended the independence of the civilized tribes, for though now citizens of Oklahoma, they were preyed upon by the whites, many reduced to dire poverty, often by frauds sanctioned by the local courts. In spite of all this they are still strong in numbers, the Cherokee about 75,000; the Choctaw, 40,000; the Creeks, 20,000; the Chickasaws, 9000; and the Seminoles, about 3000.

In closing this brief sketch we must recognize these Indians as different in history from many of the others we have met. Their capacity for taking over civilization is obvious. Officially and individually, the whites did many things to thwart their efforts. They were stigmatized as bloodthirsty, dirty, filthy, pagan, lazy and worthless. In spite of all this and with great patience, they weathered every crisis, often at frightful cost. Yet possibly, just because they did not live up to this stigma, did not keep the United States Army busy year after year, they are rarely mentioned in the history books and their great men are forgotten. Had they spent their leisure time burning white homes, taken frightful toll in white lives, and at last sulked on reservations, their descendants could have been the heroes of the movie and the joy of the tourist. Yet it is far better as we find it, since these civilized tribes can point to distinguished members of Congress and other celebrities as proof that they have achieved the level of identity with all good citizens of the United States.

The Seminole

When the Seminole of Florida are mentioned, we think of a people always hiding in trackless swamps in the Everglades country. But they went into these swamps to save their lives, not from choice. Their original home seems to have been in southern Georgia and adjacent Florida. As white settlements increased in Georgia, they withdrew into Florida instead of retreating westward. Also, remember that Florida was then Spanish territory and, as such, was held for military purposes rather than for economic development. Thus the territory had some attraction for the Seminole, at least enabling them to escape from oppression by the colony of Georgia and later by the United States. For a time they were secure in this asylum. After the Creek had been defeated, in 1813, many were forced to move west, but others joined the Seminole in Florida, so swelling their numbers that they became almost entirely a Muskhogean-speaking people. The United States began "an undeclared war" by invading Spanish Florida and Andrew Jackson, now famous and powerful, set out to seize the Seminole. The bone of contention, the real undoing of these Indians, was Negro slavery. The Creek and Cherokee owned slaves, and their right to them was not seriously disputed, but slaves sometimes escaped from servitude by crossing the Spanish boundary. The universal hospitality of the Indian guaranteed them shelter with the Seminole, and though they were, in a sense, accepted as slaves, their lot there was much more fortunate than in Georgia or Alabama. Naturally, the owners of these fugitives sought to recover their slaves, but when they crossed the line illegally to take them by force, the Seminole, backed by the Spaniards, treated them as bandits and foreign invaders, which they were. So, in 1816, the Army and Navy of the United States violated all precedent by invading a nation with whom they were at peace. In a sudden raid nearly three hundred Seminole, men, women and children of all ages, were killed outright and a large number wounded. This started something. The outcome was that Spain sold Florida to the United States in 1819, the treaty pledging the purchaser to respect the rights of the Indians and to deal justly with them. No one can claim that the United States expected to keep this promise.

From now on, the lot of the Seminole was to be anything but enviable. The slave catcher was to have a free hand; any Negro, any mixed offspring or even any pure Indian they could capture could be sold in the slave markets of Georgia, Alabama or anywhere else. The Seminole became fugitives, armed themselves, hid in the swamps and defended themselves as best they could against these bandits. So affairs went from bad to worse until 1834, when the United States tried to force the Seminole to leave Florida for Oklahoma. They would have yielded to the inevitable if, at the last moment, they had not been told that no one of Negro descent would be permitted to go, but would be sold into slavery. This meant tearing families apart, taking children from mothers, something no people will accept without protest. So the Seminole fled to the swamps, and a war was on. And a real war it was. For seven years troops entered the swamps only to meet defeat, in some cases annihilation. Seven generals failed, some of the best in the regular army. Bloodhounds were tried, but the Indians outwitted them.

At last the United States admitted defeat. It had tried force and likewise base treachery. Osceola, one of the great Seminole leaders, was encouraged to come to a peace conference, under guarantee of safe conduct, but was promptly knocked on the head, bound and thrown into a dungeon. Don't forget that all this was the work of the army under direct orders from the President of the United States. It was defended as justifiable in a war against savages. Yet all this accomplished was to stiffen the resistance of the Seminole and make it impossible to negotiate peace. However, finally realizing the futility of trying to exterminate the Seminole, military operations ceased, and peace negotiations were begun. In the end the Seminole chiefs ag eed to go to Oklahoma, where many of them now live, but an indefinite number refused to leave their refuge, kept out of sight except now and then to meet a trader. Thus they lived and prospered, teaching their children that the white man was "a beast and his ways poison," stubbornly resisting any of the aid offered by the later established Bureau of Indian Affairs; in recent years, however, they have accepted the educational and other services. They are now famous as "the tribe which never surrendered," and are known for their brightly colored appliquéd cloth, used to manufacture skirts and other items, lucrative in the tourist trade.

Chapter XIV

THE SIOUAN FAMILY

THE western front of the Algonkin faced the powerful Siouan Family. The Mississippi River was the western boundary of the United States in 1800, but in 1803 Jefferson negotiated a treaty with the French which extended the boundary to include the prairies and the plains, practically the entire buffalo range. It so happened that the boundary between the Algonkin and the Sioux was that same river. From Tennessee to the Gulf, the Muskhogean held the east bank, while the Siouan Family held the west bank as far south as Louisiana, where the Caddo held the river front. In terms of modern military science, the position of the Sioux had little to commend it, except that it had a river as the eastern front. Flanking the Sioux on the south and covering their rear northward to Nebraska were the Caddo. The Algonkin not only held the east bank of the Mississippi, north from Tennessee, but flanked the Sioux on the north, in what is now Canada, circled their position, occupying their rear, reaching down to Nebraska and thus connecting with the Caddo. In other words, the Sioux were completely enveloped by the Algonkin, Muskhogean and Caddo families. True, there were a few Siouan stragglers on the Atlantic coast, suggesting that at some remote time, long before 1492, either the Algonkin, Iroquois or Muskhogean had driven a wedge through Siouan territory. The Iroquois could have done it on their northern drive, which, in turn, almost split the eastern Algonkin into two divisions. Again, there is reason to believe that the Algonkin once held all the territory north of the 38th parallel, westward to the Rocky Mountains, and that the Sioux forced their way up the Missouri Valley, from the south, splitting the west-

THE HOKAN-SIOUAN STOCK: THE SIOUAN FAMILY

Dakota Tribes
Eastern Dakota
Santee Dakota (Little Crow)
Teton Dakota
  Blackfeet Sioux
  Brulé (Spotted Tail)
  Hunkpapa (Sitting Bull)
  Miniconjou
  Oglala
   (Red Cloud, Crazy Horse)
  Sans Arc
  Two-Kettle
Yankton Dakota (Waneta)

Upper Missouri
Mandan
Hidatsa
Crow

Others
Assiniboin
Winnebago
Biloxi

Lower Missouri
Iowa
Missouri
Osage
Quapaw
Ponca
Omaha
Oto
Kansas

*Virginia and
  North Carolina*
Saponi
Tutelo
Monacan
Manahoac
Catawba

ern Algonkin. No one knows whether this is what actually happened; the map merely suggests something like it. What we do know is that when the first Frenchman paddled down the Mississippi in a canoe, the Sioux held the west bank, as they still did in 1800. In fact, for some time they had held the Algonkin back on three fronts. It was their bold resistance that stopped Iroquois aggression at the Mississippi and later made it impossible for the Algonkin in the Ohio country to escape the wrath of the advancing frontier by retiring across the Mississippi. This is why the Algonkin made their last stand in Indiana and Ohio.

The Dakota

In the popular mind, Sioux symbolizes war, horses and buffalo, as exemplified in the Dakota, the true name for the most powerful member of the family. In the literature of the last century and even now the word Sioux (Dakota) seems dynamic, because among our fathers it meant something commanding attention. Once I saw a man standing before a museum case containing Dakota Indian objects, muttering to himself and, every now and then, shaking his fist as if defying someone inside the case. I learned upon inquiry that he had lived in the Dakota country. He held up a hand with a finger missing, explaining that he had lost it from an arrow shot at him by a raiding Dakota. He was fortunate, for many men of his generation fared worse. Among the associations clustering around the word Dakota are the Custer Massacre, buffalo-hunting horse Indians, great chiefs like Sitting Bull, Crazy Horse, Man-Afraid-of-His-Horse, American Horse, etc., red stone pipes, large camp circles of shining white tepees, painted buffalo robes bearing rayed sun figures, magnificent eagle-feather headdresses and fine fringed shirts.

The Dakota were the heroes of the original Wild West shows; Longfellow's Minnehaha belonged to the family, and such fine musical compositions as "The Waters of Minnetonka," or "Red Wing," immortalize Dakota music; and finally, the Dakota is the ideal of the artist. Tall, slender, with small hands and feet but sinewy body, strong features, high cheekbones and a beaked nose—the Indian of the nickel—all these characteristics may be seen in the Dakota or some of their hybrids. We expect all Indians to wear the Dakota costume, so that no matter what the tribe, all modern Indians appear in it. It is the conventional formal dress of the contemporary Indian, but it was devised by members of the Siouan Family and popularized by the Dakota. When a new President is inaugurated in

Washington, a few Indians ride in the procession wearing the traditional costume of the Dakota. The painter or the illustrator knows that if he presents a conventionalized figure in the Dakota style of dress, man or woman, it will spell Indian. It is a kind of picture writing. This is why we see paintings of the Pilgrims landing at the famous rock, greeted by Indians dressed like Dakota, or again Indians receiving Henry Hudson at Manhattan in the same kind of clothes, or Pocahontas in the wedding dress of a Dakota bride. All absurdities, except that we understand this to be art's way of telling us that Indians are being depicted.

Buffalo Bill was a great showman, the first to capitalize the popularity of the Indian. He chose his Indians from the Dakota and, both in America and Europe, persistently spread their fame, with drooping eagle-feather headdress and sharp features, so that young and old rarely imagine there are any other kind of Indians. Therefore it behooves us to look a little deeper into the history of the Siouan Family of which they are a part.

The speech of the Siouan Family is one of the most pleasing to the European ear. Of course, by this time the reader is aware that we have in mind a family of languages. The Dakota have many subdivisions, but they can talk with each other; this is not the case among the other members of the Siouan Family. Before 1850 some missionaries devised an English alphabet for the Dakota and began to teach its writing in their schools. Some of the old folks learned it and soon were writing letters to friends in other tribes. They did not progress as rapidly as did the Cherokee and the Choctaw, but still, before the end of the nineteenth century, they were becoming literate.

As we have said, it is a pleasing language with many soft consonants. Difficult, harsh consonants are frequent in most other Indian languages, making them difficult for the European to learn. Minnesota is a Dakota word meaning waters many. The word Dakota means friends, or allies, their own name for themselves. The term tepee means the place where one lives, or home, and has been adopted by Europeans as the name for a well-known type of tent. The Dakota language is still spoken and written by more than forty thousand persons and will probably live for a long time, since the Dakota are increasing rapidly.

Even a passing acquaintance with Indians compels one to learn a lot of new names. The main body of the Dakota were the Teton—now immortalized as the name of a national park and a range of mountains. Seven main divisions of the Teton were recognized, spoken of figuratively as the seven tribal council fires. There was no real federation like the league of the Iroquois, but they always recognized that they were close kin and, as a rule, they did not fight with each other. The names of the seven Teton-Dakota divisions, or subtribes, are: Blackfeet, Brulé, Hunkpapa, Miniconjou, Oglala, Sans Arc, Two-Kettle. Of these, the Oglala were the strongest in numbers and so take a prominent place in history; probably because they were numerous enough to dominate in the wars with the whites.

The Assiniboin

Sometimes these Indians are spoken of as the Dakota-Assiniboin group. Similarity of speech justifies this, but actually they were enemies of long standing. Years ago the writer observed that the Teton boasted of having taken more Assiniboin scalps than from any other enemy tribe. Likewise, the Assiniboin looked upon the Teton as their chief enemy. How this started does not matter, for once the vicious circle of a feud was formed it lasted a century or two. The Assiniboin expanded into the plains of Canada and over the border of the United States into North Dakota and Montana by 1830. At that time they were well supplied with guns and horses and well able to hold their own. Probably it was about this time that they became the enemies of the Teton and all the other Dakota. One reason for this may be that the Assiniboin were close friends of the Algonkin, skirting the Dakota on the east and north. Between these Algonkin (the Ojibway and Cree) and the Dakota there had been a feud of long standing, the Dakota holding a large part of the buffalo country as their own and fighting off all intruders. The Algonkin wanted buffalo, while the Dakota wanted to keep them for their own use. It all looks like an economic war, something we can understand. Yet, so far as we can see, the Assiniboin, the Ojibway and the Cree on the one hand and the Dakota on the other thought of the feud in terms of horses, captives and scalps, symbols of glory and social distinction.

About 1840 smallpox swept the Assiniboin; some observers of the time placed their losses at seventy-five per cent. As a military power in the Plains, they were reduced to a negligible remnant. The Algonkin Cree took their place, thus extending the territory of that family and presenting a strong front against the Dakota. The smallpox of that year did not trouble the Dakota, but the Cree soon restored the balance of power in the North.

How the Teton Lived

Since the Teton are the most powerful division of the Dakota, we shall sketch their mode of life. Our definite knowledge of them dates from about 1800, when they were living upon buffalo flesh and using skin tepees. Some of the other divisions of the Dakota raised maize, lived in rectangular bark cabins, used birchbark canoes, and in many minor traits of life resembled the woodland Algonkin to the east of their range. But these wild western Teton were always milling around from one favorite camping ground to another, raiding even the camps of their near relatives, the Assiniboin, Crow, Iowa, Omaha and Mandan. Their domestic economy was based upon the buffalo; his flesh was used for food, his bones for tools, ornaments and arrow points, his horns for spoons and small containers, his dewclaws and hoofs for rattles, his hair was twisted into ropes for horses, tendons for thread, skins for robes, tepees, moccasins, etc. They even used skin for binding and joining where we would use nails. They made serviceable knives from buffalo ribs, and one must admire the genius of their women in finding new uses for by-products of the buffalo hunt. Many useful bags were fashioned from buffalo rawhide, their surfaces ornamented in pleasing geometric patterns in red, yellow, black, blue and green. Some of the buffalo robes were handsomely painted on the flesh side, and as the fur side was usually worn next to the body, these paintings gave a decorative effect. A robe or two was the most important part of every Teton's wardrobe. If a man had a good robe to drape his body, a breechcloth and a serviceable pair of moccasins, he was equipped for any kind of weather. Hats and gloves were unknown: leggings, shirts and minor parts of costume were for ornamental purposes rather than for everyday use. Early observers speak of Indians going about in the coldest winter weather—and many people know how cold a winter day can be in North and South Dakota —wearing nothing more than a robe, breechcloth and moccasins. The women wore a loose skin dress instead of a breechcloth, but otherwise dressed like the men. Young buffalo calves furnished robes for the little folks, older calves for larger children, etc. By a little selective killing among the wild herds, a run of robe sizes could be had from which a person of any age could be fitted.

As may be expected, the buffalo had a place in Teton magic, art and religion. Buffalo were a puzzling phenomenon to the Indians. Often, the rolling grassland around a Teton camp was thickly dotted with them; again not an animal was in sight. The Indians, in common with most human beings, believed that there was something supernatural back of it all. They thought vaguely of a grand buffalo who ruled over all the unseen and who was human enough either to take pity on man or to retaliate. Rituals were performed and prayers made that the buffalo be plentiful, and when they were scarce, the praying, singing and rituals were intensified. The Indians often apologized to the Great Unseen Buffalo for killing the real animals and exercised care not to be wasteful, for an angry power could quickly bring starvation.

They loved horses, but did not eat them. They preferred to get them by raiding rather than by other methods. There were wild herds of horses in the southern plains, but the Teton, like most of their northern neighbors, preferred to steal horses already broken to riding. Almost from the first, the western Indians stole horses from the Spanish settlements; later, from the French and the English. Tribes near the settlements got them first, then more distant tribes stole these same horses, so that, in a short time, an individual horse could reach Canada. All of the Plains Indians taught their youth that one of the most laudable acts was to steal the horses of a stranger. An Indian brought up under such a regime would be troubled by a guilty conscience if he passed a chance to steal a horse. Of course, such behavior kept the Indians embroiled with the settlers and, more than anything else, marked them for slaughter. From the white point of view, they were bandits and treated accordingly.

In an Indian camp there were usually horses enough for all, women and children included. Baggage which was formerly carried upon the backs of women, girls and dogs was now packed by horses or drawn upon an A-shaped drag frame, which the French called a travois. If Teton women ever made pottery, they forgot the art after the horse came into use. In due time trade kettles were available, but meat could be roasted over the open fire, and upon occasion stone boiling was used. Porcupine-quillwork as trimming for pipestems, bags, dress moccasins and shirts was formerly common, but was soon displaced by beads from the trader's stock. In museum collections the beadwork of the Teton is conspicuous for its artistic quality. The designs were highly geometric, not only in bead and quillwork but in the painting on rawhide bags and on women's robes. The art of the men was inferior, but since the man's art was always realistic, whereas women's art was geometric, it is difficult to judge fairly.

We have said that horse stealing was a passion; parties of adventurous men set off on such expeditions with great frequency. An almost equal urge was to kill men. Both were frequently attempted in the same raid, and great social acclaim went to the man returning with both scalps and horses. The highest rating went to the warrior who was first to strike an enemy, either with his bare hands or with a "coup stick" (from the French word for blow). Often they carried symbols of such achievements on their persons. One Teton the writer knew carried a cane of his own make upon which were marks to show that two Assiniboin, one Crow and one Ojibway had lost their scalps by his hand. When in formal dress, his war shirt bore the conventional signs that he had stolen many horses. We heard of many Teton who surpassed this record. There is nothing unusual in this: among us the general recounts his medals, the college professor his degrees and other honors. Whatever the culture of a people, great value is usually placed upon that which is rewarded by badges of distinction.

In common with some of their neighbors, the Teton practiced a curious sacrifice, so spectacular that the first reports from white observers were received with great skepticism. Deeply set in their scheme of the unseen was the idea of self-torture and the offering of flesh to the sun and other sources of supernatural power. The Dakota and some of their relatives were frankly selfish in their sacrifices, the supplicant seeking individual superiority to escape death and to overcome enemies. The price he paid he considered high, so high that only a few strong-willed men each year offered themselves. Yet this does not imply that there were no noble and admirable ideals associated with these sacrifices, for there were. The whites have no monopoly of such sincerity and virtue.

The procedure varied, the best-known being the thrusting of a sharpened stick through the skin, around which a stout cord was fastened. The end of the line was tied to a post and the victim required to release himself, if at all, by tearing himself free. While tied up in this way, he danced, sang songs, prayed, cried out to the unseen power to pity him and give him power. If the supplicant fainted from exhaustion and pain, the expected climax was reached, for in such a state he would be in communion with the gods. One could undertake such tortures at any time, but the usual time was during the greatest tribal festival, the Sun Dance. Shortly after the Teton were placed upon reservations, such sacrifices were prohibited by the government and eventually suppressed. Occasionally a single individual performed this sacrifice secretly (the last Wissler was informed about took place in the early 1930s, not by a Teton but by a man from a neighboring tribe). Yet such practices are not unique, for religious enthusiasts in New Mexico still lacerate their bodies; many non-literate peoples in one way or another cut and mutilate themselves with fanatical frenzy. Yet human sacrifice was repugnant to the Teton. They lauded the man who tortured himself in the Sun Dance, but considered suicide and forceful sacrificial killing as criminal.

Among the Teton there were philosophers of no mean order who reflected upon things as experienced, sought explanations in terms of causes and looked for the signs of a unified system embracing the universe. They gave numbers a place in the mysteries, placing all powers in a hierarchy of fours. Thus over all was a unit of four powers, sometimes thought of as a whole, at other times as of four parts. Each of these four was, in turn, composed of four powers, and so on down. As one would say, over all is the great four, the highest level of being; upon a lower level are the four times four powers; upon the next lower level four times sixteen, etc. Upon such a foundation was built a detailed explanation of the universe, too complex for us to consider here.

History of the Eastern Dakota

In 1650 there were no white men in the land of the Dakota. Their country comprised the southern half of

Minnesota and all of South Dakota. On the east the Mississippi separated them from the Algonkin with whom they were at war. Algonkin tribes held northern Minnesota; in North Dakota were the powerful village tribes, Mandan, Hidatsa and Arikara—all more or less hostile. Nor were they on friendly terms with their western and southern neighbors. We have noted how the relentless Six Nations pursued the remnants of the Huron and Erie to the banks of the Mississippi, on crossing which they were kindly received by the Dakota, who defied the Six Nations. Traders had not yet come among the Dakota, so they were still equipped with bows and arrows, whereas the Huron brought guns with them. Being better armed, the Huron became arrogant and finally abused their privileges as guests, by openly ridiculing the bow-using Dakota as "back numbers." This was the last straw; the Dakota turned upon the Huron, destroyed all they could lay hands upon; the remainder saved themselves by flight, recrossing the Mississippi and hiding out again in Algonkin country.

The French gradually extended their contacts to include the Dakota, but were slow in establishing trading posts among them. However, by long and hazardous journeys to forts at Mackinac and even further east, they managed to acquire a few guns, making it easier to repel the better-armed Algonkin, especially the Ojibway or Chippewa, their most aggressive enemies. In 1727 the Dakota joined the Algonkin Sauk and Fox tribes in a brief war with the French who bought peace with them by establishing traders in their country and equipping them with guns. The effect of this was to intensify the Dakota-Ojibway war which continued until about 1850, more than two hundred years in all. Perhaps we should call it the Two Hundred Years' War. In Europe the Thirty Years' War was considered a record, but that is nothing as compared with the Dakota-Ojibway war.

In 1763 Canada became British territory, a change which puzzled the Dakota, but they finally accepted it wholeheartedly, becoming loyal subjects. They were too far away to know much about the War for Independence, and their never-ending struggle with the Ojibway kept them out of the Algonkin war with the United States. Yet American traders began to enter their country, and a few settlers filtered in among their southern relatives, making them aware that two different white nations were on their borders. When in 1803 the territory west of the Mississippi was purchased by the United States, they were again confused and disturbed. They were a proud, free people who regarded the British as friends and allies, so what right had the United States to claim their lands and to object when they raised the British flag over their villages? However, it seems that a few Dakota sensed the situation and announced their intention of favoring the United States, probably because that government was smashing the power and arrogance of the Algonkin. Yet most of the Dakota were pro-British. Tecumseh pleaded with them to cease fighting the Ojibway and join in the struggle against the United States, and succeeded so far that when the War of 1812 began, a few Dakota joined Tecumseh's brigade in the British Army. Of these, a few individuals were active, but the rank and file hesitated and soon returned to their homes. The British way of fighting was strange to them, and they were still suspicious of the Algonkin and Huron with whom they were brigaded. And to make matters worse, the British did not trust them. In fact, the coldness of the British and their failure to gain victories in the Great Lakes country split the Dakota into two divisions, pro-United States and pro-British. The United States whites encouraged their Indian friends to suspect the good intentions of the pro-British Indians, developing thereby a good deal of bad feeling which might have led to bloodshed after the War of 1812 if the British had not turned a cold shoulder to their Dakota allies.

In 1815 the United States called a conference, inviting all the chiefs, whether friendly or not. Most of them came to this grand council, where, after due deliberation, they declared their loyalty and their intention to break off trade relations with the British. Shortly thereafter (1816) the British called a conference which all the pro-British Dakota attended, together with a few who had light-heartedly pledged their allegiance to the United States. The conference was held at Drummond Island, in Lake Huron, about one thousand miles away. The Dakota chiefs were courteously received, yet not especially honored, and but few presents were offered them. This called forth their contempt. They recounted the men lost in the War of 1812, that now the British received them coldly and were about to dismiss them with a few trifling presents. Chief Little Crow said:

"After we have fought for you, endured many hardships, lost some of our people and awakened the vengeance of our powerful neighbors, you make a peace for yourselves and leave us to obtain such terms as we can! You no longer need our services, and offer us these goods to pay us for having deserted us. But no, we will not take them; we hold them and yourselves in equal contempt!"[1]

He then kicked the bundles of presents about the room and withdrew. Others made similar speeches, after which they too withdrew, returning home well disposed toward the United States.

Waneta

The Dakota were strong in numbers; allowing for over-estimation, they numbered about ten thousand in 1800. Among so large a body of people a number of exceptional men and women are sure to come to notice. In the War of 1812 the following became prominent: Little Crow, Wapasha, Tamaha, Red Wing and Waneta. However, the hero of the War of 1812 was Waneta, born a Yanktonai about 1795. He joined the British Indian contingent and distinguished himself fighting the Americans at Forts Meigs and Stephenson, in the Ohio country. Even though

1 Doane Robinson, "A History of the Dakota or Sioux Indians," *South Dakota Historical Collections*, Vol. 2, 1904, p. 100.

the British with whom he fought were defeated, he was given the rank of captain and after the war went to England, where he was presented at court. Naturally, he returned pro-British and for a long time led that minority. His father having been treacherously killed by the Ojibway when trying to make peace with them, he swore eternal vengeance and led in the perpetual war against them. Being a fighting man and still a British soldier, he meditated war with the United States, dreaming of annexing their own territory to Canada. In 1820 he led an armed force to Fort Snelling, near Minneapolis, but first entered the fort as a friendly Indian, to study its defenses. Loyal Indians warned the commandant, so Waneta was seized and given a kind of "third degree." In Waneta's clothes were concealed a number of British medals and his commission as captain in the British Army, still in force. These were destroyed before the prisoner's eyes. In the end Waneta renounced his allegiance to England and thereafter proved himself loyal to the United States, becoming the outstanding chief, using his power wisely, keeping peace with the whites, but still fighting the Ojibway. On the northern Dakota front, the Caddoan Arikara and the Siouan Mandan and Hidatsa, weakened by disease and harassed by the Algonkin, were recognized by Waneta as allies and given his protection. In 1832 the famous artist Catlin visited the Dakota and painted Waneta's portrait, though another artist had sketched him in 1823. Waneta continued to be the leader of all the Dakota until his death in 1848. Though almost continuously at war with the Ojibway, Assiniboin, and occasionally on other fronts, he was loyal to the American whites after 1820 and maintained peace with them.

War with the United States

One thing is certain, the whites did not bring war to the Dakota. For centuries they had been schooled in arms, in surprise attacks to get away with a scalp or two. Elusiveness was their strong point. Marshaling tribe against tribe was not their way of making war, but continual petty raiding, with exasperating cunning and audacious suddenness, followed by a quick getaway was their method. These raids were never against the other Dakota tribes, but that was the limit of their friendliness, for not even other members of their own Siouan Family were safe. They harassed the Algonkin frontier persistently. The villages of the Lower Mandan and Hidatsa living along the Missouri were annoyed by these miscreants who scalped their women while they worked in the cornfields, made away with their horses and occasionally lurked by the palisades guarding their villages. The Caddo, especially the Pawnee, were kept busy retaliating.

Into this setting, the ever-advancing white frontier sent its prairie schooners and ox teams, and when homesteads were set up where the Algonkin once lived, they were, in turn, raided and harassed. Yet behind the frontier was an even stronger United States. It had won two wars with England. Wayne had smashed the power of the Algonkin in Ohio, Harrison had given them a mortal wound in Indiana, and Jackson captured the last Creek stronghold in the South. Of Indian battles there were many. Between the settlement at Jamestown in 1607 and 1814 about a hundred battles with white men are officially listed, half the total for the whole United States. This takes no note of the thousand or more raids by Indians and whites, with resulting white losses estimated at eight thousand and Indian losses of at least half that number. The United States was to wage a war with Mexico and then engage in a desperate Civil War before the Dakota were to feel the real power of the white man. Even before the Civil War was over, they made a drive against the white frontier in Minnesota, but suffered dreadfully at the hands of the troops hurled against them. A considerable number were treated as murderers and hung. But the real struggle was yet to come. Railroads were built across the country, telegraph lines strung, river craft improved, all to the disadvantage of the Dakota. On the other hand, the Indians had become thoroughgoing horse-men, swift in attack and retreat. They were often better armed than the soldiers sent against them, because local white traders were selling them the latest repeating rifles when such were available. Yet, more ironical still, the government, in accordance with its treaty promises, pre-sented them with arms and especially with ammunition, theoretically for hunting, but actually enabling them to stock up for a struggle with that same government.

Around 1840 the frontier of settlements reached the Upper Mississippi country. Before this, Dakota contacts with white culture had been based on mutual interest, and for almost two hundred years peaceful intercourse had prevailed. They were still free tribes, maintaining their morale by skirmishing with other Indians, but had raised their standard of living by taking over from the whites many luxuries, such as horses, guns, knives, cloth-ing, etc. A minority had become stock raisers and farmers, but the majority were still buffalo hunters. They gloried in their allegiance to the United States and proudly un-furled the Stars and Stripes on all public occasions. But now the stage was being set for a less peaceful scene, settlers were demanding some of the Indian land. Already the buffalo were leaving the Mississippi River, gradually bringing about a westward movement among the Dakota themselves.

In 1851 the Eastern Dakota agreed to give up most of their land in Minnesota; it had been their home for ages, and for two hundred years they had sacrificed many lives in defending it against the Ojibway. Naturally they were reluctant to give it up, but for the sake of peace they did so and moved on. Yet the white frontier was soon at their doors again, inviting friction and misunderstanding. The terms of the last treaty were openly violated. The chiefs did their best to calm their people and maintain peace, but in 1856 a hotheaded band killed, scalped and raped in a white settlement. The main body of the Dakota put pressure on the offenders, and the affair blew over. In 1859 the Santee division reluctantly gave up more land

in Minnesota and went on a reservation. Irritation and
doubt were now voiced around every Eastern Dakota
fireside. The frontier had come between them and the
Ojibway, putting an end to that long-standing war, but
now that same frontier threatened them. The explosion
came in 1862, when a band of hostiles swept through
settlements in the valley of the Minnesota River; no one
was spared, an old-time massacre was under way. A few
women were taken captive and subjected to the usual
abuses. War was now inevitable. Many Dakota, formerly
friendly to the whites, now joined the hostiles, so they
were able to put about fifteen hundred men in line. Generals Sibley and Sully began operations against the Indians
at once, but the Civil War was under way and few troops
were available, making it necessary to raise volunteers,
but even raw troops, led and supported by veterans from
the front, put the Indians to disadvantage. Further, improvements in artillery made fighting more difficult for
the Dakota than it had been for the eastern Algonkin, so
notwithstanding their numbers the Dakota gained no real
victories. Most of the Indians participating in the outbreak
were soon captured, tried for murder, and thirty-eight
were hanged at Mankato.

This was impressive enough, but later, when a small
Dakota war party murdered some settlers, a squad of
cavalry captured and executed them upon the spot. This
threw all the Dakota into a panic. The troops relentlessly
pursued the different bands as far as the Missouri River,
forcing peace in 1865.

History of the Teton

In later times the Teton became the dominant division of
the Dakota. Fix in your mind the Black Hills, a detached
group of mountains rising upward in the plains, as the
center of the Teton domain. Eastward, they held the
country to the Missouri; southward, to the Platte in Ne-

braska; westward, in Wyoming to the Teton Mountains; and northward, to the Yellowstone.

While the Eastern Dakota were holding off the Ojibway and making friends with the whites, the Teton grew strong and more warlike. They became thoroughgoing horse Indians before 1800, ceased all attempts to raise maize, and discontinued the use of pottery. They tolerated the Algonkin Cheyenne who adopted a similar mode of life, even taking them under their protection for a time, but made war on the Crow, the Pawnee and every other western tribe they met.

Until 1849 no white people disturbed the Teton, except traders who were in the main welcomed, but now the Gold Rush to California filled the trail along the Platte with ox trains and horse herds. These alarmed the Teton. They began to pillage these wagon trains and not infrequently killed and scalped the travelers. They participated in the famous Laramie Treaty of 1851, promising not to molest the trail, but even if the chiefs were sincere in their efforts for peace, their young men were not to be restrained. The net result of these continued depredations was an increase in the garrison at Fort Laramie and the construction of other forts. Thus, in 1855, General Harney appeared suddenly with a large force, took the Teton by surprise and crushed a large camp, inflicting great loss. As Harney stayed in the country and the Teton feared other reprisals, all was quiet for a time.

Harney seems to have been a man of vision as well as sense. He conceived a plan to organize a native police force and set up a tribal government under the direction of the United States. There is every reason to believe that the plan would have worked and changed Teton history for the better, but this was not to be. Where Indians are concerned, always expect the worst! No one in Washington would even consider the plan. But events were marching on. A new Teton leader was coming of age, who, under the name of Red Cloud, was destined to play a major role in the next war. The Minnesota outbreak in 1862 and the ensuing campaign stirred the Teton to commit new atrocities. Again the Nebraska trail ran blood. The evidence indicates that Red Cloud was the leader. The situation was further complicated by surveys for a railroad which the Teton opposed as contrary to the last treaty. Red Cloud was a soldier, not a statesman or politician. About three thousand men were available, and in so far as Indian traditions permitted, he organized this man power and strengthened Indian tactics.

The response to these new atrocities was to send more troops. Since the center of Teton concentration seemed to be the Powder River or the Big Horn country of northern Wyoming and adjacent Montana, a small detachment of troops built Fort Phil Kearny, south of the present city of Sheridan. It was clear to the Teton that a chain of forts was to be built extending to the Yellowstone, which would put them under complete subjection. At once Red Cloud hurled his men against the new fort, Phil Kearny, and later against Fort Fetterman, standing between it and Laramie. The advantage in numbers lay with Red Cloud, but even a crude palisade defended by a few cannon and regular soldiers balked him. He tried to draw the small garrison into an ambush, but failed. Now and then a few soldiers would be caught outside, but still the forts held.

The next year Red Cloud met with a surprise. He had concentrated his entire force just south of the present town of Sheridan for a heroic effort against Fort Kearny. About the end of July 1867 a small detachment of soldiers came out from the fort to cut wood. They camped upon a knoll, removed the wagon boxes and laid them in a circle for shelter, in case of need. On August 2 some Indians attacked the party, but they took refuge in the breastwork of wagon boxes. Red Cloud brought up his reserves. Behind the wagon boxes were thirty-two white men with plenty of ammunition and the newly invented breech-loading rifles. For the first time the Indians were to meet these rifles in the hands of expert marksmen. Red Cloud ordered his men to charge, but their losses were so terrific that they turned back. Time after time they charged, only to fail. The fire was too deadly. Note that

Red Cloud was a general, he stayed in the rear. Had he led either of these charges, he would most certainly have been among the slain. While Red Cloud was holding a council as to what to do next, word came that a rescue force was coming from the garrison. At this point the fight was stopped. One source placed the Indian loss at several hundred, but later accounts have agreed that only six were killed and six wounded. The engagement is known as the Wagon Box Fight, the sight of which may be seen near Highway No. 87.

Desultory fighting continued, but the forts survived. The Teton were discouraged and ready to talk peace; they negotiated a treaty in 1868, which Red Cloud finally signed in 1869. The Teton won in one particular: the forts in northern Wyoming were abandoned and the troops concentrated at Fort Laramie. Thus they were granted everything they asked for and gave nothing in return. Of course, the real point at issue remained: the ever-advancing frontier. Later Red Cloud was taken to Washington and publicly received in New York. Upon his return he retired to the Pine Ridge Reservation in South Dakota, his military career ended.

All was quiet on the Teton front for a while, but soon gold was discovered in the Black Hills, territory guaranteed to the Teton by treaty. To control the rush and prevent flagrant violations of the treaty, troops moved in to build forts. There was considerable friction, but the matter was smoothed over, chiefly because there were no buffalo in that rough country, so none of the Teton wanted to live there. In 1875–76 the Teton and other Dakota tribes were given permission to leave their reserves to hunt buffalo in the Big Horn country, in northern Wyoming. When their leave expired they refused to return. Naturally the Army was called upon to bring them back. This was what the Indians expected, for once again they were determined to try conclusions with the Army. Then followed the campaign in which Custer was surprised and his small command annihilated. The Indian leaders were Gall, Crazy Horse and others, but the dominating figure was Sitting Bull. Red Cloud seems to have been at his home on the reservation. After the Custer affair, Sitting Bull is said to have remarked gloomily, "Now the soldiers will give us no rest." He had no illusions as to the power of the United States. More troops arrived, and in time all the Indians were rounded up, except Sitting Bull and Gall, who escaped with their bands into Canada. Canada did not want them; the Canadian Indians objected to giving them land; the United States did not want them back, so their position was anything but satisfactory. Sitting Bull loudly proclaimed that he was an English subject, that his people had accepted English rule after the French and Indian War and had never recognized the authority of the United States, but this false claim made no impression upon Canada. These Indians were looked upon as dangerous intruders and troublemakers. Soon small groups began to slip back across the line to their proper reservations in Dakota, and eventually Sitting Bull surrendered to the United States. A few of the Dakota liked Canada well enough to stay; their descendants are now considered regular Canadian Indians. Here the chapter ends. Please note that though under Red Cloud something resembling a real military campaign was carried out by Indians, that was exceptional. After Custer was wiped out, the Indians dispersed, though they were still strong enough to have defeated the remaining troops. What the Reverend Pond wrote many years before is true of most Indian fighting; he stated that during the period of 1835-45, when, as usual, the Dakota and Ojibway were at war, his record showed that the Dakota suffered only 88 casualties, the Ojibway 129. In both instances more than half were women and children. This would mean roughly eight to ten per year in populations of several thousand. A majority of the war parties returned empty-handed, not because they saw no one, but because the surprising of even a lone individual or two was regarded as too hazardous. A real fight was to be avoided if possible. Pond says:

It was not the practice of the Indians, after taking one

or more scalps, to go on in further quest of more, or to remain in the enemy's country after being discovered.[2]

So either a victory or a defeat was regarded by Indians as the end to a play. Each party was expected to withdraw and return to their homes. In due time they would try it again.

The Great Depression

Around 1885 the Indians of the plains in the United States and Canada were faced with a crisis. The buffalo were no more. This meant, not merely hunger, but the absence of materials for adequate clothing and housing. A tepee of buffalo skins was a warm house in winter, and a good buffalo robe was sure protection against the cold winds. With the passing of the buffalo these went also. It was then not merely a food shortage, but an economic collapse —hard times with a vengeance. The government rushed in rations of crackers, flour, salt pork and cattle; few Indians starved to death, but they disliked these new foods, none tasted like fresh, juicy buffalo meat. They were forced to live in tepees covered with thin cloth, and good wool blankets were too expensive for them. The reports of Indian agents on file in Washington tell tragic tales of suffering, colds and an accelerated death rate. Young children were the hardest hit. The Indian leaders were discouraged, sullen and resentful. With the buffalo gone and raiding for horses prohibited, there was nothing to be done but sit about in idleness awaiting the slowly coming bounty of the government.

The Teton Dakota felt the pinch acutely. A few years back they had annihilated Custer's cavalry, but this only hastened the end. Now Nature herself had turned against them. Their leaders saw no future, except in trying to farm in a country ill adapted to agriculture. Anyway,

[2] Rev. Pond, quoted in Robinson, *op. cit.*, p. 113.

farming was woman's work and, according to their traditions, disgraceful for men. They longed for the return of the buffalo and the good old days. Then came a ray of hope. Rumor had it that far out in Nevada lived an Indian who could see into the future, who could speak to the dead, etc. Possibly he could point the way out of the present dilemma. So a committee of chiefs was sent out to investigate. They returned convinced—whether by this medium or the workings of their own imaginations, we do not know; but soon many of the Teton Indians went into induced trances after which they told of a world filled with buffalo and free of white men.

A few leaders preached the coming of an Indian Messiah, who would sweep the white people away and restore the country to the Indians. The white people began to speak of this as the Ghost Dance Religion, possibly because the Indians danced until they fell into trances, thought they talked with the ghosts of the dead and believed in a Messiah. Soon agitators were sent to other reservations, and delegates from other tribes came to inspect these new religious ceremonies. The emotional pitch was high and becoming more and more intense. Friendly Indians, skeptical of the promise of these new leaders, informed the agents and other white people that a revolt was under way, that a general massacre was possible. The alarm spread to the surrounding towns and cities, whose citizens began to expect the worst. The government mobilized large bodies of troops near the important reservations influenced by this new movement. The Teton of Pine Ridge Reservation were in the center of the disturbance and the most likely to make trouble, so bodies of troops began to move in upon them from all sides. The great Teton leader, Sitting Bull, living on a nearby reservation, was killed while resisting arrest. A skirmish or two, with considerable loss on both sides, ended the affair. The Indians were disarmed and cowed. Thus ended the last outbreak of the Dakota; it was little more than a gesture, and only a relatively small number of the Teton participated.

The two outstanding leaders in this religious movement, and the most militant, were Short Bull and Kicking Bear, relatively young men. Both were good pleaders, of commanding but stern personalities. They were sincere followers of the new faith and ready to lead the Indians against the whites. After the collapse of the movement, they withdrew to different parts of the reservation, where they lived quietly with their respective bands. Short Bull seems to have been the abler of the two and quietly followed the precepts of the Ghost Dance Religion for a long time. His band remained the most conservative and the most pagan, yet gave the officials the least trouble.

The Hidatsa and the Crow

The Crow now live in Montana. The French knew them as Plains people under the name "handsome men." Many early travelers were impressed by their bearing, fine physique and elegant costume. The latter, however, was of the prevailing Plains style, but merely better made and with an artistic touch. They loved these fine clothes and, above all, long hair. In an ingenious way they attached strands of hair to lengthen their own locks, until they sometimes dragged on the ground. No wonder early observers called them the Beau Brummells of the Indian world. Bodmer, the artist, visited them in 1833, making a few spirited drawings. These Crow were a thoroughgoing Plains people, not differing greatly from the Teton, but incidentally their enemies.

The Hidatsa, so closely similar to the Crow in speech that they must have been a single people at no remote date, lived in earth-covered houses, made pottery, raised corn and vegetables. There are many reasons for guessing that the Hidatsa way of life, the way of the southern Siouans, is the old way and that the Crow, Teton and Assiniboin, not long before white men came, were living according to this old way, but that the open plains lured them to take to tepees, abandon pottery and finally to become thoroughgoing horse Indians.

The Hidatsa were sometimes called Big Bellies, or the Gros Ventre of the Missouri, to distinguish them from the Atsina, or Fall Indians, also called Big Bellies. At other times the Crow, because of their obvious close relationship to the Hidatsa, were spoken of as Big Bellies of the Prairies. This confusion of names still bothers the historian. And as if this were not bad enough, the Hidatsa were called Minnitari by the Dakota; the first part of the name means water, the ending has something to do with crossing the water or being on the other side. Since the Hidatsa villages were on the bank of the Missouri, this is apt enough.

The Mandan

The Hidatsa villages were near Knife River, a branch of the Missouri in North Dakota. South of them, near the present city of Bismarck, were the villages of the Mandan, the most celebrated of all. Like the Natchez who were a great center of culture and influence on the Lower Mississippi, the Mandan were a center for the upper Missouri. The Teton called them the Miwahtoni and usually mentioned them in terms of respect. The pioneer fur traders in Canada heard of them through other Indians and came to admire. Later, Lewis and Clark were also impressed. By and by, Catlin, the first great painter of Indians, came to make them famous on canvas and in literature. From school days we recall Catlin's drawings of the Great Chief Matotope. He must have been an outstanding individual, which means there were other great chiefs to give the background to his greatness. Then came Maximilian with the artist Bodmer. The latter's sketches and Maximilian's account of Mandan ceremonies are classics, and the Mandan were worthy of both. They performed impressive religious pageants full of symbolism. They maintained a number of ritualistic societies for men and women. Those for men were graded by age, so that a member passed from one to another, according to his qualifications. These societies were copied by many tribes, as the Teton, the Crow, Arapaho, Cheyenne, Assiniboin and others.

But evil days were ahead for the Mandan. They were to feel the blight of the white man's culture, for before the frontier reached their villages, smallpox and cholera swept the Indian country. These scourges were bad enough among the nomadic peoples, but once the villages became infected, the losses were terrific. In 1750 there were nine large Mandan villages, but a half century later there were only two, and finally, in 1837, the sixteen hundred souls remaining were all but wiped out by another smallpox epidemic. Less than fifty survived and joined the surviving Hidatsa, with whom their descendants still live.

When the Mandan were first heard of by white men, there were among them a few albinos, or individuals with straw-colored hair and pale skin. Writers of the time jumped to the conclusion that here were the descendants of a white race. The superculture of the Mandan was cited as additional proof that they were Europeans. According to one writer they were a long-lost colony of Welshmen who, according to tradition, once sailed away from their homeland into the mysterious West. Of course, this was absurd, but one Welshman asserted that he had visited this tribe and found them able to speak Welsh; yet, since no other traveler found them able to speak anything but Mandan, we know there was no foundation to that tale.

The Southern Siouans

It remains to take note of some other distinguished Siouans; the Osage, Omaha, Iowa, Kansas, Oto, Missouri and Winnebago. These were in part agriculturalists but also hunted buffalo and deer. They made little use of tepees, except when on the march, most of them living in large oven-shaped houses covered with earth. As these houses could not be moved, their villages had a certain permanency. Some of these tribes maintained two villages, one for summer use, near fertile land where corn, pumpkins and beans were raised; the other for winter, near an adequate supply of firewood. In general, they were considered more civilized than the Teton, but a study of their respective cultures indicates that this may or may not be true. If raising a small amount of vegetable food distinguished a tribe as civilized, then these tribes were superior to the Teton. But the Eastern Dakota were farmers, too. The ritualistic ceremonies of the Osage and the Omaha, for example, impress one as a little more elaborate than those of the Teton, but, in general, there were many similarities between all these Siouan peoples.

The Osage grew suddenly rich because the lands given them in Oklahoma produced oil. For a time, at least, they enjoyed the greatest per capita income of any people in the world.

It would not be fair to close this chapter without mentioning the now nearly extinct Siouan-speaking tribes living in Virginia and the Carolinas just about the time French and English ships began to sail up and down the Atlantic coast. Some of the tribe names recorded in early history are Saponi, Tutelo, Monacan, Manahoac and Catawba. These tribes were hard pressed by Iroquois and Muskhogean Indians, when Europeans appeared upon the scene. The picture we get is that of a once-numerous, powerful Siouan-speaking block of tribes holding Virginia and the Carolinas. To the west, along the Mississippi and up the Missouri, the Siouan tribes we have just reviewed were even then a large group of relatives destined to carry on valiantly, to survive white conquest, and to constitute one of the largest and most influential bodies of contemporary Indians.

Some Distant Relatives

At this point it may be of interest to reaffirm the relationship which many linguists believe to exist between Iroquois, Caddo, Muskhogee and Sioux. These linguists would further include a number of small tribes such as the Yuchi, the Chitimacha and the Tonkawa along the Gulf Coast in Louisiana and Texas; and finally, in California and Lower California, such tribes as Yana, Karok, Shasta, Yuki, Pomo and Yuma (in Arizona), a group to which the name Hokan has been given. This gives a kind of superfamily tree, or a stock, as we have noted, suggesting possibly that the major early home for these families was the southeastern United States, and that at one time they held the whole southern half of the United States, from California to the Atlantic.

Now we must take leave of the Siouan Family, in many respects the best known. Their strongest members were a proud, haughty people. They had great faith in themselves, teaching their young that they were superior to all other peoples and nations, that all others were inferior and lived only by their sufferance. They were handsome and fit. They believed in war, after the Indian fashion. One of their war songs is a lament for those who are so unfortunate as to die in bed. There are many, many books dealing with their history; biographies have been written of their great men. What more should a people want?

They were characterized by strong faces, with the familiar profile of the buffalo nickel. The objects which most clearly remind one of the Dakota and other Siouans are the red stone pipe, the beautiful eagle-feather war bonnet, the tepee and the self-torture of the Sun Dance. The rose-colored stone known as catlinite or pipestone comes from a quarry in Minnesota and was looked upon as symbolic of living flesh and blood and so sacred. All pipes made of this stone were fit for offering smoke to the gods and for cementing friendships. We have spoken of the tepee, the feather headdress and the war bonnet of the curio collector; these are familiar enough. The self-torture referred to moves us to horror, rather than admiration, but it was the self-torture of fanatical religious zeal and not cruelty imposed upon unwilling victims. All Indians believe that the gods can be moved to pity, if one be willing to suffer pain and anguish long enough. So they attached thongs to strips of their own skin by which they dragged buffalo skulls, or fastened the thongs to the center pole in a Sun Dance, dancing and pulling back until the strips of skin holding these thongs were torn out. If the supplicant fainted from the pain, so much the better, for then the gods would appear to him and give him protection and power. Finally, every prominent Dakota man could show scars on his breasts and back produced in this way. He was proud of them, because they certified to his worthiness of supernatural guidance.

Chapter XV

THE PENUTIAN FAMILIES

In California and northward are a number of small families which linguists believe to be related because their languages employ some of the same grammatical tricks. To the reader, the word Penutian may suggest something unimportant or trifling, but the origin of the word shows that it has no such implications. One group of these related families uses the term *uti* (two) in many combinations; the other group uses *pene* (two). So the linguists coined the term Penutian. Afterward, some linguists found what they thought were sufficient grounds for relating certain tribes in Oregon and Washington to this group, as shown in the family chart.

The Californians

About one half of California was held by Penutian-speaking peoples. Their home was the basin drained by the rivers entering San Francisco Bay, roughly from Bakersfield north to Weed. At the beginning of the nineteenth century the number of tribes ranged from two to three hundred, indicating a population of unusual density for Indians. In the older books one finds the five main tribal groups listed as separate linguistic stocks, but it is now clear that they comprise a single stock. If the reader is interested in names, the chief divisions are Maidu, Wintun, Costanoan, Miwok and Yokuts. Their culture is often spoken of as the typical Californian. Certainly their mode of life is more uniform than is usual among American Indians, possibly because they live in a compact body and in a rather homogeneous environment. Every people on a

THE PENUTIAN FAMILIES

California Tribes
Miwok
Costanoan
Yokuts
Maidu
Wintun

Klamath-Modoc
Klamath
Modoc

Cayuse-Molale
Cayuse
Molale

Chinook
Wasco
Wishram
Chinook

Shahaptin
Nez Percé (Chief Joseph)
Klikitat
Umatilla
Yakima
Wallawalla
Palouse
Warm Springs, or Tenino

Mexican
Mixe
Zoque
Huave

primitive level must solve the problem of living by learning how to use the raw materials their habitat offers for exploitation, and since these Californians lived in a fairly uniform area, the same pattern of economic life would suffice. It is not far wrong to say that the Penutian lived on acorns. To us this may seem ridiculous, for the bitter, puckering taste of an acorn should convince anyone that such a nut was not designed for man's food. Among the doubtful ingredients of the acorn is a heavy charge of tannic acid which, taken in quantity, becomes a poison. The California Indians were aware of all this, but since acorns were abundant they sought and found a way of treating them to make a rich, nutritious food.

The process is more complicated than that by which we transfer wheat into bread. The acorns are gathered, in season, and stored in bins or small structures erected at convenient places. The next job is to hull as many as may be wanted for immediate consumption. Then the kernels are pounded with stone mortars and sifted or winnowed until a fine yellow meal is produced. Next, a shallow pit is scooped out in clean sand and the meal spread over the bottom and the sides. Warm water is then poured in, which percolates through the meal into the sand below, taking with it some of the tannic acid and other bitter materials. This process of leaching continues until the mushy meal is satisfactory to the taste. When sufficiently dry, the meal may be removed in chunks. From this bread is made.

Though these Indians were regarded by some as of simple culture, they possessed one cardinal virtue: they stored food for the future, and thus seldom went hungry. They also hunted deer and small game, and gathered many seeds, roots and vegetables, which were available most of the year. In fact, California was a kind of Indian paradise where food of some kind was always at hand and the climate comfortable. Archaeologists tell us there has been little change in the economic life of the aboriginal Californians since the arrival of the first immigrants several thousand years ago, a state of affairs quite different from that observed in other parts of the United States. Possibly these Penutians are the most ancient immigrants into California, but if they were later invaders, they soon adopted the food habits of those they conquered, and settled down to enjoy the even security of life which the California living technique guaranteed. Perhaps too successful a technique of living under primitive conditions and an even tenure of economic security inhibit all important social changes. We wonder whether these Californian Penutians had the most perfect adjustment to environment of any Indian tribe and were never troubled by reformers, depressions and revolutions. It looks that way, anyhow.

Then we often hear that of all United States Indians the Californians followed the simplest form of life. They were loosely organized, not overfond of fighting and little given to roving habits. They usually went barefoot, wore little clothing and, aside from basektry, did not develop much in the way of art. In contrast to the Hopi and Zuni

Pueblos, or even an Iroquois village, they fall well below par. The same can be said of their mythology and their ceremonies, which, in the main, seem weak in ideas and dramatic quality. In short, they seem to have some of the characteristics we expect to find among the underprivileged. Yet they maintained a relatively dense population, with neither the starvation nor lowered vitality that is found on poverty levels. The whites despised them for all this and hurried them toward extinction.

The Modoc

In southern Oregon were two related tribes—Klamath and Modoc—the latter destined to a place in history because they put up a fight. Their contact with the whites began after the settlement of Oregon, around 1830; after a moderate amount of friction both the Klamath and Modoc accepted a reservation, where their survivors still live. The Modoc were not satisfied. In 1870 they ran away to the open country along the California boundary, refusing all requests that they return.

Finally, in 1872, the government ordered them to take up residence on the Klamath Reservation at once. This they refused to do and, under the leadership of Kintpuash, known to the whites as Captain Jack, defeated a detachment of troops sent out to move them. Then the Indians did the usual thing: they killed white settlers and burned farm buildings, finally taking refuge in a rough country known as the Lava Beds. This was an ideal place for Indian fighting, so a small body of troops sent against them was defeated. The white mediators now went into action. At first the Modoc were conciliatory, but when they had the peace commission in their power, they made the mistake of killing them. A military campaign resulted. After resisting for a time, the Indians stole out of their position, led the troops into a trap and worsted them, but in a second encounter their best leader was killed. This proved fatal to their cause, because the Modoc then split into two divisions, each hostile to the other. The military campaign was now in full swing, so all the Modoc were soon prisoners of war. Captain Jack and several other leaders were tried for the murder of the peace commissioners, convicted and hanged.

The Chinook

The word Chinook has a place in the vocabulary of the well-informed. Originally the name of an Indian tribe near the mouth of the Columbia River, it gave a name to the warm winds blowing inland and influencing the climate even as far to the east as Montana and Alberta. Then a trade language evolved, a combination of Indian, English, Spanish and French, once used all over the northwestern United States and even in Canada. This language came to notice early in 1800 and was studied in 1841 by the famous linguist Hale. At that time the Chinook jargon was limited to three hundred words, but in 1894 approximated a thousand words. About half these words were of English origin.

The Nez Percé

The name Shahaptin is probably strange to the reader, but the best-known tribes in this family are the Klikitat, Umatilla, Yakima, Wallawalla and Nez Percé. The last are the most famous, the "stuck-noses," so called because it was their custom to pierce the septum of the nose for ornaments and rings. It was a convenient characterization, since in the Indian sign language the Nez Percé could be designated by passing the extended index finger under the nose. Anyone could guess what that meant. Some time in 1700 the Nez Percé became thoroughgoing horse Indians, as did several other tribes in the region; many habits and crafts of the bison-hunting Plains Indians were taken over until some of the Shahaptin camps were at least reminiscent of the picturesque nomadic Plains culture.

They made no pottery, but were stone boilers, as were their neighbors on the north. As may be expected, they made fine baskets. This was, in fact, their chief craft. Some years ago collectors prized the baskets of the Klikitat especially, as a visit to any well-stocked museum will show. The Nez Percé specialized in soft bags woven in basketry techniques. Both coiled and twined baskets were produced in the area, their unique feature being a method of ornamentation designated as imbrication. Books on Indian basketry explain these difficult matters. The Nez Percé did no other weaving except rabbitskin blankets, if these can be called woven. If rabbitskins are cut into long strips, so twisted as to make fluffy fur cords, and then loosely woven into a rectangular piece, the result will be a light warm fur blanket or robe. Otherwise, these Indians were clothed in deerskins.

The country of the Nez Percé was rich in vegetable foods, especially edible roots. In fact root digging is a characteristic of most tribes inhabiting parts of Washington, Oregon and Montana. The most important was camas, a bulbous root gathered in large quantities and roasted in pits. When not eaten at once, the roasted bulbs were pounded into a mush, made into loaves, cooked again, then stored for future use. The roots of the kouse were available when camas could not be harvested. There were many other edible roots, as bitterroot, carum, wild carrot, etc. The country of the Nez Percé was also rich in wild berries which, sun-dried, formed an important food reserve. About the only wild seed used was that of the sunflower. In times of extreme food shortage, lichens, the inner bark of trees, pine nuts, etc., were also eaten.

The tributaries of the Columbia River and the many small rivers draining into the Pacific Ocean are the favorite egg-laying waters for salmon. When the time for such egg laying approaches, the fish crowd into the mouths of these rivers and rapidly ascend to the very headwaters of all branches. These "runs," as they are called, are exciting times. While the "runs" are seasonal, the precise hour for the salmon to appear varies. Three varieties of salmon ran in the streams accessible to the Nez Percé, and since they did not run at the same time, there were several periods during the year when a lot of fish could be had for the taking. At such times the surplus fish were dried, smoked and stored for the future. Many neighbors of the Nez Percé pounded their dried fish into a kind of meal which could be mixed with a flour made by pounding dried roots, but the Nez Percé rarely mixed pounded dried fish with their root meal.

The common way of fishing was to stand on the bank, or in the stream, with a long-handled fish spear or three-pointed gig. In large streams the fish were speared from canoes. At regular fishing places platforms were built in the water, upon which the fishers stood with their spears. Hooks were not used, but dip nets, net traps and seines were known. Weirs of large size were often combined with screen traps in which the salmon were caught.

Horses probably reached the Nez Percé early in 1700 and had about the same effect upon their housing habits as in the case of buffalo-hunting Indians. The tepee used by the Plains Indians was always used by the Nez Percé when traveling with horses. As a permanent residence, a long, many-family house was the traditional type. This was an A-shaped structure, composed of a framework of poles covered with mats. The top was open so that smoke from the long row of family fires down the middle could escape into the open air.

We do not know much about how the Nez Percé dressed before white days, but, when first known, the men wore moccasins, leggings, breechcloth, shirt and blanket. These were of deer, elk and buffalo skins, and so remind us of Indians generally, except that Nez Percé men seem to have worn full dress regularly instead of on gala occasions, as among many other tribes. The women dressed in skins, too, wearing long loose gowns similar to the Plains Indian style.

It is a curious fact that in the valley of the Columbia

River the methods of using the horse were the same as in the plains, and that along with this went a similarity in dress, house furnishings and the use of the tepee.

Few white men entered this country before 1800. The Salish Flathead first came into fame by sending messengers to St. Louis with a petition that a priest be sent to them. The chief reason for this was that some Iroquois hunters from New York State, following the fur trade west, and doubtless hoping to escape the pinch of white settlements, made their home with the Flathead. Some of these Iroquois were Catholics and, feeling the need of a priest to baptize their children, induced the Flathead to take this unusual step. Father de Smet accepted the invitation and met with unusual success. His influence over the surrounding tribes was extraordinary, as his biography demonstrates.

In 1840 the famous Whitman set up a mission near Wallawalla, in the country of the Shahaptin, but seven years later the Cayuse Indians burned the mission, killing Whitman and his family. The site of this tragedy is now a national shrine.

Chief Joseph

An Indian known to white people as Chief Joseph is the outstanding personality in the history of the Nez Percé. Indeed, he may be said to have rescued this tribe from oblivion by skilled leadership in an unsuccessful war with the United States. He won the first skirmish, but from then until the end was in full retreat. The retreat is what intrigues us, the wonder being that he had military genius enough to escape annihilation.

The date of his birth is uncertain, but he died September 21, 1904. In 1875 he was a man of maturity, a recognized leader, probably thirty-five years old. He had some education, some knowledge of English and the ways of white people. In 1863 his people had entered into a treaty by which they agreed to give up roaming about and settle on a reservation near Fort Lapwai. When it came to a final decision, they were reluctant to move, and temporized until about 1877, when the Indian agent ordered them to comply. A part of the tribe did so, but Joseph's people refused. Joseph himself recommended compliance, but his followers favored resistance. Trouble was precipitated by a few Indians killing settlers; in one raid twenty-one whites were massacred. Joseph knew that now war was inevitable, that his people had begun it, nor did he seem reluctant to assume the leadership. To all appearances he was enthusiastically for it. He seemed to be blind to the vast power of the United States government and the relentless way in which it had pursued the Dakota after Custer's defeat. Anyway, his followers were sure they could defeat all the troops sent against them. Joseph took up a strong position in White Bird Canyon near the Salmon River, Idaho. On June 16, 1877, a small detachment of United States troops rashly attacked, but were forced to retreat with relatively heavy loss.

So Joseph won. The history of Indian fighting shows that after a victory the enemy retreats and both sides consider the affair settled for a time, at least, and go their separate ways, the victors to dance over the scalps and recount their deeds. Perhaps Joseph knew better, but was helpless. On the other hand, he may have been too thoroughly conditioned in his youth to think anything else possible. Anyway, the Indians left their strong position, retiring to the Clear Water River near Kamia, Idaho.

Soon a larger body of troops under General Howard came upon him. Joseph had to give battle, but was outfought. He seems to have realized that from now on his only chance lay in keeping ahead of the pursuing troops, turning upon advance and scouting parties when he had a chance to overwhelm them. He was well equipped with horses, well armed, and well supplied with ammunition. The whole band was with him—women, children, the aged, the sick and the wounded. His advantage lay in knowing the country and how to live by game killed on the way.

Joseph headed for Yellowstone Park. Passing through it, his men kidnaped a party of tourists (later let them escape), then turned toward Montana. There were several skirmishes between Joseph's rear guard and outriders from Howard's troops, but nothing decisive, except that every loss to the Indians was Howard's gain.

Just west of Billings, Montana, General Sturgis, in charge of the cavalry, caught up with Joseph, but he escaped in flight. Joseph planned to reach the Musselshell River and, if still pursued, to continue north into Canada. As usual Howard had with him a body of Indian scouts who, in one way and another, got information as to Joseph's plans.

It so happened that near what is now Miles City, Montana, was a body of troops under General Miles. He was ordered to intercept the Indians. So when Joseph and his weary followers reached a point near the Bear Paw Mountains, south of the town of Chinook on Milk River, he found a new army blocking his way. General Howard was close upon his heels, so at last Joseph found himself in a trap. In fact General Miles surprised him, rushed his camp and captured most of his horses. Yet the Indians dug rifle pits and prepared to fight.

Neither Howard nor Miles wished to exterminate his band, so they gave Joseph time to consider a surrender. His final speech is recorded as follows:

"Tell General Howard I know his heart. What he told me before, I have in my heart. I am tired of fighting. Our chiefs are killed. Looking Glass is dead. Toohoolhoolzote is dead. The old men are all dead. It is the young men who say yes or no. He who led the young men is dead. It is cold and we have no blankets. The little children are freezing to death. My people, some of them, have run away to the hills and have no blankets, no food. No one knows where they are—perhaps freezing to death. I want to have time to look for my children and see how many I can find. Maybe I shall find them among the dead. Hear me, my chiefs. I am tired. My heart is sick and sad. From

where the sun now stands I will fight no more forever.[1]

Joseph had made a masterly retreat of about one thousand miles. Yet he was doomed from the start. Had he entered Canada, his fate would not have been improved, for that country had enough Indians on its hands. After surrendering, he was not permitted to return to the reservation he refused in 1877, but was carried to Oklahoma as a prisoner of war. Some of his party were returned to the reservation, but after many years Joseph and his most faithful followers were sent to the Colville Reservation, in Washington, where he died in 1904.

[1] As recorded in Francis Haines, *The Nez Percés; Tribesmen of the Columbia Plateau,* Norman, Oklahoma, 1955, p. 280.

North Pacific Coast: Alaska and Canada

Haida	Tlingit	Taku
Eyak	Auk	Tongas
Ahtena, Copper River	Chilkat	Yakutat
Eyak	Sitka	

ATHAPASCANS

Northern: Interior Alaska, and Canada

(Listed alphabetically; most of these tribes are north and west of the area shown on the map, pp. 64–65.)

Bear Lake, or Satudene	Nabesna, or Upper Tanana
Beaver, or Tsattine	Nicola, or Stuwihamuk
Carrier, or Takulli	Sarsi, or Sarsee
Chilcotin, or Tsilkotin	Sekani, or Tsekahne
Chipewyan	Slave
Dogrib, or Thlingchattine	Tahltan
Han, or Hankutchin	Tanaina, or Kenai, Knaia-
Hare, or Kawchodinne	khotana
Ingalik	Tanana, or Lower Tanana
Kaska, or Nahane	Tsesaut
Koyukon, or Unakhotana,	Tutchone, or Tutchone-
Tenas	kutchin
Kutchin, or Loucheux,	Yellowknife, or Tatsanottine,
Dindjie	Copperknife
Mountain, or Tsethaottine	

Pacific Coast: Washington, Oregon, California

Kwalhioqua	Hupa, also Chilula, Tlelding,
Tlatskanai	and Whilkut
Chastacosta, also Coquille,	Wailaki, also Kato, Lassik,
Galice, Tututni, Umpqua	Mattole, Nongatl, and
Tolowa, and Chetco	Kinkyone

Southern: Arizona, New Mexico and Oklahoma

Navaho

Kiowa Apache, in Oklahoma

Apache: Jicarilla, Lipan, Mescalero, Warm Springs (Victorio), Chiricahua (Geronimo), Western Apache, including the San Carlos, White Mountain, Cibecue, Tonto

Chapter XVI

THE NADENE FAMILIES

WE turn now to northwestern Canada, the great belt of forests, chiefly conifers, stretching from north of Lake Superior into Alaska. On the north these forests thin out into the Arctic tundra, beyond which lie the Eskimo. On the south the Algonkin Cree spread along the margins between these forests and the grasslands of southern Canada, but the forests and a part of the tundra were held by a division of another great stock, the Nadene. Scattered over the western half of the United States are many tribes, all more or less divergent members of this group: nineteen in Washington, Oregon and California; nine or more in Arizona and New Mexico; and finally, the so-called Kiowa Apache in the plains. The strongest group of all is the Navaho in Arizona and New Mexico, now numbering over eighty thousand.

Returning to the North, language experts tell us that the Tlingit and Haida are also distant relatives of this group. So, in number and range of territory, the Nadene people rank near the top. A unique feature is the way in which the detached tribes are scattered in the United States. In Canada they form a compact, continuous body of people, as do the Algonkin, but in the United States they are scattered down the Pacific coast and into the Southwest, with two stragglers out in the plains. Looking at the map, one cannot help wondering whether these outlying tribes are merely stragglers, or whether they are remnants of a large southern extension of the Nadene into Washington and Oregon and into the northern plains, their continuity finally being broken by the Algonkin, Siouan and other intruders. Probably we shall never know the answer to this question. Some writers claim that the

Nadene are the last immigrants from Asia, but, if so, they have been here for a long time. If students of language should find peoples in Asia speaking such a language, everyone would recognize the probability of a recent origin for this family; but until we know more than we do now, the question stands unanswered.

Treating briefly a few of the stragglers, we will meet these families in four main groups: the totem-pole makers of the North Pacific coast; the Athapascan hunters in the Canadian forests; and in New Mexico and Arizona, the Apache and the Navaho.

The Totem-Pole Makers

Every educated person knows something about totem poles, those bold expressive carvings on large tree trunks, queer animal and human forms piled one upon another, intriguing tourists and museum visitors and moving them to wonder what is the meaning of it all. There were artists of no mean ability among the totem-pole makers, who carved house posts, beams, great wooden masks and many small objects. Totem poles are merely the most conspicuous of their carvings. The ideas back of these totem poles are far from obvious, because there is nothing quite like these carvings in the culture history of Europe. The best we can do is to compare them with family coats of arms; yet there is nothing really heraldic in the idea. Roughly stated, these wood-carving tribes are divided into clans. One is born into a clan and so can do nothing about it. Born to the Raven Clan, for example, a Raven he is, and custom decides into what clan he may marry and to what clan his offspring belong. Each clan cherishes a mythology in which the original clan ancestor is named. Strangely enough, among many non-literate people such groups of relatives are believed to have a kind of animal-human ancestor, and so we meet with such clan names as bear, wolf, whale, raven, owl, and beaver. The doings of the mythical clan ancestor are cherished as hero tales to the glorification of their descendants. Here we have the basis for a clan or family emblem. A tribe or village might contain many clans, intermarriage between which would continually cross and combine ancestors, as was the case under the system of heraldry in Europe, to the end that a given household of totem-pole makers could boast a long list of these mythical heroes. These might be carved upon a tree trunk and set up in front of the house—thus a totem pole.

Such poles were used by most of the Indians from Vancouver Island, northward through the country of the Tlingit in southern Alaska; but as we are writing about the Indians of the United States and Alaska, rather than of Canada, we shall give chief attention to the Tlingit.

If the reader turns to a map of southern Alaska, a group of islands flanking inlets into the coast will attract his attention. Tourists sail among these islands in summer to admire the mountains rising on every hand. Geologists tell us that even these islands are mountains, the valleys around which are submerged and now covered by the sea. As one goes northward, the coast becomes more regular at or near Cook Inlet, where the country of the Tlingit ends. The Tlingit are coast dwellers; their idea of a village is a row of houses near the shore, all facing the water. When first discovered, they lived in fifty or more villages grouped under some fourteen dialectic or tribal divisions, and were estimated to number about ten thousand souls.

The shores are lined with great cedar trees, whose wood is fine-grained, splits straight and is a delight to work. Even the inner bark can be shredded, twisted into string and woven into mats and capes. These grand trees appealed to both the poetical and the practical in Tlingit nature, and so the cedar tree may be taken as the keynote to their culture. Instead of totem-pole makers, we might better call them men of the cedar forest. They were master craftsmen in primitive lumbering; they knew how to fell these great trees, cut them into logs and split out planks, all with crude tools of bone and stone. Their houses were of planks. To begin a house, they set up two heavy posts or tree trunks, about twelve feet high and six feet apart. Another pair were set up opposite these, at any distance up to sixty feet, according to the size of the house desired. Two long beams were then fitted to the tops of these posts. These beams supported the roof, the comb of which ran parallel and above them. The walls of the house were formed of split planks, set upright; finally, boards covered the roof. The house fires were up and down the middle, and the smoke was let out by moving one of the roof boards with a pole. A large number of people, all relatives, occupied such a house. The living apartments were on platforms around its sides. After all, this is not so primitive and reminds one of the great halls of the Saxons in England. The totem pole stood in front of the house, and the four large posts inside might be carved in the same way.

The Tlingit were a seafaring people. All their boats were dugouts. They did not build boats with planks and ribs, perhaps because cedar trees were large enough to furnish dugouts over sixty feet long. Such large boats were usually reserved for war. Smaller boats were always at hand for fishing and short journeys. Even the large boats were paddled like canoes; rowlocks were not a part of their equipment. The Tlingit seem to have used sails for the larger boats, as did the Eskimo. They fished and hunted seals and sea otter. Stranded whales were welcome, but occasionally they tried to harpoon them. The climate being moist and mild, they needed little clothing and usually went barefoot. The men often went about without even a breechcloth; the women wore a short apron of cedarbark. Robes of woven bark, wild goat or dog hair were common. When first visited by white men, many of them wore robes of sea otter, in exchange for which they were promptly offered trade blankets worth but a fraction of the value of the sea otter robes they displaced.

The Chilkat, a division of the Tlingit, wove curious capes with long fringes, known to collectors as Chilkat blankets. They bear queer designs which at first seem to be geometric, but upon closer inspection prove to be the representation of animals, birds and fish similar to the paintings on house fronts. Fine baskets of spruce root, handsomely decorated in color, were made by most of the Tlingit. As stated in an earlier chapter of this book, the Indians of the Pacific coast were stone boilers, so, as would be expected, the Tlingit boiled food in wooden boxes and baskets with stones heated in the open fire. In the Tlingit home, good housekeeping required that cooking stones be kept in the open fire, hot and ready for the cook. As may be expected, the Tlingit made no pottery, nor were they very quick to adopt the metal kettles offered them in trade, probably because the food tasted better when boiled with stones.

Elaborate ceremonies were the order of the day. Large wooden masks representing their ancestors and other supernatural heroes were worn on such occasions. Elaborately carved wooden rattles representing birds and other living creatures were carried in the hands of dancers. The shaman, or medicine man, was an important person in this society; at death his head might be cut off and placed in the wooden box where he kept his magical equipment, and then hidden away in a dark, dry cave. Such boxes have found their way into museums, where they are on display.

In common with the other totem-pole makers we have met, the Tlingit practiced the "potlatch." In the popular mind this word stands for any kind of a feast, when gifts are made, but the true "potlatch" was not so simple as that. Specifically, the term implies the giving of a feast and the distribution of a large amount of property. Among the Tlingit a special feast was given after a death; as a kind of memorial to the deceased there would be a great "giveaway" of slaves and all kinds of property. Of course, the near relatives were expected to furnish the property to be given away. In later years trade blankets were considered the conventional gift, and in anticipation of need a household would save them, often in large numbers. Of course, giving away such property lays a kind of obligation upon the recipient to make returns on occasion. His social position may stand or fall according to performance in this respect; a miser would get nowhere.

The totem-pole makers never had a real war with the white people, made no great retreat into the west because they already lived on the margin of the continent: their houses were built upon the shore of the ocean, they found most of their living in the sea, which the white men could not fence up and say, "This is mine"; nor did the white man deny them room for their villages; in fact they were always willing to give them the necessary land. So, in general, the totem-pole makers were allowed to live and to pursue most of their old occupations. The greatest achievement of these people was their art; they were master wood carvers, as a visit to any large museum collection will show. Go to one of these exhibits, sit down comfortably, and note the skillful way in which these artists have handled their figures. At first all may be grotesque and strange, but by and by one begins to understand that here the traditions of a people and the less material parts of their culture are expressing themselves in a heroic way. For they did things on a grand scale; their houses were large, with massive pillars and beams; their canoes, though of a single log, were often sixty feet long, and their totem poles were gigantic. Their country produced enormous cedar trees, and it was in the scale of these great trunks that the builders and wood carvers worked. If the best thing a people can do is to produce a distinctive art, then these Indians may be called great.

It may be true that the white man spared them; but his culture did not. It engulfed the totem-pole makers' villages; their children began to go to the white man's school, later to find jobs in fishing and other white man's work and so, little by little, the traditions weakened. No longer was it a joy to have a great carved house post or a totem pole, and worse, few young men tried their hand at it. Today that art is all but dead. Thus these Indians are on the road to civilization like the others. Yet we should not feel too regretful. All great art runs its course, especially when it flowers as the climax in a culture. It would have died anyway, for it appears to have reached its zenith under the stimulus of the early contacts with white men; not that its content was derived from white culture, for from all we can see this art is wholly indigenous. The great cedar trees invited them to express what they had come to feel and believe, and they accepted the challenge. Rather better than most peoples, they adjusted their lives to this one outstanding feature of nature and so naturally achieved a great art. Fortunately, a few of our museums have many of their masterpieces; otherwise, the medium being wood, all would have perished.

Yes, the Tlingit were a great people, but they too were real human beings. Their social scheme included slaves, common people and aristocrats. The slaves may have enjoyed some privileges; they may not have labored fifteen hours a day, but their masters looked upon them as so much property to be given away or bargained for. Upon occasion, to show how wealthy he was, the owner of slaves would club some of them to death in public; in other words, he was rich enough to destroy property. Collectors of curios are proud if they own a "slave killer," the implement used for such killings. Yet this is not all, for sometimes, when building one of their great houses, slaves would be knocked on the head and cast into the hole before the post was set into it. This was human sacrifice. Of course, similar things were done in other parts of the world; even in parts of medieval Europe children were sacrificed to make bridges safe.

The Northern Hunters

If any one thing can tag a people, it is *babiche;* of all Indians the Athapascans are the most addicted to its use. Every traveling kit and every cabin was marked by a skein of this dependable string, an untwisted thong, or ribbon, often unbelievably narrow and of amazing length, cut with machinelike exactness. A tanned caribou or deerskin was laid flat, then cut spirally with a sharp knife. Only a practiced eye and steady hand could produce a string of even width. This *babiche*, as it was called, was used for lacing snowshoes, making nets and bags and for all kinds of binding. Naturally, no hunter went abroad without a skein of this ever-ready *babiche* in his kit. So we are justified in saying that you will know your Athapascan by his *babiche*, and if you have the feel for fine handwork, go to a museum and gaze at the best examples of this craft.

These *babiche* people lived in the interior of western Canada, the Great Northwest and Alaska. They are an inland people, ranging north to the Arctic Circle. From Cook's Inlet on the west the Eskimo held the entire Alaskan coast and then ranged eastward to Hudson Bay, thence around Labrador. West of Hudson Bay are the Athapascans. They were an inland people because the Eskimo formed a barrier between them and the sea. The respect was mutual; the Athapascans feared the Eskimo, and vice versa. Each seemed to think the other inhuman antagonists. In Labrador the Eskimo kept the Algonkin inland. There is something impressive in this. Dame Nature may have had much to do with it, for between the bleak Arctic coast and the inland forests lies a belt of tundra, an inhospitable country for man in winter and not particularly inviting in summer. The Eskimo wintered on the seashore, in fact often on the ice, while the Indians took shelter in the forest. In summer each might venture into the tundra for game, but they seldom met, except in battle, which made each of them more or less a mystery to the other. Nor were the Athapascans always at peace with each other. It is the same old story, for the assumed peaceful past some writers stress to encourage the belief that killing human beings is something civilization brought into the world is an example of wishful thinking. Archaeologists can show us that some of the earliest men were killers. Certainly, the early accounts of Canadian fur traders reveal nothing resembling a paradise in these northern forests. For example, read Hearne's account as an eyewitness to an Indian massacre, how even though a girl clung to him, begging to be spared, she was torn away to be murdered.

There are, even now, few white men in the territory of the Athapascans, so few that we lack good information as to the number of tribal divisions and the details of their lives. We suppose climatic conditions have deterred students of Indians from wintering among them. It may not have occurred to the reader that until tribal names are standardized there will be a confusion of tribes in history and literature. The names most often encountered in books on Canadian tribes are Chipewyan, Yellowknife, Dogrib, Hare, Ingalik, Carriers, Beaver and Slaves, mostly living between the Rocky Mountains and Hudson Bay. Among the names used for those of the Yukon country are Khotana, Kutchin and Loucheux. No one of these tribes stands out above the others, so a rough general account of them must suffice. The Hudson Bay traders first came in contact with those east of the Mackenzie, particularly with the Chipewyan, but as soon as the Cree were well armed they raided the Athapascan country, making away with the poor natives and establishing trapping camps in the best localities for furs. Fortunately for the Athapascans, the Algonkin Cree found the Far North too cold in winter, so they contented themselves with their first gains, ceasing to war upon their neighbors. As few white settlers invaded these northern forests, there were no white and Indian wars. Most of these Indians still make their own living in their own way, by hunting, fishing and trapping.

The aboriginal culture of these peoples can be characterized as that of caribou hunters. To about the same degree that certain Plains Indians lived upon the buffalo, these hunters depended upon this wild member of the reindeer family. There are several kinds of caribou, but the best-known are those which live in the forests in winter, yet migrate in great herds to summer feeding grounds on the tundra beyond the Arctic Circle. When they reach the Eskimo country, many of them are taken for their skins and flesh; the Athapascans follow them out into the tundra, but after killing their quota, await their return in the autumn. They, too, need their skins for winter clothing. However, there are other species of deer and even moose in their forests, all of which contribute to Athapascan economy.

Snowshoes are indispensable in winter. The toboggan is widely used, but usually pulled by the hunter himself. In summer, birchbark canoes are common, but what distinguishes these Indians is the "ever-ready *babiche.*" Their women show no interest in pottery, contenting themselves with making containers of skin and bark. Most of their spare time must be given to making skin clothing, for the need is great. Some of them were skillful in weaving arm and leg bands of sinew thread, interlaced with porcupine quills. The cleverness of this technique and the beauty of the product are worth seeing.

Almost every great Indian family made some contribution to the world's way of living. The Algonkin gave maple sugar, lye-hominy, the birchbark canoe and the game of lacrosse. The Muskhogean gave us corn pone and yams. The Athapascans of the northern forests gave us the toboggan and the snowshoe. If they did not originate them, they brought them to a high state of perfection. Both these handy appliances are used by the whites. To such perfection did they bring snowshoes that they made them in rights and lefts. Also, they made them long and graceful, incorporating some of the features of a ski. To see a hunter in his graceful warm fur clothing, on his streamlined snowshoes, with his ski-pole-like staff, a long neat toboggan trailing behind him, is to fix in memory a picture never to be forgotten.

The Stragglers in the Plains

Two small tribes, the Sarsi and the Kiowa Apache, hold a prominent place in Indian history, not because they did anything in particular, but because they were found far from home. Some time before known to white men the Sarsi came down across the Saskatchewan River and took over the habits of the bison hunters. Apparently they enjoyed some kind of protection from the powerful Algonkin Blackfoot tribes in whose territory they were living when discovered. Their mode of life and even their ceremonies closely parallel the Blackfoot, suggesting that they were always weak in numbers and so followed in the footsteps of their powerful neighbors. We use the Blackfoot name for them, which seems to mean "no good," though that may have no literal significance. It may mean little more than that they were regarded as a weak group needing friends. They retained their independence, but some of them learned to speak Blackfoot, possibly because the latter were not interested in learning to speak Sarsi. Occasionally the Sarsi came down into Montana, but they always regarded Canada as their home and, finally, were settled upon a small reservation near Calgary. In recent years their proximity to a large city hastened the collapse of their tribal life, so that their future is uncertain.

The Kiowa Apache, as the name suggests, were first found under the protection of the Kiowa, a then-powerful bison-hunting tribe. Like the Sarsi, their mode of life closely followed that of their protectors. Whether they split from the Apache of the south and took to the plains, or whether they came down from Canada, as did the Sarsi, no one knows, but like the latter they stuck to their original speech, thus enabling us to identify them as Athapascans.

The Apache

To older readers the word Apache calls up visions of relentless raiding and killing. The French use the word to mean the worst kind of robbers and assassins. This may sound harsh when applied to the living Apache in New Mexico and Arizona, but history bears testimony to their former raiding habits. The name Apache applies to some eight or more tribes, all closely related in speech and so

9. INDIAN LIFE IN CALIFORNIA— The women in the center of the foreground are hulling acorns and grinding them into meal. In the distance women are making baskets. *Painted by A. A. Jansson.*

10. TOTEM POLES

11. A NAVAHO WOMAN SPINNING SHEEP WOOL

12. PUEBLO INDIANS PLANTING CORN – The village can be seen in the distance. The culture of these Pueblo Indians was essentially sedentary. They were agricultural, they wove cloth and made baskets, while their pottery was of a high type. They inhabited dwellings that were permanent, and gathered in communities sufficiently large to be called cities by the early explorers. Even today some of the old pueblos are inhabited as they have been for centuries. *Painted by A. A. Jansson.*

probably springing from a single wandering group of immigrants from the north. They were in the country when the Spaniards arrived in New Mexico, and some of them, at least, were then raiding the Pueblo villages and the agricultural tribes of Arizona. They soon took to horses, acquired firearms and became more predatory than ever. They raided the Spanish settlements for horses and other plunder, occasionally taking scalps. In 1837 their incessant raids, south of what is now Arizona, so annoyed the Spanish settlements in Mexico that a bounty was offered for their scalps. The Apache retaliated in kind, open war prevailing for forty years, or until the United States took over the Southwest. The Apache war did not cease then, but was directed at the United States and neighboring Indian tribes.

Finally, in 1864, both Mexico and the United States threatened a drive for their extermination, but this merely intensified Apache resistance. So raids and petty attacks upon settlements continued until 1871. At this point General George Crook enters the picture. By 1873 he had subdued about three thousand Indians, settling them on reservations. For a few years there was little trouble, but soon there was dissatisfaction among the Apache, and some bands broke away from the reservations to attack settlements. Some were captured, but a band under Victorio went up and down the country killing white people, now fighting off the soldiers, now eluding them. His real success was due to dodging back and forth across the Mexican boundary. At last, in 1880, Victorio was killed in a fight with Mexican troops.

Now the famous Geronimo comes upon the scene, as the new leader of the hostiles. He was born in Arizona in 1829. In the many raids in Mexico and later in the United States; he was schooled in war, for after 1850 he participated in one or more raids each year. Things went on about as usual until General Crook returned to Arizona in 1883, defeated Geronimo and placed him upon a reservation. In a few years he was out again, burning and killing. General Miles succeeded Crook, and with five thou-

sand troops tried to capture Geronimo, with his handful
of followers. The country was too rough for troops to operate in, but finally Geronimo voluntarily surrendered in
1886. This time he was treated as an incorrigible bandit,
and, with some of his followers, imprisoned in Florida.
Geronimo was kept a prisoner, at hard labor, for several
years, first in Florida, but later on a military reservation
at Fort Sill, Oklahoma. Strange to say, he became a Christian, joining the Dutch Reformed Church in 1903. He died
at the age of eighty. His was a career of blood and pillage,
if ever there was one. For more than forty years he was
raiding and fighting either in Mexico or the United States.
Hiding in rocky wastes and unexplored canyons, he defied the troops of two nations. But it was a losing game,
conditions were changing, the frontier had passed on,
leaving Geronimo and his followers engulfed in the settlements. We have seen that wherever this happened to an
Indian tribe its days of fighting were at an end.

We should like to end the story here, but even loyal
Americans should occasionally be told some of the unbe-
lievable things their government does. Would you expect
that a President of the United States would order the army
to seize several hundred women and children and sentence
them to a military prison for life? But history records the
act, so it cannot be ignored. Geronimo's people were the
Chiricahua Apache. When General Crook placed them
upon reservations, all but a few of them decided to give up
raiding and live by farming and stock raising. It was the
few irreconcilables that formed Geronimo's band; the main
body of the tribe stayed at home and took no part in raiding. Many Apache men served under Crook as United
States scouts against Geronimo. This itself should indicate
that the stay-at-home Apache were loyal to the United
States.

Yet, after Geronimo surrendered, orders were issued
from Washington to General Miles to seize all the peaceful
Chiricahua Indians and ship them to a military prison in
Florida. In the meantime a small party of their chiefs had
been invited to Washington for a conference. They were

received by the President and praised for their faithful services and loyalty to the United States. A large silver medal was given their leader, but immediately thereafter they were arrested and taken to a military prison in Florida. This sounds improbable, but the records show it to be true. The Indian men on the reservation in Arizona with 399 women and children were seized by the United States Army and shipped to a military prison in Florida. We sometimes talk about the atrocities of European nations, but we do not recall that they carried off children and confined them in military prisons. In 1890, four years after these Indians were imprisoned, public sentiment was aroused to such a pitch that Congress ordered an investigation, but it was not until 1894 that anything was done about it. In the meantime deaths among the women and children were about double the normal rate, because of unsanitary conditions, poor food, etc. Yet none of them were released in 1894, but moved to Fort Sill, Oklahoma, where the Army continued to hold them as military prisoners until 1914. Thus for twenty-eight years the innocent were kept as prisoners of the United States Army. Children born in prison were prisoners too; and if this is not stupid and absurd enough, just note that after these prisoners were taken to Fort Sill, one of the men enlisted in the United States Army, served his time and was then returned to Fort Sill, where he died a military prisoner.

After 1914 these Indians were given permission to return to their old home on the reservation. Those who chose to remain in Oklahoma were settled on a reservation in that state. The chief who received the silver medal was often heard to ask, "Why was I given a medal to wear in prison?"

The main divisions of the Apache are the Jicarilla, Mescalero, San Carlos, White Mountain and Chiricahua. The last-named were the chief raiders, the tribe of Geronimo. Their home was in southeastern Arizona. The Jicarilla were in northern New Mexico, the Mescalero in the southeastern part of the same state. All the Apache were somewhat nomadic and became horse Indians in historic time. The Jicarilla and the Mescalero used tepees when in the open country, but brush shelters when in the mountains; since similar shelters were used by the other Apache most of the time, we suspect this form of housing once prevailed among all of them. All practiced some agriculture, but placed their chief dependence on wild plants, seeds and game. They did not weave cloth, nor were they much given to making pottery; on the other hand, they made fine baskets, some of which are highly prized by collectors.

The Navaho

Everyone knows about the Navaho, picturesque in his semidesert home, famous for his unique wool blankets, fine silver jewelry and intriguing appearance. No other Indians make quite the same impression on the writer, the artist and the tourist, who all laud their pleasing pastoral life at every opportunity. Part of this may be due to the Navaho's pastoral economics, our religious traditions furnishing a background for the idealization of the shepherd. Yet some of the Navaho characteristics we most admire were acquired from the whites; Spanish missionaries taught them to raise sheep, to spin wool and to weave; the silver craft came in later. On the other hand, many of the designs used in weaving and in silverwork seem to have been their own; at least they are original and consistent, which, more than anything else, gives these people a place in the sun. Further, they are upstanding and self-confident, as befits a people who make their own way in the world.

The Navaho home is called a hogan, a term about as well known as tepee. The older type of hogan is the most interesting and reminds one of certain Nadene shelters in the north. To build a hogan, three heavy poles, forked at one end, were cut about twelve feet in length. These were set up like a tripod, the forked ends interlocking, one pole to the west, one to the north and one to the south. Two straight poles without forked ends, but similar in length, were laid against the tripod on the east side to form the doorposts. A large number of poles were then set up around the frame, forming a cone-shaped tepee-like structure. The spaces between these poles were stopped with bark and chinked with mud. There was a smoke hole at the top in the center. The entrance was through a passageway attached to the doorway, extending outward, reminding one of a storm door.

This was the old, original form of hogan. Many of those now seen and used are hexagonal, made of logs laid up like a log cabin, except that the roof is conical, drawing inward toward the smoke hole. It is a substantial dwelling, warm in winter and comfortable in summer. Since most of human life pivots around the family fire, the hogan becomes the symbol of their culture. Many Navaho now live in wooden frame houses, or the adobe buildings common to the Southwest, but the hogan remains the only building of consequence: here ceremonies must be performed, the sick are cared for and the family lives. No wonder the Navaho sometimes think of their world as merely an enlarged hogan, for they build no temples, no houses of worship. Nor do they gather into villages as do most Indians, possibly because the family herds of sheep need wide pastures. So they scatter widely, a hogan or two here, another there, often scarcely within sight of each other. Yet they maintain a high degree of culture solidarity, a fair number of ritualistic ceremonies and a satisfactory tribal government. For one thing, the population is mobile, everybody riding horses, thus providing for sufficient communication to counteract their rural isolation. There is no more picturesque sight than a troop of Navaho horsemen and -women, gracefully seated and in pleasing costume.

But what of the celebrated Navaho blanket? What we now buy is not a blanket, but a rug. We still call them blankets, because that is what they were in the old days. At that time no outsider wanted them; they were woven for home consumption and to wear as robes. The Navaho man of today buys his clothes ready-made, like the white man; his womenfolk buy cloth and make their own clothes. Instead of homemade blankets, they buy factory-made blankets, like other modern Indians. But the reader who possesses one of those old original Navaho blankets may well congratulate himself, for as a textile it possesses qualities all its own. Such blankets are still made occasionally by some ultraconservative Navaho women, but now they weave rugs to sell to white people and not to use at home. Rug weaving has become a manufacturing industry. Yet weaving is woman's work; the men have nothing to do with it. She washes the wool and prepares it for spinning, dyes the yarn, then weaves the rug. The design is visualized before she begins. Her loom is a wooden frame, usually set up out-of-doors near the hogan. That she takes pride in the craft and finds joy in it is evident to all who are so fortunate as to see her at work. When the rug is made, it is taken to the trader. Even at best, the weaver gets only a few cents an hour for her labor. The magnitude of this industry may be comprehended when we learn that nearly two million dollars' worth of rugs are produced each year. Before World War II the Navaho Arts and Crafts Guild was organized for the improvement of the craft, to study rugs in museums for new ideas in design and color, to learn techniques both new and old. The Guild has been a successful tribal enterprise, and travelers to the Navaho capital at Window Rock can examine Navaho crafts in the Guild's new building.

Portraits of Navaho women reveal silver-bead necklaces, characterized by a conventional flower symbol, said to be "a squash blossom." Three to five strands in such necklaces are not uncommon. Men wear broad leather belts bearing disks of ornate silver. The skill with which these are fashioned commands respect for the craftsman. So we should not overlook the proficiency of the silversmiths, when praising the women for their textile skills. The Navaho jeweler uses the simplest of tools and obtains his silver from Mexican coins. There is some reason to believe that the craft itself originated in Mexico, reaching the Navaho about a century ago, since some of the shapes and designs are obviously of Mexican origin.

Perhaps the reader has heard of sand painting, another art in which the Navaho man is supreme. Clean sand is spread over the floor of a hogan on which pictures are made with red, yellow and black dry colors, so deftly sifted between the thumb and finger that true lines can be run under the control of the artist. The center of the design is often a pair of lines crossing at right angles, upon which stand some tall human figures wearing masks. These, of course, are gods. Curving over all are colored bands representing the rainbow, at one end of which is the bust of a god, at the other his legs. These sand paintings often vary in form and content but have a style of their own which must be seen in its true setting to be appreciated. Nor is such a painting to be seen every day, for it is sacred, executed as part of a serious ceremony and, when the ritual has been performed, obliterated.

Like all other Indians, the Navaho approaches natural phenomena with a reverence that a white man may imagine but never understand. Maize, or corn, is to him not merely a food plant but a child of the gods; so when the Navaho farmer goes into the field with his hoe (farming is his work, not that of the woman), he feels that he is in the presence of some great mystery. The germination of the seed, the dependence upon rain, the life-giving sun, the covering of the ear and its silk, the beautiful pollen, as the life-giving principle—all are symbolized in legend, sacred song and ceremony. The white visitor to the Navaho country may not know all this, but he somehow senses the presence of an attitude different from his own, something lacking in his life. Then the unexpected beauty and charm of the Navaho country may have something to do with it. His is the largest Indian reservation, as large as the states of Massachusetts, New Hampshire and Vermont together, presenting great variety of scenery, ranging from high mountains, through desert plains to deep canyons and famous natural bridges. Among the best-known scenic spots is the Canyon de Chelly, in which, here and there, are strips of fertile land where sheep are herded, corn raised and an occasional peach orchard planted. The richly colored walls of the canyon reflect faint color tones in the deep shadows, casting a glamor over the life within. Here you may see the Navaho riding by, mounted on beautiful horses, the women with their wide graceful skirts, their slim bodies blending gracefully into the lines of the galloping horse, as if there were but one living creature instead of two. The rich purples and greens of their costumes blend with the hues of the canyon walls; the simple, unobtrusive lines of the hogan conceal its artificiality so completely that you accept it also as the work of nature. In such a peaceful setting one should see the Navaho to appreciate his contribution to human culture.

Yet, as everywhere, human life is stern and at times brutal. When the Spaniards came into the country, the Navaho lived by hunting, gathering, agriculture and raids on their Pueblo neighbors. The acquisition of sheep increased the necessity of raids, and that of horses greatly increased their mobility and the extent of their raids. Both were items not only of utility but of prestige, a point also important later in dealings with the American government. Raids were made on Pueblo and Spanish alike; the Spanish settlers retaliated by raiding the Navaho, and the war went on for two hundred years. But this was not the worst part of the story. When the Mexicans raided the Navaho they captured women and children to be held as slaves, and they encouraged other Indians to capture them for sale in the markets. Every Spanish family of any consequence possessed such slaves. Of course, the Navaho retaliated by taking Spanish and Indian captives. All this went merrily along, the Navaho more than holding their own and increasing in numbers, notwithstanding their losses, until 1849, when their territory was taken over by the United States.

At first the Navaho paid no attention to their new masters, but raided and took captives as before, though the Mexicans and other Indians were punished for raiding them. Finally it became clear that harsh measures were necessary to break the habit of two centuries of thievery and murder. Accordingly, the famous Kit Carson was commissioned to round them up, in 1863-64. He struck hard, destroyed their sheep and orchards in Canyon de Chelly, captured their horses and soon forced those he did not capture to surrender or starve. About eight thousand were rounded up, and forced on "the Long Walk" to exile at Fort Sumner in eastern New Mexico. Contemporary authorities estimated that a few thousand more were slaves scattered among the white population, and others estimated that an additional several thousand managed to escape capture or starvation, hiding in the mountains.

The exile at Fort Sumner, lasting from 1864 to 1868, was a tragedy in the life of the Navaho. The attempt was made to turn the hunters and shepherds into farmers; droughts, disease, crop failure and other difficulties beset the tribe. It was obvious that the attempt was a failure, and in 1868, the Navaho were allowed to return to a reservation in their homeland, where they still live. They promised peace, and kept it.

At heart the Navaho is a home-loving body; he reverences his cornfields and worships the rain gods of his semidesert but beautiful country. The white man's heavy hand and the Navaho's temporary captivity in a strange land brought to him the realization that the old days had passed and that the solution of living lay in another direction. The adjustment was made, and with it has come about as much peace and prosperity as falls to the lot of the average. The Navaho have responded to change, and today are among the most forward-looking of all the American Indian tribes.

The Uto-Aztecan Family

Shoshonean

Bannock, Idaho
Chemehuevi, Arizona, Nevada
Comanche, Oklahoma
Kern River, Mission, Mono
    Tribes, California

Paiute, Nevada
Penamint, Nevada
Snake, Idaho
Ute, Utah and Colorado
Wind River Shoshoni,
    Wyoming (Washakie,
    Sacajawea)

Hopi, Arizona

Pima, Papago, Arizona

The Tanoan Family

Tiwa Pueblos
    Sandia
    Isleta
    Taos
    Picuris
Towa Pueblos
    Jemez
    Pecos (abandoned)

Tewa Pueblos
    Santa Clara
    San Ildefonso (Maria)
    San Juan
    Tesuque
    Nambe
    Hano (Nampeo)
    Pojoaque

Kiowa

Nahuatlan or Aztec
    Aztec
    Cora
    Yaqui
    Opata

Maya
    Many tribes in Yucatan and Guatemala.

Chapter XVII

THE AZTEC-TANOAN FAMILIES

FIVE of the distinguished United States Indian family groups extended their domains into Canada. The next families we are to consider range from Idaho, southward into Mexico, and thence into Guatemala. They comprise what were once thought to be a number of independent families, but later linguistic study has put one after the other into the same family group and raised such suspicions about a number of others that, though suspecting some of them to be illegitimate descendants, we are justified in grouping them under one name, the Aztec-Tanoan. Geography reveals them as a highland people, seemingly preferring a terrain approaching aridity, but with fertile spots here and there susceptible to irrigation, for, in the main, they are agriculturists. In intellectual and social status they range from the highest to the lowest, as from the Maya and Aztec to the lowly "Digger Indians" of Nevada. In short, we now meet a family group composed of both rich and poor relations, not to mention a number whose parentage seems a bit irregular. No one questions the cultural supremacy of the Maya, nor are the Aztec and their predecessors much lower in rank. True, the Aztec did many shocking things, but such matters are relative. They built fine temples, wrought in gold, jade and turquoise. From maguey fiber they made a kind of paper, upon which they recorded events and official orders, made maps of the country, wrote literature, including poetry, and, on occasion, rolled tobacco in a piece of it to make a cigarette. They built roads, though all travel was on foot, made aqueducts to bring fresh water to their cities, and constructed floating gardens in a kind of Venice where small lighthouses guided the boatmen at night. In their capital they maintained a zoo, where many birds and strange animals were kept. A great people truly, they domesticated maize, cocoa and many other useful plants, which later enriched white men. They played with hollow rubber balls long before Columbus was born. The Maya knew enough of mathematics and astronomy to invent the zero (no one but a mathematician will understand how significant that discovery is) and to make corrections for the fraction of a day in the year to adjust their calendars. We do it, in a way, by the added day in February; they had another method, but it worked. Yet the temples of the Aztec were more revolting than slaughterhouses because human sacrifice was the order of the day, for which a steady stream of captives was brought in. Many of the devout Aztec offered their own blood to the gods, drawn from cuts in their tongues through which sticks and strings were sawed back and forth. And if this is not enough for the reader, he should know that when the body of a sacrificed youth was thrown down the temple stairs, it was often carried off to be eaten at a religious feast. Yet all this was done with the highest motives and in keeping with sacred symbolism of a high order. The story of Abraham offering his son as a sacrifice comes to mind here to help us understand this seeming contradiction.

There are vague traditions that the Pueblo villages in Arizona and New Mexico belonging to this family once offered human sacrifices, but we are not sure. There is another tradition that infants were fed to a captive snake, and for this there is some evidence. Yet the one clear case for human sacrifice, after the Aztec pattern, is found among the Pawnee, who are not members of this family. However, there is little reason to doubt that the Pawnee learned this from the Aztec.

The chief branches of the Aztec-Tanoan stock in the United States are the Uto-Aztecan Family, including the Shoshonean tribes now on reservations in Idaho, Wyoming and Colorado, the Shoshonean-speaking Hopi, and the Pima and Papago of Arizona; also the Tanoan Family, including the Tiwa, Tewa and Towa groups of Pueblos in Arizona and New Mexico. The Kiowas of the plains, now in Oklahoma, and certain tribes in California are also included, and some believe the Zuni of New Mexico are too. Not all students of language accept this grouping, but the languages of these tribes are related in some way, thus justifying our considering them as parts of one great family.

The Pueblo Villages

While there may be some doubt as to the legitimacy of some members of the Uto-Aztecan Family, no one questions the right of the Hopi Indians to a seat in the family circle. They are among the best-known of our western Indians and are classed with the Pueblo or village Indians.

The tourist to New Mexico and Arizona becomes familiar with the Pueblo Indians, their quaint terraced apartment houses, the picturesque costumes of the women sitting beside the highways and railroad stations to sell their pottery. The Hopi are famous for the Snake Dance, a serious ritualistic ceremony, considered necessary to induce the powers above to give them rain and good crops. Their way of handling snakes, especially rattlesnakes, has always been a mystery. Without harm to himself the dancer, with seeming carelessness, grasps the snakes in his arms and dances around with one of them in his mouth. Although it is still debatable, the truth of the matter seems to be that the poison is squeezed out, in secret, before the dance begins.

It is a striking spectacle, and a few hundred white tourists gather at the proper season to see the public part of this ceremony, the dancing with snakes in the mouth. The ritual is rather long and complicated but in outline is something like this: At least nine days are required to carry through the program at intervals of two years. Parts of the ritual are secret, known only to the priests of the cult. These priests spend the first four or five days gathering live snakes, taking every one they find, regardless of species. The captive snakes are kept in pottery vessels. Altars are then constructed, and the various ceremonies called for in the ritual are performed. On the last day the snakes are taken out of their jars and given a bath. When dry, they are brought into the village, where the dancers assemble and each in turn dances with a snake in his mouth. After sprinkling the snakes with corn meal, the priests pick them up, run out of the village and release them. The idea seems to be that the snakes will return to the rain gods, reporting that they were well received and that the people deserve sufficient rain for a good crop.

None of the other Pueblo villages in New Mexico and Arizona have this ceremony now, and it is possible that they never had it, but they do perform other ceremonies to influence the rain gods. According to some old Spanish accounts certain villages in Mexico had similar dances in which the participants appeared holding snakes, lizards and frogs in their mouths, so it may be that the Hopi snake dance is a lone survivor of what was once a widespread custom.

The traveler in Arizona is likely to receive invitations to purchase some small, interesting wooden dolls, with masked faces and bright colored garments, called *kachinas*. This is the Hopi Indian name for certain gods, or supernatural beings, who live in a mysterious country somewhere in the neighboring mountains. During the Hopi ceremonies these *kachinas* are supposed to visit the village in spirit, but are actually impersonated by masked dancers. These small wooden dolls are prepared in advance to be carried or otherwise displayed as symbols of the true *kachinas*. Each *kachina* has a name and distinctive form of dress, the total number exceeding a hundred. Some of the masked *kachina* dancers call at the homes of children to inquire into their behavior and whip them if they deserve punishment.

At present there are six Hopi villages in Arizona (Walpi, Sichumovi, Shipaulovi, Mishongnovi, Shungopovi and Oraibi). The first and the last are the most popular

THE AZTEC-TANOAN FAMILIES 239

with tourists, probably because their names are easy to pronounce.

The other group of Pueblo villages which linguists consider as a branch of the Aztec-Tanoan stock are the Tanoan, chiefly in New Mexico, now twelve in all, of which the best-known are Taos, San Juan, San Ildefonso and Isleta.

For completeness, we may mention other village Indians not yet regarded as members of this family: the Zuni villagers who may be distant members of the same family, and the seven Keresan villages, the best-known of which are Acoma, Laguna and Santo Domingo. So far, the Keresan have been considered a distinct family, but since they live much like their Uto-Aztecan neighbors we shall not consider them further.

Zuni was probably the first Pueblo village seen by white men. After Cortez conquered Mexico City and his followers began to understand the native language, they were intrigued by tales of the Seven Cities of Cibola, far to the north, the homes of a great people. To the Spanish mind a "great people" meant a nation rich in gold and other desirable materials. In 1539, Fray Marcos, accompanied, among others, by a Negro named Estevanico, and guided by Indians, arrived in the Zuni country. Estevanico went into the village to open negotiations, but for some reason was shot to death with arrows, possibly because the Zuni did not like his appearance. The good father wisely turned back, recording the event and thus making it history. The next recorded excursion into the Pueblo country was a military affair, an army headed by Coronado, who went up the Rio Grande, passing near what is now Santa Fe in 1542. The present Santa Fe was settled in 1609, making it one of our oldest cities. The Pueblos were roughly treated by Coronado's soldiers as well as by subsequent garrisons and officials, but maintained their solidarity, though forced to become nominal Catholics. However, as there were neither gold nor silver mines in the country, the Indians were not enslaved on a large scale or required to operate plantations. The Span-

ish settlers were not numerous, and the Indians, being
agriculturists, were not unduly crowded. Nevertheless
they felt the steady pinch of growing numbers. Like the
Indians of the Ohio country, one village began to confer
with another, and eventually evolved a concerted plan for
an uprising of all the villages in Arizona and New Mexico,
the purpose of which was to drive the Spaniards into
Mexico. This is known in history as the revolt of 1680.
The Indians were successful; they killed the priests and
such white men as they could lay hands upon; the others
fled. Santa Fe was captured, churches and farmhouses
were burned. The Spaniards who survived the revolt fled.
For twelve years there was peace in the area, except for
occasional Apache raids; but the Spanish government was
determined to reoccupy the country. De Vargas returned
to Santa Fe in 1692, and after announcing his authority
to forgive the Indians for the revolt, was able to secure
the support of most of the Pueblos along the Rio Grande.
He left Santa Fe, and returned to find the city occupied
by Indians, who refused to return to their pueblos. The
ensuing battle was fierce but short, and in the end the
Indians were overcome.

Then followed an interesting course of events. Out-
wardly, the Pueblo people conformed to Spanish control,
tolerated the presence of the priests, but organized a passive resistance, keeping secret all their thoughts, hiding
away to perform their ceremonies and maintaining a
conspiracy of silence. The important thing now was to
resist change, to avoid contact with white people whenever possible, and so to become fanatical in the preserva-
tion of all their old culture. The Spanish settlers and officials were not offended by what they neither knew nor
saw and were willing that the Indians should have land
enough to raise what corn and vegetables they needed.
The organized and relentless reticence of the Indians pre-
vented personal quarrels with the whites, and their obvious poverty offered no temptations to white thievery,
so there was little friction.

This even tenor of life went on through 1700 and well

into 1800, a long, tranquil period of passive resistance. Early in 1800 Mexico revolted against Spain, a struggle in which the sympathies of the Indians were with the revolutionists, since to them the Spanish authorities were the authors of all their own troubles. All they asked of the new government was to be let alone, to live in splendid isolation. When Mexico achieved her independence and while the spirit of liberty was alert, the Pueblos were formally acknowledged as self-governing towns and their lands were guaranteed. When the United States took over the territory in 1848, the government agreed to respect these rights. This obligation has been lived up to, not one hundred per cent, but to a degree exceeding that of any other Indian obligation. Even today, though the villages tolerate tourists, they preserve their aloofness, secretly govern their own people, and carry on mysterious hidden ceremonies, all of which adds to the desire of the whites to penetrate the veil. However, the Pueblos have absorbed some white culture, most of their children attend school, some modern home equipment is in use, but ceremonially and socially most of the old life remains. They are still grand masters in isolation and in preventing social change.

We have said that these villages are fairly independent. To preserve their characteristic aloofness, firm discipline is necessary. The writer heard a Pueblo man tell how he was once called before the council of his village because he had cut his hair white fashion. Having been employed for a time on a road-construction project, working with Mexicans and white labor, he had conformed to white practice. The council regarded this as a serious offense, a break with Indian tradition, and threatened him with a whipping. He admitted the act, but in defense offered a countercharge: pointing to the leather factory-made shoes of his accusers, he asked if they were Indian; then he called attention to the ready-made overalls many of them were wearing; next, he pointed to their white man's shirts, etc. He demanded that his accusers be whipped for taking over too many white ways. According to his story, the council then dropped the matter. This happened many years ago; now most of the Pueblo Indians wear their hair short. Whipping seems to have been an aboriginal mode of punishment, but they are now said to use hanging by the thumbs and other advanced European methods.

Probably because of their long passive resistance to white influence, they have few heroes known to history. Wars seem necessary to reveal such greatness. Had the Pueblos terrorized the settlements, massacred women and children, left a trail of blood and destruction behind them, they would hold a high place in history, as we know it; but they did nothing of the kind after their great outbreak in 1680. However, in recent years some of their women have found a place in history, because of their genius in the peaceful arts. The first was Nampeo, a Hopi potter. In the Hopi country are the ruins of many former villages, some quite ancient, scattered about which are fragments of a beautiful pottery with a pleasing yellow-tinted surface. While still a young woman (1890), Nampeo was intrigued by this lost art and set herself the problem of reproducing it. She was eventually successful, making pottery even more beautiful than the original. To her, pottery became an art rather than a utilitarian craft. Her work soon became famous, and although she died in 1942, other Hopi women still follow her lead.

About 1910, in the village of San Ildefonso, a young woman whose Spanish name is Maria Martinez showed a genius for pottery. Her work soon found a ready sale to dealers and tourists. In the course of time she invented a new and beautiful decorative technique in which dull black designs appear upon a highly polished black surface. Maria's skill lies in modeling and firing; her husband, Julian Martinez, painted the designs with a master hand. Maria's work has become world-famous, and she has been awarded medals for her work both here and abroad. Several younger women have shown proficiency and a school of ceramic art has grown under the leadership of Maria, just as a similar tradition was inspired by Nampeo among the Hopi.

Of all the Indians indigenous to the United States the

Pueblo Dwellers were the true agriculturists, for though many tribes of the Algonkin, Siouan, Caddoan and Muskhogean families raised corn and other food plants, they also depended largely upon hunting. We can truly characterize them as primarily hunters and secondarily farmers. On the other hand, these village Indians of New Mexico and Arizona were primarily farmers and secondarily hunters. Another peculiar distinction is that throughout the Pueblo villages men worked in the fields, whereas elsewhere in the United States agriculture was the work of women. Curiously enough, when the Pueblos were first discovered, the spinning and weaving of cotton were man's work, but women made the baskets and the pottery. Yet what most distinguishes these Indians in our minds is their peculiar type of architecture, which reached its zenith around the year 1200, or three hundred years before the Spaniards came.

What we call a pueblo is a kind of apartment house with terraced roofs, pictures of which are now familiar to everyone. Many great houses of this type are now in ruins, as Pueblo Bonito in Chaco Canyon, New Mexico, one near the town of Aztec in the same state, Cliff Palace at Mesa Verde, Colorado, and a few others. The three just mentioned have been restored in part. Pueblo Bonito contained about eight hundred rooms, was nearly seven hundred feet long and over three hundred feet wide, a ground plan which would cover several blocks in a modern city. There were five stories, each having a width of one room less than the one below it, thus creating four terraces. The original number of rooms in Cliff Palace has not been determined, but it is known that there were over two hundred. The ruin at Aztec, New Mexico, contained over five hundred rooms. Here stone, supplemented by adobe for mortar, was used for the walls. The ceilings and roofs were supported by heavy wooden beams. The construction of such a building demanded well-organized teamwork and a high degree of engineering skill. A method has been devised by which the tree rings in the beams of these ruins can be dated; according to those skilled in this technique the dates of building and repair are:

	A.D.
Pueblo Bonito	919–1130
Cliff Palace	1073–1272
Aztec	1110–1121

The later or modern Pueblo villages follow this same style of architecture, but are less imposing. The great builders lived in Pueblo Bonito, Cliff Palace and Aztec between 900 and 1200 A.D. In the Hopi village of Oraibi, in a house abandoned in 1906, a beam was found which was cut in 1370; this means that this village was in existence at that time, or at least that there was a village on the spot. There is every reason to suspect that this very house was occupied for more than five hundred years, probably the longest-occupied house in the whole of the New World. What the Spaniards found, then, was an Indian culture of long standing, but one which was in its decline, or at least one with less architectural grandeur and social energy. After Spanish domination the surviving villages determined to preserve what was left of their old culture, drew apart, and have been unusually successful in maintaining most of these ways.

The Kiowa and the Comanche

Most people who know something about Indians have heard the names Kiowa, Comanche and Shoshoni. The last two are members of the Shoshonean branch of the Uto-Aztecan Family, but while none of the tribes included under this title are really desert peoples, they occupy parts of Utah, Nevada, the arid sections of California and, to the north, parts of Oregon and Washington. The Kiowa, Comanche and some of the Shoshoni lived east of the Rocky Mountains out on the dry plains, like true buffalo Indians. We call them marginal tribes because their homelands were where the great desert country and the buffalo plains meet, a strip of dry plains in Oklahoma, Colorado, Wyoming and western Kansas. These tribes were already horse Indians when they came into history. In early literature they were indiscriminately called Snakes, at other times, Horse Indians. In early 1700 the few travelers venturing out toward the Rocky Mountains found their Indian companions worrying about the Snakes whenever they saw horse dung or abandoned camps where horses had been tied out. All tribes feared them as implacable enemies. How they came to be called Snakes in the first place is lost to history, but the name was in common use when Lewis and Clark explored the upper Missouri country. Later the name Snake was restricted to members of the family living along the Snake River in Idaho, and a few closely related tribes in Oregon. Shoshoni was then used to designate a tribal group in Wyoming and adjacent parts of Colorado and Idaho, while Kiowa and Comanche were adopted as the names for the other two tribal groups.

In the seventeenth century the Kiowa seem to have lived just west of the Black Hills, while the Shoshoni camped between them and the Rocky Mountains. Immediately south of the Kiowa were the Comanche. During the next century the Kiowa shifted to the country between Denver and Amarillo, Texas, while the Comanche took up a position south and east of Amarillo. The Shoshoni stayed in the north. Thus the three tribes formed a long line from Montana to Mexico, their backs to the Rocky Mountains and facing the plains. Theirs was a long, wide range, vigorously disputed by other buffalo-hunting tribes, but since opposition was from the east only and they were superb horsemen, they more than held their own. Mooney, the best student of Indian population, put their number at about ten thousand. Thus their combined strength was impressive. Further, they were close friends and allies.

The Comanche came into contact with the Spaniards in Mexico and Texas, raiding them for horses and mules, capturing women and children, killing the men. The

Texans struck back harder than the Mexicans, so the Comanche looked upon them as enemy Number One. The Kiowa were farther north but, jointly with the Comanche, raided into Mexico and Texas long before they came into contact with settlers from the United States.

The first treaties with the United States were made about 1830, and the disposition of the Kiowa and Comanche was to keep the peace with them, but to consider Mexico and Texas as enemies. The termination of the Mexican War in 1848 left New Mexico and Texas to the United States. This the Indians could not comprehend, so they continued to raid in those territories as before. They met the complaints of the United States with the claim that they kept the peace with it, but that New Mexico and Texas had always been their enemies and were still. On the other hand Texas, having been independent before coming into the United States, looked upon Indian affairs as her own business, declared war and sent armed men against the Indians without much regard for the policy of the United States. In spite of a treaty proclaimed in 1868, raids continued until 1874, when the United States troops took the field. There was desultory skirmishing, but the Comanche and Kiowa soon agreed to settle down on their reservations in Oklahoma and stop raiding.

Turning now to the north, we find the Shoshoni of Wyoming the dominant group. They were called Wind River Shoshoni. Their reservation in Wyoming is near the heart of their homeland. For the most part they maintained peace with the United States, and since the Dakota, Cheyenne and Arapaho were their traditional enemies, they were always ready to join the whites in their wars with those Indians.

The Ute

Close kin of the Wind River Shoshoni and the Comanche were a group of Indians known as Ute. They were not predominantly buffalo hunters, nor were they a true

Plains people, but lived west of the Kiowa and Wind River Shoshoni in the valleys among the mountain ranges of central and western Colorado, straggling over into Utah and New Mexico. Their best-known divisions were the Uintah, Yampa and Uncompahgre. Like the Comanche, they acquired horses early and terrorized the Mexican settlements and the surrounding Indians. Yet because of their geographical position outside the great arena for Indian wars with the advancing frontier, there was little real trouble with the United States government. Between 1861 and 1868 these Indians were assigned reservations in Utah, Colorado and New Mexico, and now number about two thousand.

White people generally have regarded them as hostile and rude. In times past they harassed the Navaho and the Pueblo villages. In 1879 they destroyed their agency and killed all the government employees, but when the troops came they surrendered after a skirmish or two. In 1906 some four hundred Ute decided to leave their reservation in Utah and settle upon Pine Ridge Reservation in South Dakota. As this was in defiance of orders, they were surrounded by troops, to whom they peacefully surrendered near Fort Meade, South Dakota. After an interval they asked to be returned to their own reservation.

The Diggers of the Desert

Utah, Nevada and adjoining parts of southern California make up what is known as the Great Basin. In it are Great Salt Lake and numerous small lakes without outlets, the whole area having once been an inland sea. It is now a semidesert and, though apparently once a country of marshes, was as much of a desert as now when the Shoshoni of the Great Basin came to live there. It was not a favorable country for primitive man, but it was possible to live in it, provided the Indians were willing to use small game and all kinds of vegetable food, no one plant being abundant enough to be depended upon. When the white people began to visit this country, they saw these Indians industriously seeking and digging in the ground for root plants. Thus they came to be known as "Digger Indians"; because of their apparent poverty the term became one denoting contempt. In contrast to the horse Indians, who lived luxuriously upon the buffalo, they seemed a crude, simple, dirty people. Yet they deserve our respect, because they solved the problem of existence in such a forbidding environment, were too busy feeding themselves to engage in continual war and to conduct long, involved ceremonies. A number of these tribes are best known under the group names Mono, Kern River and Mission tribes of California; the Northern and Southern Paiute of Nevada; the Gosiute in Utah.

All of these tribes, especially those living in California, are good basket makers, but do not weave cloth. Their homes were, for the most part, simple brush shelters, sometimes little more than windbreaks. In California acorns were an important food, but elsewhere wild grass seeds were gathered. Yet in the central part of the area food plants were so rare that many kinds were used, and even grasshoppers were eaten.

The Pima and the Papago

Important members of the Uto-Aztecan Family are two tribes living in southern Arizona, known as the Pima and Papago. After the Mexican War these Indians came under the jurisdiction of the United States. In the main they were a peaceful agricultural people, practiced irrigation when water was available and were quick to take to raising wheat and cattle. From all accounts they were peaceful, though they would defend themselves if attacked. After coming under the authority of the United States, they were in contact with the worst elements in frontier life and so deteriorated rapidly. Formerly, their women made fine baskets and enough pottery for their household needs, but these are now almost lost arts. The Spanish authorities had little contact with the Pima until about 1750, and it was not until about 1780 that a Spanish garrison was quartered in Tucson. Even in 1854, when the final boundary between Arizona and Mexico was established, there were few white people in the country.

Washakie and the Shoshoni

Among the great Indian personalities in history, Washakie, of the Wind River Reservation in Wyoming, claims our attention. For sixty years he was the recognized chief of the Shoshoni. The date of his birth is in doubt. According to information given by a few older Indians who claimed to have known Washakie as a boy, he was born in 1798, but the agency officials established 1804 as the most probable date. In any case he was born while the Missouri country was unexplored, or virgin Indian country. Possibly he was strapped to his cradleboard when Lewis and Clark left the Mandan village to ascend the Missouri and pass through the Shoshoni country on their way to the Pacific, guided by that now famous young Shoshoni woman, Sacajawea. It is not improbable that from his mother's back, he gazed out upon these strange white men, representatives of the race that was to try his patience but still claim his respect.

As a youth Washakie joined in the constant petty raids against his Indian neighbors and in repelling the Blackfoot, Cheyenne and Sioux. His ability soon impressed both his followers and the enemy; at least in 1840 a white observer writes that Washakie was one of three great leaders, at whose names the powerful Blackfoot quaked with fear. At about this time Washakie, now in his prime, came into contact with such distinguished whites as Jim Bridger, Father de Smet and Brigham Young. In the fifties he appears at the height of his power, with a thousand well-armed, disciplined, mounted men. He had enough horses to mount the women and children also. He was holding his own with the Blackfoot, Cheyenne and Sioux, and since the latter, especially, were at war with the whites, Washakie found himself logically allied with the United States. In the Indian wars of the seventies he rendered signal service, as in Crook's campaign when he, at the head of a picked body of his own horsemen, saved Crook's army from annihilation. He seems to have enjoyed the highest respect of the Army, was enlisted as a scout and held a commission at his death.

Among the many recorded anecdotes of this great leader we cite the one in which he demonstrated his right to lead in 1869. To most ways of thinking, he was then an old man, ready to retire, and so thought his tribesmen, because one day he overheard them saying that Washakie was too old to lead in war, that a new leader must be sought. The next day Washakie rode out of the camp; no one saw or heard of him until two months later, when he returned, bearing seven scalps which he had taken single-handed. Obviously, his successor had to perform greater deeds if Washakie was to be deposed. It was after this that he, then a man of seventy or more, took an active part in the wars with the Sioux.

Like all other tribes, the Shoshoni had their land troubles, but Washakie led in all such negotiations. He was not always happy, he met with disappointments, but through it all subordinated his emotions to his intellect, which told him that reservation life was inevitable and that the white man would dominate, that armed resistance was worse than folly. At a conference called by the governor of Wyoming in 1878, Washakie spoke as follows:

"We are right glad, sir, that you have so bravely and kindly come among us. I shall, indeed, speak to you freely of the many wrongs we have suffered at the hands of the white man. They are things to be noted and remembered. But I cannot hope to express to you the half that is in our hearts. They are too full for words.

"Disappointment; then a deep sadness; then a grief inexpressible; then, at times, a bitterness that makes us think of the rifle, the knife and the tomahawk, and

kindles in our hearts the fires of desperation—that, sir, is the story of our experience, of our wretched lives.

"The white man, who possesses this whole vast country from sea to sea, who roams over it at pleasure and lives where he likes, cannot know the cramp we feel in this little spot, with the undying remembrance of the fact, which you know as well as we, that every foot of what you proudly call America not very long ago belonged to the red man. The Great Spirit gave it to us. There was room enough for all his many tribes, and all were happy in their freedom. But the white man had, in ways we know not of, learned some things we had not learned; among them, how to make superior tools and terrible weapons, better for war than bows and arrows; and there seemed no end to the hordes of men that followed them from other lands beyond the sea.

"And so, at last, our fathers were steadily driven out, or killed, and we, their sons, but sorry remnants of tribes once mighty, are cornered in little spots of the earth all ours of right—cornered like guilty prisoners and watched by men with guns who are more than anxious to kill us off.

"Nor is this all. The white man's government promised that if we, the Shoshones, would be content with the little patch allowed us, it would keep us well supplied with everything necessary to comfortable living, and would see that no white man should cross our borders for our game or for anything that is ours. But it has not kept its word! *The white man kills our game, captures our furs, and sometimes feeds his herds upon our meadows. And your great and mighty government—oh, sir, I hesitate, for I cannot tell the half! It does not protect us in our rights. It leaves us without the promised seed, without tools for cultivating the land, without implements for harvesting our crops, without breeding animals better than ours, without the food we still lack, after all we can do, without the many comforts we cannot produce, without the schools we so much need for our children.*

"I say again, the government does not keep its word! *And so, after all we can get by cultivating the land and*

*by hunting and fishing, we are sometimes nearly starved,
and go half naked, as you see us!*

*"Knowing all this, do you wonder, sir, that we have fits
of desperation and think to be avenged?"*[1]

Here is evidence of a great man; here is the outline of
his struggle to "guide right" in the face of undeniable bad
faith and trickery on the part of those with whom was
entrusted the fate of his people. There are always many
marks of superiority in a great man, and we are not surprised to learn that Washakie could speak French and
understand English.

On February 21, 1900, Washakie died and was given a
military funeral in the cemetery at Fort Washakie; his
casket was borne upon a caisson, volleys were fired over
his grave, and taps sounded by the bugler. The inscription
over his tomb reads, "Always loyal to the Government
and to his white brothers."

Sacajawea, or Bird Woman

The most famous Indian woman is Sacajawea; artists have
made her and her exploits the theme of paintings, and
statues of her are numerous. Her career is more appealing
than that of Pocahontas and equally romantic. She was
born about 1787 in a camp of Snake or Shoshoni Indians,
who ranged in the mountainous country from Three Forks,
Montana, westward into Idaho. We know nothing of her
childhood, but assume that she grew up like any other
normal Indian girl, was pledged as the wife of a much
older man, but when about fourteen years old an Hidatsa
war party, from a village on the Missouri River in what
is now North Dakota, attacked the camp of her people,
who sought safety in flight. Sacajawea and an older girl

[1] Grace Raymond Hebard, *Washakie. An Account of Indian
Resistance of the Covered Wagon and Union Pacific Railroad
Invasions of Their Territory,* Cleveland: The Arthur H. Clark
Company.

tried to escape across the river near their camp but were captured. The war party then set out for home with their prisoners, but the older girl escaped one night, leaving the little girl, Sacajawea, a lonely captive.

She was carried to the Hidatsa village in North Dakota where resided a French-Canadian trapper and fur trader by the name of Toussaint Charbonneau. Whether for humane reasons or otherwise, this white man bought the little captive and placed her in the care of his wife, also a captive from the Shoshoni Indians, apparently not of the same tribe, but of one speaking the same language. In a way this was fortunate for the little captive girl. In 1804, when Sacajawea was about eighteen years old, Charbonneau took her for his second wife.

That same summer the expedition of Lewis and Clark arrived at the villages of the Mandan Indians near where Bismarck, North Dakota, is located. The plan was to winter here, harden the members of the party to living in the Indian country, and acquire useful information from the Indians. The reader will recall that in 1803 Jefferson bought from France the country west of the Mississippi and at once sent out this expedition to explore the territory purchased and to notify the several Indian tribes that they were now subjects of the United States. Since most of them were not aware that they belonged to anybody, the mission was delicate, to say the least. Everyone now knows how skillfully this expedition was handled, how accurately the country was mapped from North Dakota to the Pacific Ocean, and what a store of information was collected. The original journals have been published so that one can follow the expedition day by day to the Pacific and back. As historical documents these journals are unique; as human documents they are as interesting as a novel.

Next to Captains Lewis and Clark the leading character in these narratives is the Indian girl, Sacajawea. Her husband, Charbonneau, was engaged as an interpreter and guide, with the understanding that she accompany him. Statements in the Journals make it clear that Sacajawea, rather than her husband, was the person wanted to guide the expedition when it reached the country of her people, and because she knew their language, to explain to her people its object and persuade them to co-operate. Her first appearance in the Journals is merely as a wife of Charbonneau, but on February 11, 1805, Lewis writes:

About five Oclock this evening one of the wives of Charbono was delivered of a fine boy. it is worthy of remark that this was the first child this woman had boarn, and as common in such cases her labour was tedious and the pain violent;[2]

Subsequent entries show that this was Sacajawea; she was then eighteen or nineteen years old.

The expedition set out up the Missouri on April 7, Sacajawea with her six-week-old baby on her back, Indian fashion. She was the only woman in this party of men, so naturally she and the little boy are mentioned almost every day in the Journals—through whose pages the interested reader will enjoy following them. Once Charbonneau struck his wife, but was promptly disciplined by Captain Clark. As there is no other mention of such acts, we assume Charbonneau learned his lesson. On May 14, near the Yellowstone River, Sacajawea is commended for great courage and alertness in saving parts of a boat's cargo in the face of danger to herself. On June 10 she became ill, reaching the crisis on June 16; the entries in the Journals show the deep concern of both Lewis and Clark, who set down daily reports on her condition, medicines given, and so on; there can be little doubt that she was near death; but a week later we find her able to carry on her daily work. Her boy was growing nicely and in good health, a favorite with both Lewis and Clark.

On July 22 the party was nearing Three Forks, Montana, when Sacajawea recognized her home country, and

[2] Lewis and Clark, *Original Journals of the Lewis and Clark Expedition, 1804–1806,* Reuben Gold Thwaites, ed., New York, 1904, Vol. 1, p. 257.

on the 28th 'the expedition camped at the spot where she had been captured. She was now the guide, and her remarkable knowledge of the country testifies, if such testimony were now needed, to her intelligence. It was hard going through the mountains, but she knew the way to the home of her tribe, and on August 17, marching ahead of the party, she caught sight of some of her people on horseback. At once she began to dance for joy. We pass over the moving scenes of the next few weeks and her success in securing aid from her people, all of which is well presented in the daily entries in the Journals. At last, supplied with horses, the expedition set out for the Columbia, then down that river to the ocean.

One day in the expedition camp near the Pacific, Sacajawea pleaded to be allowed to go from the base camp to the seashore. Lewis writes:

Monday, January 6, 1806.
Captain Clark set out after an early breakfast with the party in two canoes as had been concerted the last evening; Charbono and his Indian woman were also of the party; the Indian woman was very importunate to be permitted to go, and was therefore indulged; she observed that she had traveled a long way with us to see the great waters, and that now that monstrous fish was also to be seen, she thought it very hard she could not be permitted to see either (she had never yet been to the Ocean). [3]

She saw the ocean and the whale. She certainly deserved this experience.

When the returning expedition reached the Mandan Indian villages on the Missouri, Lewis and Clark paid Charbonneau for his services and dismissed him, August 17, 1806. Sacajawea received nothing, but that was in keeping with the customs of the time and place. Charbonneau had bought her, so she was his woman. On the other hand, Clark leaves us in no doubt as to his appreciation of their services, for three days later (August 20,

[3] Lewis and Clark, *ibid.*, Vol. 3, pp. 314–15.

1806), on his way down the river, he wrote a friendly letter to Charbonneau, from which we quote:

You have been a long time with me and have conducted your Self in Such a manner as to gain my friendship, your woman who accompanied you that long dangerous and fatigueing rout to the Pacific Ocean and back, diserved a greater reward for her attention and Services on that rout than we had in our power to give her at the Mandans. As to your little Son (my boy Pomp) you well know my fondness for him and my anxiety to take and raise him as my own child. I once more tell you if you will bring your son Baptiest to me I will educate him and treat him as my own child—I do not forget the promis which I made to you and Shall now repeet them that you may be certain— Charbono, if you wish to live with the white people, and will come to me I will give you a piece of land and furnish you with horses, cows & hogs. . . .

Wishing you and your family great suckcess & with anxious expectations of seeing my little dancing boy Baptiest I shall remain your friend

WILLIAM CLARK.[4]

History is silent as to whether Charbonneau accepted the proposals in this letter, but five years later the traveler Brackenridge boarded a boat at St. Louis, sailing for the Mandan villages; in his journal we find this entry, dated April 2, 1811:

We had on board a Frenchman named Charboneau, with his wife, an Indian woman of the Snake nation, both of whom had accompanied Lewis and Clark to the Pacific, and were of great service. The woman, a good creature, of a mild and gentle disposition, greatly attached to the whites, whose manners and dress she tries to imitate, but she had become sickly, and longed to revisit her native country; her husband, also, who had spent many years

---

13. A CAMP OF HORSE-USING INDIANS IN THE SOUTHERN PLAINS — *Painted by Catlin, 1833.*

14. METHODS OF TRANSPORTING BAGGAGE, ORIGINALLY BY DOG, LATER BY HORSE—The Indians of the Plains trained dogs to drag tent poles and to haul baggage on frames called travois. After white men came the Indians used horses in the same way as dogs. When dogs were used the Indians walked, but after horses were available, they rode. Dogs continued in use until about 1900, so that both dogs and horses were often seen on the march.

15. MANDAN WOMEN IN A CEREMONIAL DANCE — *Drawn by Bodmer, 1834.*

16. THE DANCE OF THE HALF-SHAVED HEAD SOCIETY—MANDAN—*Drawn by Bodmer 1834*

among the Indians, had become weary of a civilized life.[5]

Nothing is said about a child, so this suggests that she and her husband had been at St. Louis and that the boy was left in the care of Clark.

Sacajawea next appears in history when a fur trader named Luttig makes the following entry in his journal:

Sunday, December 20, 1812. *Clear and moderate . . . This evening the Wife of Charbonneau, a Snake Squaw, died of a putrid fever she was a good and the best Women in the fort, aged abt 25 years she left a fine infant girl.*[6]

This, then, was the end. She was the most distinguished Indian woman in history who, at the age of nineteen, rendered such important services to the United States that her fame is now secure. More statues have been erected to her memory than to any other American woman.

A final historic document may be of interest. In the Court Records at St. Louis, August 11, 1813, Luttig was appointed guardian of two children, but later his name was crossed out and that of William Clark substituted. The court order reads as follows:

The Court appoint William Clark guardian to the infant children of Tousant Charbonneau deceased, to wit Tousant Charbonneau a boy about the age of ten years and Lisette Charbonneau a girl about one year old. The said infant children not being possessed of any property within the knowledge of the court. The said guardian is not required to give bond.[7]

[5] *Journal of a Voyage up the River Missouri; performed in Eighteen Hundred and Eleven,* Baltimore, 1816, p. 10.
[6] John C. Luttig, *Journal of a Fur-Trading Expedition on the Upper Missouri, 1812–1813.* Stella M. Drumm, ed., St. Louis, 1920, p. 106.
[7] Facsimile reproduced in John C. Luttig, *op. cit.,* facing p. 106.

This implies that Captain Clark made good on his promise to care for the little boy by also adopting his infant sister. As to what became of these children, history tells us nothing. The court record speaks of Charbonneau as deceased, but he was still alive in 1838; probably Mrs. Charbonneau was meant.

But now comes the queerest part of the story. Upon its return the Lewis and Clark expedition became instantly famous, but for a long time no one paid much attention to Sacajawea, as the heroine of the exploit, nor recognized the importance of her services. About 1875 a missionary among Washakie's people in Wyoming found an old woman by the same name who professed to be the original Sacajawea. Attentions were showered upon her, and when she died a monument was set up, bearing her name. A biography has been written identifying the life of this old woman with the young mother who accompanied Lewis and Clark. Many persons are sure these two women are one. We should like to believe it, but the records we have cited speak for themselves.

Yet it matters little whether this woman did live on. Her claim to fame rests upon the part she played in the expedition, a fact not fully recognized until about 1890, since which time ample amends have been made to her memory. Her fame is now secure. There is good evidence that she was more than an ordinary person. She must have learned a great deal from her association with the expedition, into the spirit of which she entered wholeheartedly. To leave it and to return to the drab routine of a trading post must have been something of an anticlimax; contact with her own people again broken, married to an illiterate white man, and grasping much of the significances of American life as exemplified in Lewis and Clark —how could she have been happy! But Luttig testifies to the respect shown her by the whites with whom she came in contact, and to us of this day and time her life is the most appealing of any Indian woman known to history. She deserves all the statues erected in her memory.

PART III
INDIAN LIFE IN GENERAL

THE *story of each great Indian Family line ends in the same way, complete economic or military defeat and confinement upon reservations. Most of the tribes have survived these disasters and are now increasing in numbers as they come to live more and more like their white neighbors. Practically every tribe has kept its original language alive, for many Indians speak neither English nor Spanish. Yet more and more they are becoming bilingual, English and Indian, except in the southwestern United States where they speak Indian and Spanish. It promises to be a long time before these native languages die out. The Iroquois of New York State have been in close contact with English-speaking people since 1800 and though many of them can speak English, their native tongue is the home and community language.*

Chapter XVIII

THE INDIAN WAY OF LIFE

ONE of the first things to learn about Indians is that there are many kinds of them. We first think of an Indian as living in a tepee, flashing in beadwork from moccasins to headband, wearing a gorgeous feather headdress, long braids of black hair, tomahawk, hand drum, tom-tom, scalping knife and, most important of all, a red stone pipe with a gaily decorated stem as long as your arm. This is the way we expect Indians to look in pictures, on the stage and around hotels famous for tourists. All these highly original objects are of true Indian origin, but the picture is a composite, welded together partly under white influence, and the reader now knows that this picture presents a generalized Indian, rather than the reality. If one had walked through the United States about 1600, he would have noted ever-changing styles of clothing, housing and standards of living. Speech, too, would have been different at every village or camp.

We suppose that the ancestors of the Indians to be seen on such a journey just grew in numbers and spread over the country without plan or intention. An Indian community rarely consisted of more than a hundred persons of all ages. A few such communities or bands might live together in a village or camp, but even then each band considered itself its own master and free at any time to withdraw, camp apart or join another group of such bands. When one of these bands increased to one hundred and fifty souls or more, part of it would secede and thus become a new band. The probable explanation is that when a band or community became too big, its simple, natural system of government no longer worked smoothly, and it became more difficult to kill enough game for an adequate food supply. Not infrequently, according to tradition, a quarrel or a murder was the immediate cause of separation.

For a time the new rebel band might keep in touch with the parent band but eventually become completely estranged, so that even their speech would be different, not to mention new ways of living. Leadership in such a band was largely spontaneous; what we mean is that he led who, by nature, was equipped to lead. Often there was rivalry between two or three men with powers and ambitions of leadership. When the number of people in the band became great enough to divide readily, one of these would-be leaders might move out with those willing to trust him and thus start a new band.

This procedure continued for centuries, until the land was occupied from ocean to ocean. The great Algonkin Family must have begun with a few bands who set the fundamental speech pattern, so that, in spite of all the secessions and organization of new bands, enough of the original speech framework survived to show their Algonkin origins. Some of those we have characterized as doubtful Algonkins must have split off a long time before the others.

The view we now get is of a thin, scattering population of little bands living in small camps or villages dotting the shores of streams and lakes. The camps and villages, at least, were jealous of their own freedom, even though a number of them might consider themselves collectively as a tribe and, on occasion, send a few of their head men to meet in tribal council. If a village did not agree with the decisions of the tribal council, it refused to co-operate for the time, as was its right. It was this loose, liquid, formless social and political status that made the Indian an easy prey to white penetration.

Occasionally pressure of hostile Indian bands forced villages to combine for defense, as happened when some ambitious chief rallied a number of tribes to oppose the whites, but these were usually temporary and very tenuous unions. However, a few Indian alliances endured for some time, as the Iroquois League, the Creek Confederacy and the Pawnee Republic. These were the beginnings of what might have been Indian nations, if the whites had stayed at home in Europe.

Population Density

Almost everyone wants to know how many Indians there are now and how many there were when Columbus arrived. The first question can be answered more easily than the second. Our Indian population, according to the United States Bureau of the Census, 1960, totaled 523,-591. Eskimos and Aleuts in Alaska raised the total to 552,228. A carefully prepared estimate for aboriginal United States and Alaska was a population of 1,153,000. Some scholars considered this too high, others later too low; at present, the best estimate seems to indicate an aboriginal population of between one and two million. The aboriginal population density averaged about one Indian to every three square miles; the density of the population today in the United States is nearly two hundred times greater. The white population is not evenly distributed, nor was that of the Indian. The densest Indian population areas were California and a narrow belt along the Pacific coast in Washington and Oregon. The two small localities with the maximum density were in the vicinity of San Francisco and the Pueblo villages centering in Arizona and New Mexico. The only central or eastern areas approaching the density of California, as a whole, were in southeastern Virginia and the coast belt of North Carolina. Of moderate density were (1) the southern half of New England, New Jersey, eastern Pennsylvania, Delaware and parts of Maryland; (2) Wisconsin; (3) the southern states, exclusive of Florida. All other parts of the United States varied in thinness of population.

In general, then, the Indian population was thickest near

the seacoasts, or on the eastern and western margins of the United States. This meant that the English, Dutch and French settled where the Indians were more numerous than anywhere east of California, which accounts for the bitterness of the fighting. As the eastern Indian tribes were pushed back into Kentucky, Ohio and Indiana, the population there increased, until the climax of defeat scattered the survivors.

We have mentioned the small size of Indian communities and tribes. There are some data upon the sex and age of Indians. Students of population know that mode of life has something to do with the relative number of women and men, as well as with the average age at death. A census of hunting tribes in central Canada in 1805 gave the following curious ratios, per thousand of population:

	1805	1929
Men	74	187
Women	212	244
Minors	714	569

In the population table above we have added data for some of the same tribes in 1929. The chief occupation of men in 1805 was hunting and war; in 1929, hunting alone. Hunting is obviously a dangerous occupation, and the hazard in war can be roughly estimated by comparing the ratios 74 and 187. Women were not subjected to these hazards, and the dangers of living show a tendency to lessen as they come more and more under the influence of white people.

In 1805 a band of one hundred Indians would depend upon seven adult men for food, clothing and protection. Of this seven, two or three might be too old to hunt. Under the conditions of 1929 there would be eighteen adults, so the number of hunters would have doubled. However, in 1929 the standard of Indian living was higher than in 1805, requiring that each hunter kill many more fur-bearing animals to barter for necessities and luxuries at the trading post.

In an average white community of one hundred persons in 1930, we should find twenty-eight men, twenty-seven women and forty-five minors; here twenty-eight men are available, but the standard of living is higher than that of the Indian.

One popular notion is that Indians lived longer than whites. There are no data to support this fancy. At present there are fewer old people among Indians than whites, and what data we have for the past suggest that in colonial days old Indians were scarce. On the other hand, the possible span of life seems about the same for Indians and whites, so that now and then an Indian may live to be a hundred, but the ratio will be much lower than among whites. What we mean is that relatively more old people will be found among whites.

Are the Indians Dying Out?

When we note that there are now about half as many Indians as in 1700, the decline seems shocking. Statistics show that when Indians were conquered and placed upon reservations, their death rate rose above the birth rate. This continued until about 1900, when a turn for the better was made, and since that date most of the surviving tribes are increasing at an accelerating rate: in 1901 the Indians numbered 269,388; in 1937, 337,366. The birth rate of Indians has always been high and shows little inclination to fall; but the death rate is constantly dropping, promising to become as low as that for rural whites. This means an ever-widening margin between births and deaths, from which it follows that there will be more and more Indians in the future. Statisticians in 1940 estimated the Indian population for 1960 as exceeding half a million, which it has done; it is still growing.

The Daily Round of Life

To understand a people we must know how they make their living. To provide food, clothing and shelter is essential to any kind of human existence. Other interests in life are secondary. Everywhere it seems that man is the provider and woman the cook. Whether the way of life is hunting or farming, whichever is the main dependence, that task falls to the man. When we turn to the aboriginal Indians in the United States and Canada, we find a society of hunters rather than farmers. In California, Colorado, Idaho, Montana, Nevada, Oregon, Utah, Washington and Wyoming there was no agriculture in 1492. In Arizona and New Mexico a good deal of maize was raised, but east of the Mississippi it was produced in varying amounts, at no time sufficient to sustain the Indians for even a part of the year. So if we were asked to state the economic base to Indian living as our forefathers first saw it, we would say it was hunting. This was the main industry, the output of which determined whether the population survived, was well fed, well clothed, or lived in privation and want.

In the United States and Canada it was the man's job to hunt; if vegetable food was to be gathered or a garden plot cultivated, that was woman's work. We find the only exception to this rule in Arizona and New Mexico, where young and middle-aged men worked in the fields, but some of them, at least, hunted deer and other game at intervals. So, bearing in mind that, for the most part, the Indians of history were primarily meat eaters, we see that in contrast to human life in Europe the Indians possessed no domesticated "beef" animals, but depended upon such wild animals as deer, moose, elk and bison, according to locality. The food value of these animals depended upon their size, and while exact weights are not available, the estimates or dressed carcasses are: bison, 1000 pounds, moose, 800 pounds, elk, 350 pounds, deer, 100 pounds.

It would take at least ten deer to equal a bison, but a single deer would equal a goodly number of rabbits.

It is difficult to estimate an adequate meat ration for an Indian hunter. Experts in diet have set the daily average at two pounds plus per person, but the fur traders usually counted upon four pounds per day for each man, woman and child in camp. As there was always some waste because of the irregularity of the daily supply, a minimum of four pounds is a fair figure. Suppose, then, we look in upon a band of 100 Indians who live alone in the usual way. To live comfortably, then, the hunters must take 400 pounds of meat per day, or 12,000 pounds a month. So, assuming that deer will net 100 pounds of meat per head, and that a camp of 100 Indians will require 400 pounds of meat per day, an average of four deer per day must be killed.

According to what we know of the Indian population, the number of able-bodied hunters would range from five to ten. So, under the most favorable conditions, a hunter should bag a deer every two or three days. Hunting with bow and arrows over the same territory demanded long journeys and hours of creeping carefully through the brush or waiting beside a trail for a deer to pass.

We are not unmindful that adolescents and even boys killed some small game and that the women gathered some vegetable food in season when not otherwise engaged. There might be, in storage, a small quantity of dried fruit, roots and possibly a little corn and a bag of beans, but these were for emergencies. So we can see that even if the camp were not well fed, the hunters would be busy most of the time. Then they must make their own bows and arrows and keep them in order, make snowshoes for winter, etc. If canoes were used, these were further responsibilities. Taking all this into account, as well as some allotment of time to war and defense, we see that the Indian male was not altogether a gentleman of leisure.

To comprehend the part big game animals played in Indian economics, we should note the ranges of the several species. The main kinds of common deer are the white-tail, black-tail and mule deer, which taken together covered the whole of the United States from the Atlantic to the Pacific. The deer was of first importance to the Indians east of the Mississippi and in California and northward, because there were no other large hoofed animals. So while the relative importance of deer varied from one area to another, they were available almost everywhere. The moose was important in eastern Canada, but did not range far into the United States; hence we may ignore this animal. The bison, or buffalo, on the other hand, was the main food animal between the Mississippi and the Rocky Mountains.

Since the pre-Columbian society of the United States was maintained by hunting and this was the man's job, the three R's of a boy's education were the techniques of hunting; he must major in deer or bison according to where he lived. In the Northeast, one of his minors would be moose; in the bison area, he would have two minors, elk and deer. No youth could qualify to respectability unless well trained in these hunting techniques. There is no evidence that all the graduates from the hunting school were rated A+, and as in all societies the able provider fed more than his share, but made up for it in prestige and power.

We may summarize with the remark that the desirable standard of living in aboriginal United States was based upon hunting large game, meat being the staple and the preferred food. It is recorded more than once in literature that Indians said, "When there is no meat, starvation stalks through the camp." In general, then, the basic occupation among the United States Indians was hunting large game. The only possible exception might be in the Puget Sound area, where fishing was important, and in Arizona and New Mexico, where maize was cultivated intensively. Yet, even in those areas, the hunting of deer was important.

The killing of large game not only results in food, but

many inedible by-products. For example, from deer there come:

SKIN – moccasins, thongs, clothing
HAIR – stiff hair from the tail for making ornaments and embroidery
ANTLERS – tool handles, arrow points
HOOFS – glue, rattles
DEWCLAWS – jinglers for belts and anklets and for rattles
SINEWS – for thread, bowstrings and snares
BONES – bodkins, skin-dressing tools, handles, ornaments, etc.
PAUNCH and BLADDER – for bags and containers of various kinds

These materials were always available, and so the line of least resistance would be to use them. However, the most important of these by-products are skins and sinew. The Indians looked upon deerskins as indispensable, for they were the finest available materials for clothing. Deerskins could be tanned in such a way as to make them dry soft after wetting, thus making them the equal of cloth in this important quality while superior to cloth in durability and strength. As moccasin materials they headed the list. The adoption of "buckskin" moccasins, leggings, shirts and coats by white hunters, trappers and frontiersmen is familiar to all and is sufficient evidence that deerskins possessed unusual wearing qualities. It is easy to understand, then, that all Indians, even those specializing in agriculture, hunted deer of necessity, if not for food, then for clothing.

The grasslands along the Mississippi River and westward to the Rocky Mountains were overrun with bison. They were common in parts of Kentucky and Indiana, and even found their way into Ohio, but were most numerous in the grasslands. Their food value was about equal to that of cattle. If the Indian camp of deer hunters we had in mind moved out into the bison range, the six hunters need not kill more than two or three bison per month each, to keep all the people well fed. The large, hairy bison skins were useful too, as robes, bedding and tepee covers. As bison skins were thick and coarse, they could not compete with deer- and elkskins for clothing, and since deer and elk were found thinly scattered over the grasslands, they were hunted too. Yet one hundred deerskins per year might well suffice for the entire camp.

The Indians of the bison country camped along streams whose banks, lined with trees and bushes, were the only source of fuel. Everywhere man must pitch his camp near water and fuel. There were probably enough bison in the Mississippi drainage to have supported a much larger Indian population had fuel and water been equally well distributed. However this may be, the meat supply of the bison country was luxurious. The bison grazed in large herds, which made it practical for the hunters to work in teams. Deer hunting is, at best, the game of a lone hunter who steals upon a deer in the thick woods. Bison, on the other hand, were in the open, usually in close formation, and easily seen from afar. The aboriginal Indian had neither horses nor guns, but hunted afoot. The bison were both wary and militant, skillful in keeping out of arrow range, quick to charge the hunters, if crowded. On the other hand, they could be stampeded and run into swamps or over high banks. The usual method of hunting was by stalking. One procedure was to cover the body with a wolfskin and crawl to the side of the grazing herd, then rise and shoot. Two to four hunters might get under a buffalo skin and approach the herd in the same way. To stampede a herd, a line of hunters might approach boldly and noisily. At other times the grass would be set on fire behind and on their flanks, to escape which the herd must flounder into a swamp or tumble over a cliff. All the variations in these methods are described in the special books on the subject, but what is important here is that, with teamwork, a day or two per month would keep the camp in luxury. So the men in the bison country seem to have had an easy job.

This raises the question as to what the bison hunters

did betweentimes, seeing that they enjoyed a good deal of leisure. The women, on the other hand, were well occupied, drying meat, serving meals, dressing skins, caring for children, making clothing and perhaps tending a garden. Students of population tell us that there was usually a marked excess of women in the bison country, which would have reduced the amount of work each woman must do, but even so they were busy all the time. The men gave a good deal of time to raiding and war; at home they were occupied in holding ceremonies and sitting in councils. Some authorities tell us that the bison-hunting Indians were more often at war than were the tribes that followed other modes of hunting. Perhaps that was because the bison hunters had so much time on their hands. Yet one result of this continual fighting was an increase in the death rate for men. The population table for 1805 was based upon Indians who were in large part bison hunters. The hunters for 1929 sought deer and fur-bearing animals.

Then we must not overlook the circumstances that in 1805 the bison-hunting Indians were well supplied with horses. A single hunter on a good horse could ride close to the flank of a running herd of bison and send his arrows into the hearts of the helpless animals at the rate of one or two a minute. If the herd left the region, the camp could pack its belongings on horses, mount other horses and travel at the rate of forty to fifty miles a day, until a new herd was located. No wonder the bison hunters could live in large camps and the men spend their time at war, gambling and idling about!

In most parts of the United States fishing was casual and unimportant. There were tribes who would not taste fish, but as fish were scarce in their country this made little difference. The largest area in which fishing played a leading role was the Columbia River drainage and streams in the adjacent parts of the Pacific coastal belt. These are the streams up which the salmon "run" at intervals, crowding them from bank to bank, enabling the fishermen to take them wholesale. The women cured the fish by drying and smoking, thus laying up a supply of food until the next "run." It so happens that the original Indian population of western Washington and Oregon was rated as the densest; the abundant fish supply may account for this. The other locality where fishing was prominent was in the bays of Virginia and New Jersey, where the Indians were skilled in the use of large nets of their own manufacture.

Woman's Work

Many writers have noted that almost everywhere, in all states of society, women work continuously, but at a variety of tasks, whereas men engage in violent bursts of effort at intervals. We suppose this is what is meant when the woman is called a household drudge and the man a laborer: the one career looked upon as a tragedy, the other as a glorious opportunity. Among hunting peoples, like our Indians, the sex differences in work appear in high relief. The pursuit of big game calls for great exertion, then a period of rest, but at intervals only does hunting call for the maximum output of energy. The women, on the other hand, are confronted by as many housekeeping tasks as are women everywhere—one small, recurring job after another, of which feeding and clothing make the greatest demands upon their time.

Under aboriginal conditions each woman was expected to do everything for herself and her family. She could not go to a trader to buy what she needed, so practically all that was consumed must go through her hands. All the food was prepared and served by her.

We use the past tense in speaking of Indian life, because there have been great changes, but among many contemporary tribes the lot of the Indian woman is about the same as of old. We know of Indian camps in which it is still true that every Indian woman must be adept at making clothing and keeping it in repair. She does most of the housebuilding; anyway she owns the house and so is expected to keep it in repair. When the family moves, she must carry more than her share of the family baggage.

The woman makes her own household furniture, the utensils and her own tools. She tends the fire, gathers the wood and packs it home. There are no servants, but often a grandmother can lend a hand, and little girls do their share. Again, those men who could support a second or even a third wife would naturally live upon a higher plane than in households where one woman must do everything.

If any weaving is done, the woman gathers the plants, shreds out the fiber, twists or spins the thread, makes dyes, dyes the thread, then weaves. Among the Pueblo Indians men did the spinning and weaving, but otherwise in the United States it was woman's work. In Arizona and New Mexico the men worked in the fields, but among many agricultural tribes the whole matter was delegated to the women. When the men held a ceremony, the women gathered the wood for the fire, cooked the food and served it. Finally, at a funeral they were the mourners and often dug the grave as well. No wonder an anthropologist was once moved to write a book on woman's share in primitive culture. Most of the homely but basic inventions he attributed to her, and even went so far as to say that she domesticated man and so was the civilizer. We do not know to what extent this is true, but we do know that the Indian woman did as much to make Indian life a success as did the man. She was a strong laborer, a good mechanic, a good craftsman, no mean artist, something of an architect, a farmer, a traveler, a fisherman, a trapper, a doctor, a preacher and, if need be, a leader.

The Indian did not develop great systems of transportation. In the forest country he was advanced in the use of canoes, and in the grasslands of the West he used dogs to carry and drag loads, but on land he had to walk, carry his young children and his baggage. Perhaps an undue share of this fell to women. As little girls, they had babies strapped to their backs and carried home the wood, thus growing up strong. An adult Indian woman could carry more on her back and head than most white men. The Indian man did not carry much if he could avoid it. On the march, careful watch must be kept for hostile Indians, and also game must be killed. He had enough to do in terms of the hunting and protection of his family.

In many forms of society women always have at hand a bit of sewing, twisting of thread or weaving. It was the same with the Indian woman. While the pot boiled she could repair moccasins, sew a seam in her husband's leggings, etc., and if a visitor called she might also bring some work with her. There was a good deal of co-operative labor if the task was large; for example, when a bison hunter's woman wished to make a new tepee cover. Having collected the twelve to fourteen skins needed, she would get together some food, then invite the most experienced women in camp. All would assist according to their special skill, cut and fit the skins, then do the necessary sewing. The girls, when not wholly occupied with the care of younger children, would turn to sewing or whatever other handwork was urgent.

Men and youths worked at odd moments in the same way, making new arrows, repairing the necessary ceremonial objects, etc. The old men loafed a good deal, but even they had minor craft jobs to perform, to teach boys how to shoot, narrate myths, give moral talks and attend to many other small tasks. Finally, an Indian community was a human group: a few were lazy, some stupid, some immoral, some quarrelsome, some grasping and tyrannical, some intelligent, some thrifty and some industrious.

Indian Culture Areas

During our walk across the United States we should have noticed a good many differences in dress, household economy, ways of making a living, styles of ornamentation, amusements, games and ceremonies. However, changes in these would seldom be abrupt, but would tend to grade into one another. For example, moccasins might be the same in the way the dressed skin was fitted to the foot, but differ from tribe to tribe in decoration, the shape of the uppers, etc.; finally, hard soles might be added, resulting in a very different-looking footgear. This again might continue for a time and then give way to another style. Going westward we should find tepees in use, first covered with birchbark, then with buffalo skins and finally, when we reached the Columbia River, with woven mats. At about this point tepees would disappear entirely. To generalize, we could say that neighboring tribes resemble each other.

This generalization holds especially for housing, dress, food habits, crafts, etc. It is also fair to say that the manner of living will change with the nature of the country. So we often hear Indian tribes in the United States spoken of under the following group names:

EASTERN WOODLAND AREA
Types: Iroquois, Ojibway, Delaware, Naskapi
SOUTHEASTERN AREA
Types: Creek, Yuchi, Natchez, Seminole
PLAINS AREA
Types: Dakota, Pawnee, Crow, Blackfoot
SOUTHWEST AREA
Types: Zuni, Navaho, Apache, Pima
CALIFORNIA
Types: Pomo, Yokuts, Maidu, Wintun
PLATEAU AREA
Types: Nez Percé, Spokan, Kutenai
NORTH PACIFIC COAST AREA
Types: Tlingit, Nootka

Under the several tribal names we have given brief sketches of the prominent tribes falling under these area classifications. The usefulness of the classification is that, within each area, the basic modes of life are similar.

Chapter XIX

WHEN THE WHITE MAN WENT INDIAN

WHENEVER two widely differing peoples meet, some individuals desert their own kind to live with the strangers. When a white man took to the Indian camps, or "went Indian," his people held him in contempt; but when an Indian came to live with them, the whites considered the act laudable. Whether the Indians looked upon those Indians who deserted their way of life with the same contempt, we do not know, but what little evidence there is points in that direction. It is clear that when a white man came to live with Indians, they considered it a manifestation of good sense. An important chapter in this book would be a penetrating account of Indians "going white," but we do not have the data in hand to write it. They rarely wrote books about themselves, but if a white person were found in an Indian camp his or her biography was promptly written. Yet we suppose there are some data somewhere about Indians who "went white"; at least, we hope they will be published sometime, so that the other side of the story may be heard. But perhaps the reader prefers to hear about white people who went Indian.

The European, especially the Frenchman and the Englishman, often liked the frontier so well that he spent his life in Indian camps. Once adjusted to this free hunting life, comforted by his Indian family, freed from the exacting discipline of civilization, he found a return to his people distasteful. Yet these white men rarely became completely Indianized, because their early training was that of Western people, some of whose ideals they still cherished. Those who went over completely were captives taken in childhood and brought up as Indians; they are the ones who went wholly native.

These and temporary captives are the heroes of colonial literature. Any well-stocked library can produce many of these old books, more thrilling than detective stories. There are more than a hundred titles. Among the best-known are the captivities of John Tanner, Frances Slocum, Mary Rowlandson and Mary Jameson. Frances Slocum and Mary Jameson lived out their lives as Indians, but there were hundreds of others lost to history. Frances Slocum was captured from her home in Wyoming Valley, Pennsylvania, when five years old and carried to Indiana, where she lived with Indians until she died in 1874. A monument was erected to her memory in 1899, and later the state of Indiana created the Frances Slocum State Forest.

A man by the name of Gist traveled in Ohio in 1750, leaving us a diary in which we find the following entry:

Tuesday, 15. We left Muskingum, and went W 5 M, to the White Woman's Creek, on which is a small Town; this White Woman was taken away from New England, when she was not above ten Years old, by the French Indians; She is now upwards of fifty, and has an Indian Husband and several Children—Her name is Mary Harris, she still remembers they used to be very religious in New England, and wonders how the White Men can be so wicked as she has seen them in these Woods.[1]

The historian Hanna tells us that this woman was taken at the burning of Deerfield, Massachusetts, February 29, 1704.

It had long been the Indian custom to take captives; in a raid the adult men and youths were killed on the spot, except one or two spared for torture for the entertainment of the folks at home. Old women were killed at once, but girls and young women, together with young boys, were taken captive. So it is not strange that when the Algon-

[1] William M. Darlington, *Christopher Gist's Journals*, Cleveland, 1893, p. 41.

kin of the East began to raid the white settlements, they
captured children and young men.

The object of the Algonkin Indian raider was to make
the white enemy unhappy, to burn his house, kill his livestock, scatter his possessions, scalp his women, carry off
his children and, if possible, torture him to death. In this
way he sought to shock and enrage the white man's relatives. He took care to leave behind the most hideous evi-
dences of brutality, even the revelation of his tribal identity. No wonder the settlers came to look upon the Indians
as devils and to vent their rage upon them in much the
same way, even carrying off their women and children to
be sold as slaves in the West Indies.

But let us not paint too dark a picture, for the Indian
was usually kind to his own children; in fact, he loved
them intensely; he assumed that his enemy did the same.
After he brought home the little white children, he treated
them like his own. A childless woman or one who had lost
an infant would joyfully take a little captive in her arms
and cherish it. Naturally, white families suffered acutely
from the uncertainty as to the fate of their children, just
as did the Indian mothers of old when their children were
seized by a hostile tribe. So it is natural that whenever
treaties were made after an Indian war, the chief stipula-
tion was that all captives be returned.

One of the most successul campaigns against Indians
in the Ohio country was that of the English general Bouquet, to whom we have referred before. From a narrative
of his 1764 campaign we have chosen certain extracts
respecting the return of white prisoners held by the Indians. You may recall that he drove a hard bargain with
the conquered chiefs in Ohio; to save their villages and the
lives of numerous hostages, they were given but a brief
interval in which to return all their white captives, no
matter when captured. The Indians loved these adopted
children as their own. Perhaps the shrewd general knew
this, and so turned the tables, put the Indians to torture,
not by burning at the stake, but by tearing out their heart-
strings.

One of the most touching scenes in literature is the homely account of the sorrowing Indians returning these captives:

The Indians too, as if wholly forgetting their usual savageness, bore a capital part in heightening this most affecting scene. They delivered up their beloved captives with the utmost reluctance; shed torrents of tears over them, recommending them to the care and protection of the commanding officer. Their regard to them continued all the time they remained in camp. They visited them from day to day; and brought them what corn, skins, horses and other matters, they had bestowed on them, while in their families; accompanied with other presents, and all the marks of the most sincere and tender affection. Nay, they did not stop here, but, when the army marched, some of the Indians solicited and obtained leave to accompany their former captives all the way to Fort-Pitt, and employed themselves in hunting and bringing provisions for them on the road.

What greater punishment could that old soldier, Bouquet, have meted out to these Indians? They could not have suffered more had he, in Indian fashion, tomahawked their adopted white children before their weeping eyes.

The narrative continues:

Among the children who had been carried off young, and had long lived with the Indians, it is not to be expected that any marks of joy would appear on being restored to their parents or relatives. Having been accustomed to look upon the Indians as the only connexions they had, having been tenderly treated by them, and speaking their language, it is no wonder that they considered their new state in the light of a captivity, and parted from the savages with tears.

But it must not be denied that there were even some grown persons who shewed an unwillingness to return. The Shawanese were obliged to bind several of their prisoners and force them along to the camp; and some women,

*who had been delivered up, afterwards found means to
escape and run back to the Indian towns. Some, who could
not make their escape, clung to their savage acquaintance
at parting, and continued many days in bitter lamenta-
tions, even refusing sustenance.*

*For the honour of humanity, we would suppose those
persons to have been of the lowest rank, either bred up in
ignorance and distressing penury, or who had lived so long
with the Indians as to forget all their former connections.
For easy and unconstrained as the savage life is, certainly
it could never be put in competition with the blessings of
improved life and the light of religion, by any persons
who have had the happiness of enjoying, and the capacity
of discerning, them.*[2]

The last remark is almost stupid. Frontier life was often
hard and dull for children and young women. Life in an
Indian village was probably less laborious and less encom-
passed by social isolation. Spend ten years of your early
life in an Indian camp, where you are received kindly,
with no prospect of escape, make personal attachments,
finally marry and have children, and then imagine yourself
forced to leave all this behind forever, to make a new
start. Suppose again that you had adopted an Indian child
and, after caring for it for years as your own, saw it torn
from your arms and handed over to Indians. Why should
this chronicler of the time have been surprised?

There was neither racial nor social incompatibility between Indian and white. On the frontier white men married Indian women, and we have seen that white captives
married to Indian men were reluctant to leave them. In
Europe the early tendency of scholars was to consider
the Indians as belonging to the white race. The tragic
struggle between the two was economic and political.
From the start, the Indian was the weaker. A kindly feel-

---

[2] William Smith, *Historical Account of Bouquet's Expedition
Against the Ohio Indians, in 1764,* Cincinnati, 1868, pp. 76-7,
80-1.

ing for Indians survives, except when and where there is economic competition. Intermarriage has persisted, until it is now estimated that nearly half the Indians in the United States are mixed with white blood. However, the reservation system tends to inhibit intermarriage, so the complete assimilation of the Indians may never become a reality.

The Indian as a Child of Nature

Many European philosophers, weary of wars and the arbitrary power of kings and lords, imagined that because the Indian lived a simple life, recognized no power except that of his own band and reserved great freedom of action for himself, he enjoyed ideal freedom, was always happy, and therefore lived the most desirable life. We can easily see there is an illusion here. In the abstract, there are desirable practices in the Indian way of life. He was not really a communist, but he was liberal with food. So long as he had food, he was expected to share it. That he did not always do it we learn from legends, but since in these tales the one who concealed food always came to grief, there can be no doubt that to share it was the thing to do. This is sometimes called the law of hospitality, which is, in short, that the stranger is always welcome at your fireside. However, this did not extend to private property, such as bows and arrows, one's robe, shirt, medicine bag, etc. Every member of the band went to the dinner pot when he wished, so why not hand something to the stranger? The pipe, also, was the guest's due; and having smoked with his guest, the host was a friend and must so act. Even an enemy was safe if he reached a fireside and came without threats. Food and a smoke must be given him; both host and guest were then under obligations to each other.

Yet these Indians were hunters, and when following game they were at the mercy of strangers and competing with them. The law of hunting was "tooth and claw"; to kill was the objective. Men who killed daily understood the art and were, if need be, as ready to slay a man as game. They did not shy away from the man hunt; rather they gloried in it. Such a life, one in which most men died with their clothes on, was not just what the philosopher had in mind. There was a relentless daily grind; and war whoops and death cries often roused the sleeper. There were torture and terrible privation. On the other hand, the Indian was a human being, capable of understanding much that the philosopher spoke. He was not satisfied with his own life, but sought to improve it.

Chapter XX

THREE STRANGE GIFTS FROM THE WHITE MAN

THREE things peculiar to the white man and prominent on the frontier were the gun, liquor and the horse. In the eastern forest the horse did not rise to the level of the other two, but beyond the Mississippi it was first in importance. The corresponding things the Indian offered the white man were tobacco, maize and woodcraft. It is near the truth to say that the bottle was exchanged for tobacco —the Indian offered his pipe as a token of friendship, the white man reciprocated with liquor. Simultaneously, the two races reached a common level in that the pipe and liquor became the universal passions and have so remained to this day.

The Gun

If we accept some of the stories in old books, firearms so frightened the Indians that they fell down in a faint. We have long doubted these tales, because, after all, the report of a musket is not terrifying, and Indians were brave. They were likely to be startled and surprised over the behavior of this strange weapon, but they were schooled in bravery and self-control. We know of no reason why the Australian Blacks should be more courageous than the Indians, yet when Captain Cook went ashore in boats, the natives threatened him at the water's edge until he ordered them peppered with bird shot; they retired, but quickly returned to a second attack, this time carrying shields. For this and other reasons, we suspect that the stories about Indians and guns were exaggerated. Naturally, the Indians respected these new weapons, wanting to possess them above all things. So it is not surprising that guns were, from the first, the most prized objects in the white trader's stock. Nor were the first tribes to secure them slow to realize their newly acquired power; several of them began to expand their ranges and to seek new enemies.

While the gun was a great asset to the Indian, it was, in one respect, a handicap. He could neither make a gun nor produce powder. Even keeping guns in repair was beyond his skill. With his gun out of order, he was as helpless as a layman with a stranded automobile in a uninhabited country.

For example, we find the Mohawk petitioning the Council at Albany in 1691 for a smith to reside among them to keep their arms in order. Each year thereafter petitions were filed; thus in July 1693 the request read, "Wee begge of you to let us have a Smith and a gunn stock maker in our Castle to mend our armes when they are broken."

At first it may seem strange that the Indian was so helpless in this matter of repairs. White men of the time attributed it to indolence, rather than to stupidity, but we suspect it was neither. The trouble may well have been that the Indians were unaccustomed to tools, except of the simplest kind. They had no previous experience with iron. On the other hand, Eskimo men learned quickly to repair their own guns, even reconstructing guns from parts of old ones, as may be seen in some museum collections. The Eskimo was a good mechanic, skillful with tools of his own making, and able to invent new devices when new materials fell into his hands. How he came by the urge to be mechanical in contrast to the Indian, we do not know, but he was and had been for a long, long time, before he saw white men. So whatever the cause, the Indian could become a crack shot, but was helpless when the lock of his gun went wrong. This was where the handicap lay. If he expected to use guns in war, he must lay up a reserve supply acquired by hard work in producing furs, but the worst of it was that if he went to war with the whites, he could not continue long for want of powder. In short, the Indian became dependent upon the white man for what had become an absolute necessity in his standard of living. Economically he was now in the hands of the white man; war and resistance were useless, since in the end he must make peace on terms suitable to his masters.

Yet no one blames the Indian for not accepting his situation without resistance; being human, he could not do otherwise. Some of the great Indians, the geniuses of their day, saw that through trade the white men were masters; that the Indian must labor in the forest to trap and kill and to prepare furs, while his woman tanned skins and produced surplus goods to trade for guns, powder, etc. His tasks were made harder by white competition, because the forests were soon overrun by white trappers and hunters, better organized and equipped than the Indian. They ruthlessly depleted the game and by quantity production lowered prices. All this made it increasingly difficult for the Indian to maintain his new standard of living. On the other hand, white trappers resented the competition of the Indian, while he, in turn, looked upon the trappers as trespassers upon his lands. Under such a regime the lands of the Indians dwindled, fur animals became scarcer and the trade more exacting. White trappers resorted to violence; the Indians retaliated by raiding the settlements. Yet, though many of the Indian leaders preached a return to the old ways and dreamed of a time when all white men would be swept back into the sea, never once did they advocate putting aside the gun or ceasing to buy powder. Such a sacrifice was unthinkable. Perhaps they were unaware of the inconsistency of their position. They were not unlike the contemporary reformer who dreams of a return to the good old days of the one-man shop, but expects to ride in automobiles, airplanes, use radios and telephones.

The Algonkin were good shots. They used the most improved guns, keeping up with the advance in invention.

When long rifles came into use, they also found their way into the hands of Indians. Because they were first exploited on the Kentucky frontier, they were called Kentucky rifles. During the colonial wars and even in the War of 1812, the Algonkin and the Iroquois were armed with guns superior in accuracy of fire to those used by soldiers. There is nothing strange about this, because the army is usually conservative. Even after the Civil War our regular army used single-shot Springfields to fight Indians who were armed with the latest repeating rifles and used cartridges given them by the Department of Indian Affairs, in accordance with the several treaties. To an outsider this may seem ridiculous, like one department of the government making war upon the United States Army and equipping its departmental fighting men with superior arms. Naturally this is not a fair way to look at it, for the Indians were given repeating rifles to kill buffalo for food; yet they knew what they were about, and they wanted the best guns available to use in fights with the soldiers. Just what the Indian thought about this we do not know; probably he laughed at the stupidity of the white race.

There were times when the Indian took a more realistic attitude and attempted to restrict the distribution of firearms. We have noted the argument of certain Iroquois chiefs that their guns must be kept in repair if they were to give armed support to the English against the French and to hold back the hostile Algonkin from raiding the settlements. This was fair enough. History records instances like the following: by 1800 the Blackfoot tribes in Montana and Alberta had acquired guns by trade with the posts of the Hudson Bay and other English companies east of, and later within, their territory. The Salish tribes and others, west and south of them, were without guns, so the Blackfoot raided them relentlessly. But when the traders attempted to carry the trade across the mountains to the Salish, the Blackfoot not only objected, but used force to stop them. This is the same procedure as when civilized nations blockade the enemy frontier.

However, the story of the Indian and the gun has not

yet been written. Historians write eloquently of how the introduction of gunpowder made a new Europe, made Spain, Holland, France and England world powers. It was not many years after the discovery of America before large sailing ships with heavy, tough wooden sides carried rows of cannon for offense as well as defense. Warfare on land was revolutionized by the gun. The white traders and adventurers in America found the gun indispensable, and so even today everyone wants to possess one; the framers of our Constitution took care that the right to carry one was recognized and guaranteed. The Indian was caught in this social movement and changed by it to his loss as well as his gain. It changed his mode of life more than we realize, gave him a new feeling of power and, as we have noted, set in motion economic and psychological developments that evolved too fast for the maintenance of his traditional life. It was the speed of economic and social change that confused him, rendered him relatively helpless, in spite of his skill as a marksman. He was too much of an individualist to present a united front, but even had he done so, gunpowder would have ruined him in the end.

The Horse

Another important gift to the Indian was the horse. When he first set foot upon the American continent, nature offered him this important animal, so archaeologists tell us, but it was never tamed. The early Indian hunted the wild horse for food, which may be one of the reasons why it became extinct long before white men came to America. Perhaps the Indian would have domesticated the animal had it not become extinct so soon. What would have happened then, we can but guess. With this new power of movement great nations might have arisen; but our story is far less romantic.

The early Spanish expeditions around the Gulf of Mexico brought horses into the country, and for a long time it was believed that strays from Coronado's and De Soto's sixteenth century expeditions were responsible for bands of wild horses which later stocked the country. Roe's inspection of the chronicles—many of which give statistics on numbers of horses, and details of their losses—would indicate the impossibility of populating the country by strays. It is known that horses were deliberately introduced into and bred in South America, and although the question of the wild herds of mustangs may not have satisfactorily been answered, Roe suggests that the acquisition of horses by the Indians of North America was by "direct action" on the part of the Indians, or the Spaniards and other settlers, or both. However this was accomplished, one Indian tribe after another began to ride, and before the end of the seventeenth century horse Indians were common, and a century later the Indians of the buffalo country were rarely seen afoot.

The natural habitat of the horse is grassland: he does not thrive in the forest, which may be why the great families of the East, the Algonkin, Iroquois, etc., did not make much use of him. The Muskhogean of the South used horses more, but in the grasslands where everyone rode—men, women and children—the horse developed a new order of life. Hunting the buffalo was now done by horse. Fighting also became more picturesque, for many tribes acquired horses before actual contact with white men. Horses were trained to ride beside a running buffalo until the arrows of the rider felled the animal, then to overtake another, leaving the hands of the rider free to manipulate the bow. And the Indian could ride. Riding bareback, he ran down the buffalo or fought his enemies. Like all enthusiasts he devised new tricks; he could hang from the back of the horse by one leg, throw his bow arm over the neck, reach through underneath with an arrow in the other hand, and shoot at his enemies with a minimum exposure of his own body. Writers of the time have described these astonishing feats of horsemanship. The young men were trained to bring away their dismounted and dead, reaching down and picking them up by one hand on the run and then dragging them to safety. The writer knew an Indian who claimed to have been shot from his horse but was rescued in this manner. Yet the importance of the horse lay not in fighting but in mobility. Baggage, tents, the aged and children could be transported rapidly. The changes in Indian life brought about by this new mode of travel were even greater than those produced by the automobile in our time. The increased mobility gave a broader outlook, new experiences, more leisure, and inhibited sedentary occupations. Many Indians of the grassland quit raising small patches of maize, squashes and beans, increased their ranges to five hundred miles and more a season.

We commented at length upon the inability of the Indian to produce powder and his consequent dependence upon the white man, but it was different with horses. He could propagate them himself and make such riding gear as he needed with his own hands. Had the white man withdrawn from the continent after passing the horse on to the Indian, it would not have mattered. If necessary, the Indian could replenish his stock from wild herds, nor is it likely that, once having enjoyed them, he would have voluntarily abandoned the use of horses.

The horse Indians prized guns as highly as did the tribes of the East. Primarily they wanted them for war, to hurl back the Indians of the forests now so armed. Guns spread everywhere in a kind of armament race for survival. Horse Indians preferred short guns and smoothbores. Early observers tell us how they cut off part of long gun barrels with files. In chasing buffalo the Indian carried a number of round leaden bullets in his mouth. As his horse galloped along behind the buffalo, he held the muzzle of the gun in his left hand, poured a charge of powder into it from the horn slung around his neck, then placed the muzzle to his lips, dropped a bullet into it and patted the barrel with his right hand, to settle the powder and seat the bullet. As flintlocks were used, the gun could then be aimed and discharged. With practice, such loading became so rapid that a number of buffalo could be brought down in a few minutes. In fighting, the procedure was the same. Later came the breech-loading rifle, and finally the repeating rifle, both ideal for shooting from a horse.

A few army officers have written descriptions of Indians fighting in the 1870s. Since Indians would not attack unless they outnumbered the whites, a small detachment of soldiers, seeing Indians approaching, would seek shelter on high ground, dig in if possible and wait. The Indians began by galloping single file around the soldiers and, coming within range, would fire at every exposed head or body. Usually the Indians hung from the off side of the horse, thus reducing the chance of being hit by the soldiers' fire. The line of riders would draw gradually closer, thus making their fire more effective. If their losses were not great, they eventually rode over the surviving soldiers and thus annihilated them. If, on the other hand, the fire of the soldiers was deadly, the attack would be abandoned. Several Indians have testified to the danger in attacking large bodies of infantry, because the soldiers would form into a square, drop to the ground, dig up a little earth or pile up a few stones, from behind which they could fire. If the Indians attempted to ride the soldiers down, they would rise and use the bayonet. Having no technique for foiling bayonets, the Indians would be at a disadvantage. So they preferred to attack mounted soldiers. A running fight was the usual result, an engagement in which the Indian was at his best.

We are speaking now of the grassland and Plains Indians. Environment and mode of life seem to have decided whether a tribe became thoroughgoing horse Indians or remained foot Indians. For example, in New Mexico and Arizona the village tribes made little use of horses, preferring the donkey as a pack animal. Yet the less sedentary Apache and Navaho were horse Indians. In California the horse made little headway, but in parts of Oregon, Washington and Idaho, the Salish, Shoshoni and Shahaptin were horse Indians before 1800, probably before 1750. It is significant to note that where wild horses were abundant, the Indians were mounted. The explanation seems to be that when the horses could live in a wild state, the Indian could possess them. He did not store food for them or stable them, but expected them to graze around his camp when not in use. We look upon maize as good food for horses, but the agricultural Indian regarded it as human food and never raised as much as his daily diet required. He considered the horse an animal capable of rustling for himself. In the northern latitudes the long winters presented something of a problem. The buffalo and the wild horse survived by drifting here and there where dry grass was to be found, but the domesticated horse was restricted in his movements by tying or herding. The Indian soon discovered that when snow covered the ground, horses sought shelter among the cottonwood trees bordering streams, where they could feed on twigs and bark. So they parked their herds in cottonwood groves, cut off the top branches, and even felled some of the trunks, so the horses could the more readily gnaw the bark. A few tribes like the Pawnee, Mandan, etc., used large earth-covered houses, in which a few of the best horses were stalled at night; but this was done less for humane reasons than to prevent their being stolen, not by members of their own tribe but by hostile raiders. No Indian of those days could see horses without experiencing an overwhelming desire to run off with them. Many homesteaders, pushing out into the grassland, lost their horses in night raids. Mischievous Indians would stampede and drive off their oxen, not because they wanted them, but for prestige. They were adept at creeping into the camps of sleeping travelers and driving away their livestock. Greatest acclaim went to the man who could steal a mount from under its owner's nose. United States troops frequently lost all their mounts in spite of their sentries.

Liquor

There were few prohibitionists in colonial days, but all good citizens were for barring liquor from the Indian. They considered it on a par with providing children with gunpowder and matches. The explorers felt no particular responsibility for the welfare of the Indians, so some of them were moved to amuse themselves by making the Indians drunk. There are stories about how Henry Hudson permitted a few Indians to board his ship and gave one of them a drink of knockout caliber, whereupon the native fell to the deck unconscious, later assuring his astonished countrymen that he had visited the land of the spirits, where he experienced the delights of a different order of existence. Thereafter every Indian was ready to take a drink at any and all times. We are even told that the word Manhattan means "the place of the first big drunk."

There may be an increment of fact in this Henry Hudson story, for it is certain that all along the frontier Indians were soon clamoring for liquor. Alcohol was something new. No United States Indian had discovered distilled alcohol, so there were no rules of experience to guide him. His notion of how to consume liquor was to get drunk as fast as possible. He had no feeling for the white man's way of allowing himself to be teased by the presence of liquor and showing his power of control in not taking enough to get drunk. We suppose that with most peoples drinking liquor is a social matter, the chief enjoyment coming from the community spirit in sharing it. The Indians always shared food—that was fundamental with him—and when a keg of liquor was available all the assemblage began to work up their emotions preparatory to a grand debauch. Soon most inhibitions vanished, leading to clashes of arms and often to murder.

As we have said, all the whites knew this, for the colonies and their home governments all made pronounce-

ments and passed laws. Most of the traders knew that
liquor was a handicap in the fur trade. The resulting
demoralization and idleness reduced the quantity of furs
produced. Further, whereas at first the Indian usually paid
his debts, now many of them took their furs to the dis-
honest whisky trader to exchange for a few kegs, which
when consumed left them in debt to the honest trader
and without supplies for the winter trapping. Thus a
vicious circle was formed in which the honest trader was
caught; to survive, he too plied the Indian with liquor.

Some of the clearest pictures of Indian debauchery are
to be found in the journal of Alexander Henry. During his
stay at one small trading post, 1800–07, he records in his
journal seventy-seven large gatherings of Indians for drinking, with a total of sixty-five injuries to individual Indians,
ranging from death to permanent injuries and slight
wounds. He speaks of the noisy fighting, lewd advances,
and the screams of frightened children totally neglected
by their mothers or even trampled under the feet of the
revelers. The following quotation is informative:

*I sincerely believe that competitive trade among the
Saulteurs is the greatest slavery a person of any feeling
can undergo. A common dram-shop in a civilized country
is a paradise compared to the Indian trade, where two or
more different interests are striving to obtain the greater
share of the Indians' hunts—particularly among the Saulteurs, who are always ready to take advantage of the
situation by disposing of their skins and furs to the highest
bidder. No ties, former favors, or services rendered, will
induce them to give up their skins for one penny less than
they can get elsewhere. Gratitude is a stranger to them;
grant them a favor to-day, and to-morrow they will suppose it their due. Love of liquor is their ruling passion, and
when intoxicated they will commit any crime to obtain
more drink.[1]
But the Indians totally neglect their ancient customs;*

[1] Henry and Thompson, *op. cit.*, Vol. 2, p. 452.

and to what can this degeneracy be ascribed but to their intercourse with us, particularly as they are so unfortunate as to have a continual succession of opposition parties to teach them roguery and destroy both mind and body with that pernicious article, rum? What a different set of people they would be, were there not a drop of liquor in the country! If a murder is committed among the Saulteurs, it is always in a drinking match.[2]

When a hardheaded fur trader makes such remarks, they must be accepted as understating the situation.

The evils of the later liquor traffic are illustrated in the history of Montana, where white bootleggers induced Indians to steal cattle and horses, prostitute their women, defy the authority of their chiefs and disregard all the moral teachings of their people. Such a breakdown could mean little more than extinction. However, the honest white men of Montana Territory finally took matters into their own hands and by harsh measures put this illegal trade under rigid control before the Indians were completely wiped out.

When Indian reservations became the order of the day, those in charge of such reservations were usually powerless to prevent white bootleggers from selling to the Indians. Remember that hunting had ceased and raiding for plunder and scalps was under the ban, leaving the men with no occupation. Liquor promised a way of release. The reports of agents on file in the Indian Office in Washington are filled with laments from the time of the first President down to the present. Many of the terms used, such as "bootlegger," "whisky runner," etc., originated in the illegal trade with Indians.

So the liquor trade is an ugly page in history, from the day when Henry Hudson made Indians drunk in Manhattan to the present. In early days laws and prohibitions were promulgated; in 1670 Massachusetts legislated prohibition for the Indian, the other colonies, territories and

[2] *Ibid.,* Vol. 1, p. 209.

states following in order of their establishment. Yet during the same period the English and French governments sought to win the allegiance of the strong Indian tribes by frequent generous gifts of liquor. Many times the older, wiser Indians protested, but their words fell upon deaf ears, and the majority of their Indian followers secretly petitioned the whites for more and more liquor. The pitiful appeal of the Delaware in 1698 probably states the case fairly. In a council between New Jersey colony and the Delaware Indians, a chief said:

"We know it to be hurtful to us to drink it. We know it, but if people will sell it to us, we so love it that we cannot refuse it. But when we drink it, it makes us mad; we do not know what we are doing; we abuse one another; we throw one another in fire. Through drinking, seven score of our people have been killed."

A Long Island Indian once appealed to Peter Stuyvesant:

"Even your own people, though used to your liquors, fight with knives and commit follies when drunk. You ought not to sell brandy to the Indians to make them crazy, for they are not accustomed to it. To prevent all mischief, we wish you to sell no more fire-water to our braves."[3]

Incidentally, the pre-Columbian Aztecs had a liquor problem. Long before Columbus was born, some native discovered that a strong liquor, or pulque, could be made from the juice of the maguey plant. Tradition tells us that this intoxicating drink was soon so popular that the total demoralization of society was threatened. Then the rulers of the country instituted harsh measures to curb intoxication, finally resorting to capital punishment. Yet they did not suppress secret traffic in pulque. When

[3] William Christie Macleod, *The American Indian Frontier*, New York, 1928, p. 34.

Cortez conquered the Aztecs he abolished all the old laws, among them those prohibiting the drinking of pulque. Immediately intoxication increased so alarmingly that the Spanish rulers re-enacted the old laws against intoxication. One unique feature of the ancient Aztec liquor laws was that the aged of both sexes could be drunk as often as they liked.

Tobacco was probably less harmful to the whites than liquor to the Indians, but the former swept over Europe at an astonishing rate. The white man was immediately as crazy about tobacco as the Indian about liquor, and neither laws nor executions deterred them. This is a convenient place to deal with one question frequently asked: Did the Indians of the United States have knowledge of intoxicants before 1492? The answer is that there is no evidence that they had knowledge of distilled liquors, but they did know something of fermented liquids which may be designated as beers and wines. It is inconceivable that they should not have discovered what fermentation could do to vegetable and fruit juices, and there are plenty of data to indicate that the maize- and cassava-growing Indians of South America and the West Indies made mildly intoxicating liquors from these plants. Even Columbus states that the natives he met on his first voyage made one drink from maize and another from cassava. We have mentioned the more violent fermented pulque of Mexico. The knowledge of pulque and maize liquor found its way into Arizona and New Mexico, where the Pima, Papago and the various Apache tribes occasionally made these liquors. Strangely enough, the Pueblo, or village Indians, seem not to have made such drinks, nor are there any good data to show that any other Indians in the United States used them. We naturally guess that the Apache and their neighbors learned the trick from Mexico, but that the Pueblo villages refused to adopt the custom, nor did they pass it on to their northern neighbors.

The Pima and Apache drank on certain ceremonial occasions; at other times no liquor was made. Whether the other Indians of the United States ever had such drinks, we do not know, but when they did get liquor from the whites they made the occasion a social one; in other words, a grand drunk for men and women of all ages.

It appears further that it is only among organized societies that we can expect the production of liquor in quantity, so that persons may be drunk for long periods. Hunting Indians are too busy at their necessary occupations to make liquor, and the communities were too small to delegate persons to devote themselves to its production. Mexico and Peru were organized states in which differentiation of labor, periods of leisure, etc., made the production of such luxuries easy. The Pueblo Indians could have done it, but they gave attention to other matters. Since most of the Indians in the United States were still hunters in the main and lived in small, self-contained communities, they were free from drunkenness, chiefly because the production of liquor was incompatible with survival.

Chapter XXI

THE MYSTERY OF THE INDIAN MIND

THE white man defeated the Indian, traded with him, sometimes married his women, usually held his opinions and ways in contempt, but never understood him. The colonists were impressed by the dignity and poise of the Indians who sat or stood in an atmosphere of calm, their faces unexpressive but not forbidding. The Indians were grand masters in the art of listening, never interrupting or manifesting much emotion while a speaker discoursed. Yet when it came their turn, they proceeded in a fine manner, often rising to high levels of oratory. When a visitor called, they sat in silence for an interval. This led to the saying that Indians were taciturn, unemotional and strong-willed, a mistake in a way, for they were merely living up to an ideal. They were trained to act so and to abhor any other kind of behavior. They posed when in company, as their social code required. It was with the Algonkin that the colonists made most of their contacts, and from the literature we infer that this family led in this form of etiquette, with the Iroquois a close second.

The Indian walk would put the slouching gait of the white man to shame; it was on a level with the best military standards. The Plains Indians, some of whom belonged to the Algonkin Family, were also given to these ideals. The writer, visiting Indians in the West, used to enjoy watching the important old men walk, for the younger generation were taking on the awkwardness of the whites.

"Indian file" has become a common term in our language, but must be seen to be understood. Catlin painted Iowa Indians on the march, a canvas which conveys the spirit of such a file: dignity, grace of movement and, above all, silence. In pioneer days many a white scout caught sight of such a row of moving figures proceeding with silent tread, the stillness and dignity of the marchers making their approach more ominous.

All this was in keeping with the ideals of the dance. Most people imagine that when an Indian dances, he merely jumps around without order or design, but nothing could be more erroneous. Their dances were rigidly fixed in pattern and called for the precision and art that come with long training. Naturally, they were not all of equal skill. Ritualistic dancing called for acting, in which many were expert. We have seen dances in which a scout tracking an enemy is imitated. Without breaking the conventional dance steps, the food kettle is sighted as the foe; then the charge upon the unsuspecting victim, the blow, the scalping, the whoop of triumph, etc., are all as vividly portrayed as upon any civilized stage. No wonder these Indians appeared dignified; they knew how to act the part. And though, relatively speaking, nudists, they were scrupulously exact in dress, according to their mode. A single feather might be worn, but its droop was adjusted with exactness according to the best aesthetic standards. Not all appeared equally immaculate, for the lazy, the old and the infirm, as everywhere in the world, were more or less unkempt.

As may be anticipated, Indians loved formality, else how could they exercise their skill in posing? Everything important must be accompanied by the proper flourishes. Thus, a man may be chosen to offer a pipe to the Powers Above, just as in one of our churches a person might be called upon to collect the customary offering, but instead of proceeding directly to where the pipe lies, he may pass around the assembly in a counter-clockwise manner, pausing for a time at each of the four cardinal points. Once in front of the pipe, he does not reach for it at once but, after a pause, approaches and then retreats; only upon the fourth advance does he pick it up. He holds it in his hands, prays over it and then proceeds to the fire for the lighting, which again calls for a series of evolutions. Finally the pipe must be offered to each of the four cardinal points, to the earth and to the heavens, as the ritual may require. All these movements must be carried through with all the grace and skill he can command, for though the audience gives no sign, they appraise him critically. In due time he will know their verdict.

A veteran fur trader among the northwestern Algonkin gives a graphic, though unsympathetic, account of the Indians' way of trading:

Every movement of the Slaves [Blackfoot] is a parade. When coming in to trade, young men are sent on ahead to inform us of their approach and demand a bit of tobacco for each principal man or head of a family. Six inches of our twist tobacco is commonly sent, neatly done up in paper, to which is tied a small piece of vermilion, both being considered tokens of friendship. The young men are treated to a glass of liquor, four inches of tobacco, and a small paper of vermilion, with which they immediately return to their friends. The tobacco is delivered, and a smoking-match takes place, while the messengers relate the news of the place and give an account of their reception. This ceremony being concluded, they move on their journey in one long string. On the day of their arrival the men assemble at a convenient spot in sight of the fort, where they make a fire and smoke; during which time the women and children come to the fort and erect their tents near the stockades. Observing that business to be nearly completed, the men rise and move toward the fort in Indian file, the principal chief taking the lead, the others falling in according to rank or precedence, derived from the number of scalps taken in war. The master of the place is always expected to go out and shake hands with them at a short distance from the gates, and the further he goes to meet them, the greater the compliment.

The principal chief frequently advances, leading a horse by a line, which he delivers to the trader after shaking hands. This is considered as a present, and sometimes the horse has a small parcel of furs or skins on his back to enhance the value of the gift. The owner often wears a handsomely painted robe, which he takes off his own back to cover the trader. His dressed fox-skin cap may be added, and this he must be allowed to adjust upon the trader's head. His ceremonies being over, if there be any other individuals inclined to make a present, they rise up and cover the trader with their robes, and if they have a fox-skin worth presenting, it is adjusted on the top of the first one. Thus, when a large party arrives, the trader often finds himself covered with eight or ten heavy robes, and wears on his head as many fox-skins. All this he must endure, and sit with a serious countenance until the principal smoking ceremonies are over, when he is at liberty to order the robes and skins [put] into the storehouse. It is always expected, however, that these presents will be paid for, even to double their value. . . . The drinking-match continues all day and until about midnight, when they all fall asleep, and next morning finds them sober. . . . The next day, when they trade, we pay them for their previous presents. But if what we offer for the horse does not answer the owner's expectations, he demands the horse, and it must be delivered up to him. Altercation is useless, for he gets sullen, and walks away with his horse. But a present of skins and furs is never demanded to be returned; whatever is offered for it being accepted. If a flag has been brought in, it is returned to the owner on his departure, tied up with a few yards of gartering, to which is attached a foot of tobacco. They seldom remain longer than one day at our forts. The women are all sent off first, while the men remain to smoke with the trader, and put him out of all patience by begging. The women being all gone, each man gets four or five balls and powder, about four inches of tobacco, and a dram.[1]

Now the reader can understand why an Indian council, or the making of a peace treaty, might drag on for days.

[1] Henry and Thompson, *op. cit.*, Vol. 2, pp. 728–31.

In due time the pioneers came to understand this as the Indian's way of showing respect and veneration. Yet most white men found it a bore to sit through a long ceremony. They lacked the necessary background to realize that such a ceremony is like a drama which must be visualized by the audience to be enjoyed. The Algonkin used little in the way of stage effects; neither did the Pawnee or the Sioux. Masks were almost unknown to them; their audiences were expected to know that a bear, a monster or whatever else, was to be imagined and enjoyed. This made their ceremonies subjective rather than objective. Again, the important parts of a ritual were sung rather than declaimed, so that if proper stage settings had been provided the performance would have been an opera. In fact, some of the great operas we treasure are nothing more than the primitive pagan stories of our savage ancestors glossed over and presented in appropriate stage settings. To an Indian they would mean little, because he knew nothing of the beliefs and ideals behind them, and yet he might, for all that, understand the opera better than many white people who sit through it, because he sensed the spirit of it. The Iroquois Indians used some masks, the terrifying false faces one sees in museums. Again, the Pueblo Indians staged masked ceremonies on a considerable scale, but the climax was reached by the totem-pole makers, who used huge masks, the mouths of which opened, and who flapped their wings, etc. Most Indian dramas were staged at night around a fire which gave a kind of tableau effect, thus adding greatly to the illusions of the great masks. Sometimes the lighting was manipulated by throwing some quick-burning fuel on the fire at the right moment to be most effective. The Asiatics still depend upon the mask for stage effects, and some of our Indians continue the practice, but for the most part they depend entirely upon the imagination of the observers.

We suppose that every people produced great orators, even in the Stone Age. The Indians had orators, too, who, because of their poise and dignity of bearing, impressed the colonist and the pioneer, though they could not understand a word that was spoken. When they did come to understand, it was the beautiful figurative speech that held their attention. These Indians understood nature, the ways of the birds, animals, winds and the storm as no white men knew them, and from this source drew their metaphors and similes. Even when translated by a none-too-skillful interpreter, the discourse of a great Indian orator was still a masterpiece. The contact of Indians and whites offered many occasions for oratory. Conferences preceding the making of peace treaties were serious occasions, and the Indians' plight was pitiful enough to produce great bursts of eloquence. Nor was the Indian weak in sarcasm and humor, when he thought such were appropriate.

Yet, more than anything else, the skill with which the Indian concealed his curiosity made him a mystery. I recall visiting an Indian family before I knew much about their ways, but enough not to be embarrassed. I found them in a tepee, raised the door flap, entered and took a seat in the place reserved for guests. No one looked up or said a word. A child was present, but it too kept quiet. I took out my notebook and began to write. After an interval of ten minutes or more, my host took up a pipe, filled it and, after lighting it, passed it to me. After a few circuits of the pipe my host began a monologue, expressing his pleasure that I should have seen fit to honor him with a visit. When sure that he had finished, I made a similar talk, not as good as his because it was far less natural. By and by we heard a galloping horse approaching. There were expressions of surprise from the woman and the child. Even my host stopped to listen. The woman peeped out and said it was the medicine man, Horned Owl. My host laughed and began a "take-off" on his manner; we all laughed, but at a warning "sh-sh" from the woman, set our faces in silence and received the old man just as I had been received. Not all Indians follow this procedure—the customs of their tribe may not require it—but most of them know how to hold their tongues and can maintain a "poker face" under the most adverse conditions. It is hoped that the above incident will convey the idea that even we have mannerisms which deny what we feel, and that at heart the Indian is as human as we are; he may be angry, full of curiosity, moved to laughter, but to be mannerly will conceal it, and all the appreciation he gets from the white man is to be considered a mystery like the Sphinx.

Perhaps it never occurred to you that the white man puzzled the Indian. To his way of thinking, the white man was rude and lacking in good manners. He was selfish and refused to share food, clothing, etc., even when he had an abundance. He scoffed at the most sacred ideas of the Indian and blasphemed the Powers Above. True, the Indian respected his power to furnish metal tools and, above all, powder, ball and guns—they were the great magic beyond the power of the Indian to produce. Yet, in the forest, on the trail, the Indian was superior; he taught the white man woodcraft and how to raise corn, beans, squashes and tobacco; how to build and use birchbark canoes, snowshoes and the toboggan and to play lacrosse. The medicine men taught him their formulas for the use of plants and many other beliefs respecting luck and health, thereby enriching colonial folklore. Even today, when a patent-medicine man mounts a box at the street corner, claiming to have the original remedies discovered by the Indians, he not only gets an appreciative audience but finds ready purchasers.

It was a different world the Indian lived in. We spend our time on paved roads and cross streams on bridges. We have cleared away the forests, dried up the swamps and destroyed much of the interesting wildlife of the country. Much of the native flora has been swept away to make room for crops, meadows and golf courses. Surrounding ourselves by all sorts of mechanical aids, we have forgotten nature as the Indian knew it. He was at home in the forest; we are afraid. So much of our world is man-made that we think in terms of mechanics, a world which we manipulate and control. With the Indian it was different. He saw living creatures on every hand; he spied upon them until he knew their ways; he marveled at their skill in eluding him, their humanlike ways and his inability to communicate with them. He felt the forest as a living thing; the trees were to him almost as persons, and the winds were the breath of some great unseen supernatural. When the storm clouds rolled, the thunder pealed, the tornado crashed through the trees, he felt the presence of powers upon the highest level of creative and destructive force. As he walked abroad, he felt himself in the presence of living things conscious of his existence, who could speak to him, if they chose, and at any time change his fortunes for good or ill. To them he turned for guidance and wisdom.

Yet we are not to think of the Indian as in perpetual fear. We ride in automobiles without cringing, but know that the danger is great. Rather, the Indian proceeds reverently. He feels his inferiority, his utter helplessness in the face of nature. Nothing he does with his hands and feet seems to matter: famine comes upon him unheralded, the grim reaper of death lurks beside the trail, sickness grips his body. None of these things can he foresee or understand. It is significant to note that when an Indian prayed, he humbled himself, often crying out to the all-powerful unseen to have pity on him, to help him, etc. Of course, civilized man humbles himself before his God, but often his humility is formal, whereas the Indian's is sincere; he knows that he is helpless in the hands of nature and so asks for pity.

On the other hand, when speaking in terms of the great powers of nature, the Indian expresses confidence in the supernatural. When he seeks wisdom and light, he goes out alone and, deep in the presence of nature, opens his mind and heart. He may fast and even tear his flesh, crying out, "Oh, pity me! Oh, pity me!"—believing that the unseen powers are human and that they may be moved to grant him security and power. To the chosen few, powers were given, so he believed. The literature of anthropology records many such claims. Thus, after fasting and torturing himself for a long time, a man, usually an adolescent, may hear a voice, and in the darkness a shape may appear. It may be an animal, a bird or even a tree, but eventually becomes a human being, addressing the supplicant with an inquiry as to why he is crying there. If his request is granted, instructions are given the supplicant, songs are taught him and certain injunctions laid upon him. The grant of power may be immunity from disease or from injury in war, or power to heal the sick. Such powers are usually specific and not general.

This is the pattern for dispensations of power. A bond or pledge is made by which the individual in question is linked to a particular unseen power and upon whom he may call in case of need. The song and the formula are passwords, so to speak, which reach the ear of the unseen. If the vision were that of a bear which spoke as a man, then that animal becomes the symbol of power, and the fortunate recipient may carry about with him an image of a bear, a claw, bone or piece of skin. White people speak of this as a guardian spirit, or a protecting spirit, sometimes called a totem. In popular writing an Indian is supposed to sing a death song when the end seems to be near. The name is inappropriate, because it refers to the song taught him by his protector and is really an appeal to be saved. He is playing his last card.

A frequent question is: Does the Indian really believe he saw the apparition, heard what was said and the songs that he learned? One may as well ask any faith healer or fanatic if he is sincere, or any of our neighbors who believe in omens. We have always found the Indian sincere in his belief that nature is animated, alive with unseen powers; he is surprised that anyone in his right mind should doubt it. His wise men expounded the philosophy that every happening was preceded by a related event and that, if one knew just what to do, he could manipulate the order of events to a more beneficent end. An Indian with some education once told the writer that, so far as he knew, no living Indian knew how to perform real magic, but he was convinced that, in former years, there were members of his tribe who did know how to change the order of nature. This is always the human way, to put faith in the ancients, to the disparagement of our contemporaries.

Notwithstanding all we have said, the Indian possessed his share of common sense. When his experience showed that the same result always followed an event, he ceased to worry much about it. He even doubted that the unseen powers paid much attention to it either, except when they wanted to punish somebody. He refused to believe that man could prevent heavy objects from sinking in the water, or fire from burning, etc. But when the antecedent event was hidden, he believed he was helpless unless some superhuman being interposed. Yet he was human enough to seek a way to do it himself. He experimented with charms, incantations and the like, because the traditions of his people claimed such things had worked in the past. And before we condemn him, let us remember how often we, when baffled, fall back upon these same primitive methods.

That the medicine men were always honest, no one maintains. Among their professional secrets were tricks to fool their patients and the public. They knew they were deceptive tricks, but on the other hand, believed that they resulted in cures. One of the widespread methods of treating disease was to pretend to suck something out of the body of the sufferer. By sleight-of-hand the doctor could make it appear that a shell, a pebble, or even a small live animal was so drawn out of the sick man's body. This would be exhibited as the cause of the trouble, and it followed that now all would be well with the patient. The suggestive power of the procedure is obvious and should have worked wonders in many cases.

A favorite expression of the Indian orator was that he knew only the ways of his fathers and that they were good ways. So does the white man follow the ways of his ancestors, but is seldom conscious of it. He made a mystery of the Indian because he was less observing. On the other hand, the Indian knew a great deal about the white man, owing to his habit of watching things in nature and to his acquired patience. Not that the white man ceased to puzzle him—far from it—but he understood much better than we what it meant to have different traditions and different ancestry. He knew that neighboring tribes had dissimilar beliefs and somewhat different customs, all of which he respected as his own. He was thus far more tolerant than the white man. He was willing that the white man should believe as he liked; he would not scoff at Christian religious services, but resented the intolerant attitude of the white man. As an Indian once remarked, he could go to the white man's church and worship with him sincerely; next, he could go to a pagan ceremony and believe in it; there was good in both. However, the Indians' troubles with the white man were not of this order, but a struggle for the right to live and possess their own homes.

The chances are that the human mind is much the same everywhere. Yet people do not think alike about what they see and feel. It is because the Indian expresses strange and unexpected ideas that we think his mind incomprehensible. He sees his god in everything around him and is shocked at the white man's blindness to what is obvious and at his consequent brazen sacrilege. On the other hand, the white man stands aghast at the queer logic of the Indian mind in holding a person accountable for events entirely beyond his control.

As an example, we cite the diary of Rudolph Kurz, an artist who traveled among the Indians of the Missouri, 1846–52. When he arrived at Fort Berthold on the Missouri, cholera and other ills were afflicting the Indians. Catlin, the first great Indian painter, came up the river in 1834, and shortly thereafter many Indians died. Then came Bodmer, another artist, and again illness and death swept through the Indian villages. Now came Kurz and the cholera. He had no more than settled in the fort than his life was in danger. He was advised to keep all paper and colors out of sight and for a time was hidden in a room. Later he stole away to Fort Union, farther up the river, and here too the Indians recognized him as the evil genius. Also, he wore spectacles, which was further evidence of his evil powers. Even at Fort Union his life was in danger until the pestilence died out.

All this first surprises the white man, then excites his contempt. To him it is absurd. What he cannot comprehend is that the Indian, at times so sensible, should at other times be so stupid. However, the mystery about the Indian mind may lie in such misunderstandings.

Chapter XXII

LIFE ON A RESERVATION

TODAY most of the Indians live on reservations. The original meaning of this word was that certain lands from the public domain were set aside, or reserved, for the exclusive use of Indians. We use the word in the same way for seats in a circus, or a convention hall; some are reserved, the remaining seats are free, so that when the doors are opened the public rushes in, the best seats go to the early comer, the swift and the strong. By this time the reader knows how transient were all agreements with the various tribes, how in the beginning an ample tract of hunting land was reserved for the use of each tribe in perpetuity, but as soon as the white men had taken all the free lands, they wanted the Indian lands, actually invaded them, started another war or induced the government to revoke the agreement, as the case might be. The net result was the reduction of these reserved lands by a half or more. Two or three such reductions made a concentration camp out of a reservation. The argument of the whites was that the Indian would not farm, so he needed no land.

The best to be said for this policy of progressive seizure of Indian lands is that it brought the Indian to the concentration camp gradually. As we look backward now, the procedure seems like a deliberately planned fraud, but that may be too harsh a verdict, for we have no reason to doubt the sincerity of the white men who negotiated the treaties; doubtless it did not occur to them that the country would be settled so quickly. It was the fatalistic march of events that nullified treaties. Jefferson may have glimpsed the future when he bought the lands west of the Mississippi known as the Louisiana Purchase, but most of his critics could see no real use for this wilderness. None of them dreamed that it would soon be crossed by railroads and telegraph lines, because such were not then in existence. But even if the leaders of the time had thought of such a gradual conditioning of the Indians to living on reservations, it would have been much like the old folk saying that a frog can live in boiling water if the heat is applied slowly enough.

When the Indians were rounded up and placed on reservations, as we know them, the white people always seemed surprised that sickness and death threatened their extermination; but there should have been no surprise, for even when white people are put into such camps the death rate rises. For one of our western reservations, it was reported that the death rate during the first two years rose to more than ten per cent of the population. Had this rate continued, the tribe would have been extinct in about fifteen years. If you ask whether such loss of life was avoidable, the answer might be yes and no. Deaths could have been reduced somewhat by proper food and medical attendance, but even so the death rate would have been very high. Contracts were entered into with private individuals to furnish sufficient rations for these Indians, but much of the food delivered was condemned stuff bought for a song; this was rectified in time, but not until it had taken its toll in deaths, especially among children. Then came measles, diphtheria, etc., to carry away their quotas. Finally came tuberculosis. Many adults died from homesickness and despair. A number of young men, seeing no desirable future, committed suicide. That is the picture seen possibly at its worst. No matter what was done or how skillfully, the loss of life would have been tragic. War took its toll, though as a rule white losses were greater. Even in such decisive white victories as Fallen Timbers and Tippecanoe, the Indians suffered fewer losses than the whites. Their great losses came with concentration upon reservations; there is where they met with real defeat, economic, political, social and biological. Had the Four Horsemen been a part of their mythology, their prophets would have seen them galloping along on the clouds when the trail led to a reservation.

Most of the existing reservations are west of the Mississippi. There are still a few in the East, such as the Cherokee in North Carolina, Seminole in Florida and Choctaw in Mississippi. There is a concentration of Indians in Wisconsin and Minnesota—mostly Ojibway (Chippewa), but also the Menomini, Potawatomi and Oneida in the former, and the Ojibway (Chippewa) and Sioux in the latter—a total of almost thirty thousand Indians. Not all of these, however, live on reservations. There are many self-supporting communities of Indians in most of the states east of the Mississippi. In many of our large cities some Indians live as self-supporting citizens, sometimes by exploiting their past, as painters, actors, artists' models, singers or lecturers. So while it is our habit to think of Indians as belonging to the Great West, we should not forget the Indians in our midst. The total number of Indians living in states east of the Mississippi in 1960 was ninety-seven thousand—almost as many in states with no federal reservations (over forty-three thousand) as in states in which there are federal reservations. Once the director of a local Indian pageant addressed Wissler to know the cost of bringing Indians from the West to participate in it. He was able to render real service by informing the writer of the letter that within seventy-five miles of the place where the pageant was to be given was a sizable self-supporting community of Indians who would doubtless be glad to assist. Not everyone lives so near Indians now, but no doubt they are much nearer than one thinks.

West of the Mississippi are many reservations varying in size from that of the Navaho, of about twenty-five thousand square miles (larger than Connecticut, Rhode Island, Massachusetts and New Jersey combined), to tiny plots of a square mile or two in California and elsewhere. In all, there were approximately ninety agencies in 1938, the actual number of reservations being somewhat larger. The agencies have been reduced in number in the past two decades, and the Bureau of Indian Affairs listed forty-four in 1961, with an additional dozen field offices. If, however, all areas occupied by Indian groups and maintained for them are considered as reservations (whether so called or not), the total number of these areas in 1962 came to almost three hundred.

These areas varied so greatly in size that to describe one typical of the whole of the United States is impossible. Tribal groups ranged from two or three hundred persons to those of twenty thousand or more. Some of the Plains tribes included about two thousand persons. When first concentrated, they lived in tepees or other simple, easily movable structures; most of them had horses, an inordinate number of dogs, some cloth clothing, kettles, knives, axes and firearms. By modern standards of living, today they would be considered destitute.

When Indians were first placed upon such a reservation, the man in charge was often a political favorite from the East who knew nothing about Indians or the handling of concentration camps. True, there was a Department of Indian Affairs in Washington from which the agent, as he was called, received instructions, but that did not help much. The agent was provided with a clerk or two, a stableman, a blacksmith and a farmer. There was usually a doctor. If there was a government school on the reservation, this had a superintendent and a number of teachers. The agent was in charge of the reservation, represented the government and possessed and exercised the powers of a dictator. He could put Indians into prison, determine their sentences, break up families, take children from their parents, decide where an Indian should place his residence, and prescribe his daily routine. He could do all of these things and sometimes did, but usually was content with keeping the Indians on the reservation and preventing them from killing each other and white officials. He employed a few English-speaking Indians as interpreters and assistant clerks and for light labor. He was authorized to maintain a police force of

Indians and to appoint two or three Indians as judges, though he had a veto over all their acts.

As you may now surmise, an agency was quite a busy place. With government money the agent bought large stores of food, clothing, hardware, farm machinery, harness, hay, oats, etc., which he stored in warehouses for issue to the Indians as he thought best. He bought cattle by the trainload to feed his Indians and to try to set them up in the cattle business. He built roads on the reservation and sometimes fenced it, employing Indian labor when possible. If the agent was so inclined, he could collect large sums as rake-offs on these purchases. The records show that many agents did.

Yet our picture of the agency would be incomplete if we stopped here. Two or more white men would be given a license to trade or to open general stores at the agency. Here they would offer all kinds of goods, ranging from candy to farm wagons. Any Indian who found work with the agent took his pay check to one of the stores, where he was charged high prices for what he bought. Here also he could trade in some of his horses, if there were any left, or if he had cattle, turn in some of them, the agent permitting. We should add a postmaster, though one of the traders might hold that office. Finally, there would be a Catholic mission and two or more Protestant churches. From all this it appears that a number of white men with their families lived around the agency over which the agent ruled. As a rule the white personnel changed rapidly. All were in the prime of life, the only exceptions being an occasional doctor or a missionary, both poor in material things but rich in experience.

We turn now to the Indians, the victims of white culture expansion, the prisoners of war, as it were. The three or four old men, the real leaders, the effective personalities which came to the top in the course of time, usually accepted a treaty in good faith and urged their tribe to be patient and submissive; but when the agent seemed unjust and defaulted on the terms of the agreement, they were not slow to harangue him and to ask that the Great Father in Washington be notified of their plight. Younger and more radical Indians would join in the protest and often threaten violence. In a way, the first agents deserved more than they were paid, since they were surrounded by resentful, hungry Indians within whom were bottled up emotions seeking outlets in violence. True, a small garrison was kept nearby to which the agent could point as a threat, but when Indians acted, it was unexpectedly and quickly. The agent knew he must depend upon himself. Cowardly agents ran away at the first evidence of danger and resigned, but most of them proved to be men of courage who stood by for a time. An Indian told the writer of an agent who was the bravest man his people ever saw; he had refused to grant petitions made to him until a mob assembled. He went out to reason with them, was surrounded by angry men with painted faces, with knives in their hands. They flashed these weapons around his head, stuck their points against his breast, but he emphatically refused their requests on the ground that he was carrying out orders from Washington and intended to enforce them. Perhaps these Indians were merely trying to scare him, but in any event he was brave and resourceful. Again, an agency clerk, long in the service, told how an agent, sitting alone in his office, was surprised by a prominent Indian who presented a cocked rifle, stating in broken English that he intended to shoot. The agent calmly began a conversation, a clerk in the next room heard what was being said, stole out, secured a rifle, and coming up suddenly from behind, ordered the irate Indian to put down his gun. He did, was disarmed, severely reprimanded for his conduct but given his freedom. Other incidents could be cited, but none are necessary; the mere logic of the situation is sufficient to indicate the dangers to be met. Yet relatively few agents or clerks were killed, even when there was an outbreak.

The agents' instructions were to get the Indians to live in wooden or log houses as soon as possible; to force them to give up their original forms of shelter. The other point upon which they were to be insistent was that the Indian wear what was called "citizen dress." Also, every Indian man was to begin farming at once. We forgot to mention one matter which the Department of Indian Affairs thought most important of all: every Indian man must cut his hair short and give up braids. No Indian could be employed by the agent until he had his hair cut—that was the rule. The Indians so resented this rule that it was not enforced, except in case of regular employment. It sounds a little strange to us that such an unessential thing should be given first place, but we can sense the point. It would humble the Indian and give him pain, for he took pride in his hair; and to the white man long hair was the symbol of Indian ways, so he wanted to blot out the symbol and then believe he had civilized the Indian. In those days a civilized man was expected to wear a beard; we wonder why the pulling out of face hair by Indians was not ruled out too, and the Indian required to wear a beard even though it would have been a sorry, straggling affair.

At first the agent built log houses for a few Indians and furnished them with stoves, beds and chairs. Each year the agents' reports noted the number of new houses built, but it was a long time before even half the Indians had such houses. They were supposed to be sanitary and healthful, and it was believed that their use would lower the soaring death rate. Well, the death rate fell slowly, as was natural, but for years was still too high, and tuberculosis increased fast. By and by the doctors learned that tuberculosis patients did better in tents and even out-of-doors; so, finally, the Indians were ordered to move out of their log cabins and again take to tepees and tents. Is this humor or tragedy?

Upon many reservations today there are log cabins still, but many Indians live in good frame houses, well furnished. Many houses have electricity, and it is common in many places to see a washing machine or other electric appliance prominently placed, and a television aerial on the roof.

The Indian man was urged to plow up the land, sow

wheat and raise "civilized" crops. He preferred his own plant food, such as maize, beans and squashes, but government policy turned against the old ways. He was expected not only to raise food, as had been the custom of many tribes, but to lay up money in the bank. Considering that a large part of our own population at that time had nothing in the bank, the expectation was ill-founded. The hunting tribes who had never raised food resisted the idea of farming, perhaps more than the others, and, outside of Arizona and New Mexico, raising a crop was considered women's work. Here was the hurdle. The Indian man was told he must do woman's work; that was an insult. Even the agent would have been fighting mad if some dictator had tried to make him do woman's work. Yet farming is now done on reservations where there is good soil, and livestock is raised; most Indians are self-supporting, either by these means or, more often by wage work; they have sources of income as varied as anyone else in the United States. In recent years, the Bureau of Indian Affairs has established a program for industrial development on the reservations: companies are urged to build plants on the reservations, thereby giving not only construction work but a source of wages to the local tribe.

In the past the Indian's chief grievance was the government. It exercised absolute control, so the only outlets for his social and political emotions were appeals, protests and denunciations. Thus he became an expert in such vociferous activities and a chronic complainer. Under the regime to which the Indian was subjected from the first, the agent was a harsh and often unintentionally brutal ruler. Even today, some feel some resentment over white "domination." So it was to be expected that when a reservation Indian opened his mouth he would inveigh against the government. That was about all he could do. The agent usually listened respectfully to the protests of the leading men, made vague replies and promised to write to Washington, but since his own orders came from Washington there was little he could do about it. The fundamental difficulty lay in our Indian policy of placing

Indian farmers upon the same independent competitive basis as white farmers. The white man brought up under such conditions saw no reason why the Indian should not succeed, if he set his hand to it. The agent was ready to see to it that he received instruction and advice. The difficulty lay not here, but in the fact that the Indian had lived under a different kind of economic and social system, one in which there was no capital, no permanent ownership of land, but in which hospitality and free giving were the rule. Between these ideals and the rugged individualism of white society there could be no compromise. The only surprising thing about the situation is that the Indian survived at all. The original idea of the government was to allot farms to the Indians and, as soon as they came to know something about farming, turn them loose as citizens; but rugged individualistic white men soon had their farms and demanded that the government take care of the Indian as before. In time the idea of allotting lands was abandoned; subsequent policy was to encourage the Indians to farm upon lands held by the government and under the agent's control. This put a stop to the rampant taking of Indian lands, and encouraged tribal identity. This too underwent reversal, after World War II, and during the 1950s the government's Indian policy again included the reduction of Indian-held lands, and an attempt to remove the federal government from having much to do with Indians in any way. Many federal programs were transferred to other departments (such as the Indian health program to the Public Health Service).

Such shifting back and forth has long continued. Even in colonial times the attempts of Indians to live like the white man were beset by fears and failures. Late in the eighteenth century a group of Mohegan Indians in Connecticut was urged to become civilized and seemingly made an honest effort, as revealed in a petition to the state government:

To the Most Honorable Assembly of the State of Connecticut Conv'd at Hartford May 14, 1789.

Your Good old Steady Friends and Brethern the Mohegan Tribe of Indians Sendeth Greeting:

We beg Leave to lay our Concerns and Burdens at Your Excellencies Feet. The Times are Exceedingly Alter'd, Yea the Times have turn'd everything Upside down, or rather we have Chang'd the good Times, Chiefly by the help of the White People, For in Times past our Fore-Fathers lived in Peace, Love and great harmony, and had everything in Great planty. When they Wanted meat they would just run into the Bush a little ways with their Weapons and would Soon bring home good venison, Racoon, Bear and Fowl. If they Choose to have Fish, they Wo'd only go to the River or along the Sea Shore and they wou'd presently fill their Cannoous With Veriety of Fish, Both Scaled and shell Fish, and they had abundance of Nuts, Wild Fruit, Ground Nuts and Ground Beans, and they planted but little corn and Beans and they kept no Cattle or Horses for they needed none—And they had no Contention about their lands, it lay in Common to them all, and they had but one large dish and they Cou'd all eat together in Peace and Love—But alas, it is not so now, all our Fishing, Hunting and Fowling is entirely gone, And we have now begun to Work on our Land, keep Cattle, Horses and Hogs And we Build Houses and fence in Lots, And now we plainly See that one Dish and one Fire will not do any longer for us—Some few there are Stronger than others and they will keep off the poor, weake, the halt and the Blind, And Will take the Dish to themselves. Yea, they will rather Call White People and Molattoes to eat With them out of our Dish, and poor Widows and Orphans Must be pushed one side and there they Must Set a Craying, Starving and die.

And so We are now Come to our Good Brethern of the Assembly With Hearts full of Sorrow and Grief for Immediate help—And therefore our most humble and Earnest Request and Petition is That our Dish of Suckuttush may be equally divided amongst us, that every one may have his own little dish by himself, that he may eat Quietly and do With his Dish as he pleases; and let every one have his own Fire.

Your Excellencies Compliance and Assistance at This Time will make our poor hearts very Glad and thankful.

This is the most humble Request and Petition of Your True Friend & Brethern Mohegan Indians,

  By the Hands of our Brothers

    Harry x Quaduaquid, his mark
    Robert Ashpo.[1]

Could anything be more illuminating! The rugged individualism of that day thwarted the Indian as it did much later.

In order that the Indian may receive recognition for his efforts to live by farming, the human side of the picture should be presented. Notwithstanding that many were fearful of offending nature by tearing up the ground with plows, some of them set their hands to this new and strange tool. Upon several reservations the chiefs began with great enthusiasm for the new way of life, putting in crops under the agent's guidance; but all was not easy going, for drought took its toll, and many good crops were destroyed by grasshoppers. One such failure not only discouraged the inexperienced Indian but weakened his faith in his right to try the white man's way. At the outset he had had some misgivings, but now it seemed to him that nature was against him. The unseen powers were no longer friendly. To the white farmer, however, this was merely a matter of chance; his traditions said that occasionally crops would fail, but what of it? He had been taught to believe that success was sure if he had the will to go ahead; that the failure of the crop was a matter of chance. Failure aroused his fighting spirit to make another and still another effort. Nothing like this sustained the Indian; there was no accumulated experience of his fathers to bear upon the case; he had little reason to believe there would be success next time or any other time.

[1] Original in the Connecticut State Library.

In a way he was right; to pass directly from hunting to real farming was an impossible task, and white men were foolish to think that it was easy or merely a matter of will. In their case it was a matter of will, but they were totally ignorant of the existence of a background of tradition and training which made it possible for their own wills to operate. Put yourself in the Indian's place, if you can. An oppressive government of foreigners had conquered him, but on several occasions had recognized his ownership of the land and promised him full return for it; so why should the foreigner not make good by furnishing him food and clothing when he needed such things? According to the bargain, he had traded his lands for his keep, so why venture upon such a dubious enterprise as farming?

There have been many changes in the last generation specifically, both in patterns and conceptions of Indian life, most of which have been the growing pains from which the Indian will hopefully be able to take his place beside the non-Indian Americans in equality and harmony. Some of the misconceptions include the belief that all Indians are alike; we have seen that they are not—there is no Indian typical of all. In physical appearance they are as varied as any other peoples: some are tall, some are short, others are light, or dark in skin color, though their hair is almost uniformly glossy black and straight, and baldness is all but unknown. Body and facial hair is scant, and the latter is customarily pulled out. Face paint was sometimes used; red was the prevailing color. For those Indians now living in cities and towns, the use of cosmetics by women is by personal choice, as for any American.

Not all Indians lived in tepees, though this dwelling was used throughout Canada east of the Rocky Mountains and in the United States between the Mississippi River and the Rocky Mountains. Tepees were usually erected on a base of three or four poles, each set in a prescribed order. Not all Indians wore feather headdresses. These, however, because of their spectacular appearance, have often been attributed to peoples who never saw them until they became associated with the "typical Indian."

Neither did all Indians take scalps. The distribution of scalping is a controversial point. There is reason to believe that scalping was practiced by a number of tribes before 1492. Frequently the whole head was taken. In the early Indian wars of the Atlantic coast it was practiced by both Indians and whites and thus followed the advancing frontier westward. However, there is strong evidence that the Plains Indians scalped long before they came into contact with the whites.

To do a fine job of scalping, the scalper would rush among the enemy, strike down a victim, make a circular cut in the skin around the crown of the head, raise the edge of the skin at one side, seize this with the teeth, tear it loose, wave the trophy, holding it by the hair, and run back quickly. Unless this could be done within a fraction of a minute, the scalper was liable to be killed. Upon reaching home, the scalp was given to a woman who stretched it in a hoop to dry and then carried it on a pole in the victory dance.

Geometric designs on pots, baskets and cloth, often believed to have symbolic meaning, do not. Most of the true symbolism in Indian art was realistic and not geometric. The textiles and pottery designs (geometric) were the work of women; rarely did they try to draw pictures. Many of the geometric designs on baskets and beadwork had names so that they could be talked about, as tepeepattern, tree, leaf, mountain, etc., but when these designs were used they did not stand for religious ideas, prayers or wishes for good luck. However, they were sometimes used in that way. The only way to know about this is to have information from the woman who made them. So, in general, most of the time the designs seen on baskets, beadwork, etc., are strictly ornamental, but occasionally they are used symbolically. One tribe conspicuous for such symbolic use of designs is the Arapaho.

Shell wampum, though widely used as money in trade between Indians and whites along the Atlantic and Pacific coasts, was rarely used elsewhere. Most of the Indian trade was by barter.

People have sometimes wondered if the chief always ruled the tribe. Among the Plains tribes, no Indian seems to have possessed arbitrary absolute power. A council of elders (usually, but by no means always, men) often recognized one of its number as the leader, and frequently looked to him to see that its rulings were enforced. Often, however, each small band recognized its own leader, a situation which led to difficulties in dealings with the government: a chief recognized by the government was not always recognized by the tribe as such. Small wonder that treaties were broken on both sides.

Such a background as this has contributed to the often strained relations which have prevailed for the last century and more. Government policy has swung like a pendulum from support to non-support as we have seen. World War II may have brought about a change in this respect as it did in many others. Numerous Indians took part and served their country well—in communications they were often essential; two Indians could speak their native tongue without fearing enemy understanding.

After the war, however, many returning veterans found themselves in a paradoxical situation: they no longer occupied the same position they once held in their own villages; neither were they part of the white American community around them. On the one hand they were heroes, particularly in areas where they were so far in the minority as to constitute no "Indian problem." On the other hand, both in their own communities and especially elsewhere, they were still Indians, looked on as inferior by the prejudiced. In spite of the citizenship act passed in 1924, it was not until 1948 that Indians were fully franchised by state law, and it will be the middle of the 1960s before the federal civil liberties statute is passed to insure the enforcement of this franchise.

Similarly, though the American Indian could fight for his country, he was prohibited from purchasing liquor. It was available on the black market. Though the Indian was reputed not to be able to hold his liquor, it is likely that conditions of surreptitious purchase and quick consumption (to hide the evidence) contributed to the reputation for drunkenness. It was not until 1953 that this situation changed, and the Indian was able to purchase liquor legally.

Also after World War II, in 1946, the Indian Claims Commission was set up to consider claims against the United States. This Commission has considered over 850 claims since its establishment and has sometimes been viewed as the "conscience" of the government for past mistakes—the usurping of Indian lands without adequate compensation during the height of the westward expansion, for example. In terms of settling claims, this Commission has a long and arduous task; many of the claims brought before the Commission many years ago are still unsettled, although in 1964 alone, a total of 38.5 million dollars was awarded to eight tribes. A side effect of the Claims Commission may be beneficial. In the process of establishing "fact," historians, anthropologists and tribal elders alike are required to contribute their knowledge of the people in question, and the recorded testimony may produce the most accurate—if many-sided—history of early America yet known.

Educating the American Indian has long been considered a problem for the federal and state governments and others, and many different programs have been tried. Many churches have established mission schools, many of which still operate. Other educational facilities which have been established include government boarding schools, an early experiment which has not been wholly successful, as the children were taken away from family and tribal life. Day schools for Indians have also been established, and finally, where possible, the Indian children attend public schools. Language particularly has been a problem here, for English is the native tongue for only a few of the children.

There is another aspect of "being Indian" which is now under consideration. Many groups wish to preserve their

Indian identity, while others do not. The question of "Indian: to be or not to be" is one of great controversy not only for government policy, and among veterans, but among the groups themselves. This is hardly a new question, and during the latter part of the last century many Indian villages were split by such problems; the Hopi village of Oraibi was sufficiently divided that in 1906 one group left and founded the village of Hotevilla. Factional strife has also disrupted other Indian pueblos, and other Indian groups. The Fox, for instance, have split into two groups, one living on lands which they have purchased in Iowa, the other on the Sauk and Fox reservation in Oklahoma. Differences within the same tribal group have not always resulted in a split for political reasons; but in many groups the economic variation is great. The Navaho tribe is among the richest of the United States tribes, but many of the Navaho people are among the poorest; by the same token, the Ojibway (Chippewa) at Lac du Flambeau, who for a long time have been supplying man power for an electronics firm in Wisconsin, are among the more wealthy individuals, while their neighbors are still gathering wild rice. In northern cities, where there are few Indians, one of Indian blood is sometimes looked upon as a hero; in other areas, where they are numerous, however, he may be looked down upon as the scum of the earth. All in all, the pattern of Indian life in the United States has become much more complex and variegated than was the case a generation and more ago.

Chapter XXIII

DID THE INDIAN LIVE IN VAIN?

WHEN we look back over the spectacle of Indian annihilation, the ruthless advance of the frontier crushing out the lives of Indians on every hand, though sacrificing a lot of white blood to achieve this end, we moved to ask: Did the Indian live in vain? Was all that he did, struggled for, fought for, for ten thousand years to be obliterated in three centuries? Was it misplaced charity on the part of the victors to put their helpless victims on reservations, to be wasted by disease, hunger and poverty, and later do everything possible to keep them alive merely to live as minorities? These and many other questions may rise to disturb our peace of mind, but there are no satisfactory answers; there are, however, many misconceptions. We can look at the record to see what the Indian has achieved, and what he has contributed to the American way of life.

Our task will be made easier if we first call to mind the historic outline of the achievements of the Old World. The economic structure of Old World civilization rests upon wheat, cattle, horse, wheel, plow, linen, writing and printing, iron and alcohol, among others.

Turning to the New World, we find a somewhat similar list of fundamentals, such as maize, potato, dog, tumpline (pack strap), cotton, tobacco and manioc.

There is a kind of parallelism here, and there are contrasts, too. The Indian civilizations of Mexico and Peru were based upon agriculture, with maize as the most important food, whereas wheat was the leading cereal in the Old World. Cotton was the leading textile fiber; in Europe it was linen. The only Indians devising systems of writing comparable to those of the Old World were the Maya of Yucatan and certain tribes in the Valley of Mexico, notably the Aztec. The Peruvians, with all their genius in other directions, failed to devise a scheme of writing. Printing was unknown in the New World.

Perhaps the most astonishing thing is the absence of the wheel in New World culture. The nearest approach to it was the spindle for spinning and the use of rolling hoops in games. Even New World potters never got the idea of a potter's wheel. When Indian craftsmen wanted to bore a hole, they rolled the drill shaft back and forth between the palms of their hands. The Eskimo and a few Indians of Canada used a bow to turn such a shaft, but even this reciprocated back and forth, like the hand drill. The use of a rotating wheel or disk in transportation was not dreamed of, but wheeled toys were known in the Valley of Mexico. Note also that there were no animals in the New World suitable for draft until horses were introduced; dogs were sometimes used, but because of their size their usefulness was limited, and one can only imagine the attempt to harness a wild buffalo bull.

Iron tools were unknown in the New World, though iron ores were at hand. Copper was used extensively in Peru and Mexico and worked in the United States by hammering. Gold, silver, tin, platinum and lead were used. All the tribes between the United States and Chile were expert in working gold and silver. In Peru, bronze was made by melting copper and tin in the same furnace. A visit to a well-stocked museum will show that the metal workers of these tribes had little to learn from Europeans. These pre-Columbian metallurgists knew how to draw wire; the finest specimen known has a diameter of about 0.008 of an inch. In the matter of welding they achieved standards which still excite the admiration of our own metal workers. Soldering was known. The edges on copper tools were hardened by the cold-hammering process and as a result were harder than soft iron. When this treatment was applied to bronze, it became much harder than iron.

When it was found that the pre-Columbian Indians in South America worked platinum, our metallurgists were puzzled. For example, in South America the prehistoric metal workers understood welding and soldering as in the Old World, but they combined platinum with gold in an original way. The fine grains of platinum were mixed with gold and heated. No furnace known to them could melt platinum, but the gold would melt and sinter with the platinum. By repeated heating and hammering they produced an alloy of gold and platinum which could be used for plating. Again, these New World metallurgists had a way of gilding copper, using a gold-copper alloy with a melting point so low that it could be run over the surface of heated copper.

All of which means that in the Andes country and in Central America the pre-Columbian metal workers had made discoveries not known to Europeans of the same period and had achieved most of those made by their contemporaries in the Old World.

We sometimes hear it said that the Indian lacked the genius to be an inventor, and the claim put forward that what do seem to be inventions were in some mysterious manner brought here, ready-made, from the Old World. The only weakness in this argument is that a list of useful inventions can be compiled, none of which were known to the Old World. (See table below.)

SOME IMPORTANT INVENTIONS NOT KNOWN IN THE OLD WORLD BEFORE 1492

Balsam	Maya numeral system
Chocolate	Platinum alloy
Cigar, Cigarette	Potato
Coca narcotic	Pronged cigar holder
Cochineal	Quipu
Curare	Rubber (hollow ball, etc.)
Hammock	Snow goggles
Head shrinking	Tobacco pipe
Ipecac	Toboggan
Kelp (iodine) for goiter	Tomato
Maize, and other plants	Whistling jar
Manioc grater and press	

KNOWN IN BOTH THE OLD WORLD
AND THE NEW BEFORE 1492

Barbed fishhook	Bronze
Bark cloth	Casting metals
Beam scale	Cire-perdue casting
Bee domesticated	Drum signaling
Beeswax	Fermentation of intoxicants
Blowgun	Steelyard scale
Boat sledge	Water pump
Boiled water for wounds	Writing

However, another list can be compiled of inventions known to both Indians and the Old World. The circumstances favor their independent invention by the Indian, but there will always be a lot of argument as to whether the same inventions among Indians were made independently of all ideas that were carried here. People who are anxious to prove that the Indian invented nothing make much to-do of possible shipwrecks on the coast, the idea being that one or two white men would revolutionize the life of the Indians. In such arguments people usually persist in believing what they want to believe, but we again call attention to the respectable list of inventions not known in the Old World. With respect to these, the claim of the Indian is incontestable. There are enough items in that list to demonstrate his originality.

Since we are concerned chiefly with the Indian in the United States, it will be useful to add a fuller list of achievements of the tribes treated in Part II of this volume.

Foods. Maize, popcorn, beans, squash, artichoke, sunflower seed, maple sugar, acorn meal, lye-hominy, persimmon bread, nut oil, turkey, deer, bison and pemmican.

Crafts. Buckskin, basketry, feather cloak, rabbitskin weaving, coil pottery, spinning with spindles, weaving with bar looms, chipping stone, polishing stone, porcupine quillwork, pearl beads and geometric design.

Travel. Dog travois, tumpline, birchbark canoe and dugouts, laced snowshoe, toboggan.

Housing. Wigwam, long house, earthlodge, tepee, brush shelter, plank house, lean-to and pueblo structures.

Dress. Roached head, hair braids, deer-hair headdress, feather headdress, earth paints, beardless faces, moccasins.

Narcotics. Tobacco, peyote, jimson weed, black drink and mescal.

Customs. Scalping, running the gauntlet, calumet, Indian file, sharing food, totems, guardian spirits, seeking visions, counting coups and exchanging presents.

Mythical characters. Thunderbird, horned serpent, water monster, the transformer, culture hero, the four winds, the corn maiden and the earth mother.

Borrowed Indian Words in American Speech. Hominy, moccasin, papoose, powwow, sachem, sagamore, squaw, succotash, Tammany, tepee, toboggan, tomahawk, totem, tuckahoe, tumpline, wampum and wigwam.

This list of borrowed Indian words is not complete, because our speech has been enriched by many geographical terms. Almost half of the states in our country have Indian names, and the number of cities and towns with such names is greater. Among well-known cities are: Cheyenne, Chicago, Hackensack, Kalamazoo, Kansas City, Keokuk, Minneapolis, Mobile, Muncie, Muskegon, Niagara, Omaha, Osceola, Oshkosh, Pensacola, Pontiac, Schenectady, Seattle, Tacoma, Tallahassee, Topeka and Wichita. There are many lakes and rivers bearing Indian names exclusive of English names that are translations of Indian names. Untranslated Indian names are an asset because they are musical and highly original. They also serve as memorials to the peoples, some of whom have all but passed into oblivion.

So the descendants of Indians have much to be proud of, and for those who must count all values in dollars or not at all, we suggest looking at economic tables for the yearly value of all the tobacco, maize, potatoes, tomatoes, peanuts and the other forty or more useful plants domesticated by the Indians and promptly taken over by the world. The sum of these values should impress the money-minded that the Indian contributed greatly to the well-being of the world.

BIBLIOGRAPHY

BIBLIOGRAPHY

Every well-stocked library is able to furnish a long reference list for the reader desirous of dipping deeply into this subject. Most of the eastern states have separate volumes devoted to their state histories in which a great deal of space is given to Indians. Other important sources are the serial publications of historical societies, especially those of Kansas, Minnesota, South Dakota and Wisconsin.

Another important class of publications issued in series are those of museums, research bureaus and universities: for example, the Bureau of American Ethnology, the Smithsonian Institution, in Washington; the American Museum of Natural History and the Museum of the American Indian, both in New York City; the Field Museum of Natural History, Chicago; the Peabody Museum of Harvard University; anthropological publications of the University of California, Columbia University, Yale University, Chicago University, the University of New Mexico and the University of Oklahoma, which has a particularly interesting series on the American Indian.

There are many books on the subject, including biographies of distinguished Indians, histories of separate tribes and narratives of adventure among Indians. The following books are suggestions for the reader who wishes to pursue the subject further. Many are books used in revisions; some, though out of date, are valuable for information not available elsewhere. They are arranged by the chapter to which they apply.

GENERAL WORKS

DRIVER, HAROLD E.
   1961   *Indians of North America.* Chicago: University of Chicago Press.
FENTON, WILLIAM N.
   1957   *American Indian and White Relations to 1830,* with bibliography compiled by L. H. Butterfield, Wilcomb E. Washburn and William N. Fenton. Chapel Hill: University of North Carolina Press.

JOSEPHY, ALVIN M., JR., and WILLIAM BRANDON
   1961   *The American Heritage Book of Indians.* New York:
          American Heritage Publishing Company.
LaFARGE, OLIVER
   1956   *A Pictorial History of the American Indian.* New York:
          Crown Publishers, Inc.
MURDOCK, GEORGE PETER
   1960   *Ethnographic Bibliography of North America.* 3rd ed.
          New Haven: Human Relations Area Files.
SWANTON, JOHN R.
   1952   *The Indian Tribes of North America.* Bureau of Ameri-
          can Ethnology, Bulletin 145. Washington: Smithsonian
          Institution.
UNDERHILL, RUTH MURRAY
   1953   *Red Man's America.* Chicago: University of Chicago
          Press.

ARCHAEOLOGY

MACGOWAN, KENNETH, and JOSEPH A. HESTER, JR.
   1962   *Early Man in the New World.* Revised ed. Garden
          City, New York: Anchor Natural History Library.
MARTIN, PAUL S., GEORGE I. QUIMBY, and DONALD COLLIER
   1947   *Indians Before Columbus.* Chicago: University of Chi-
          cago Press.
WORMINGTON, H. M.
   1957   *Ancient Man in North America.* 4th ed. Denver: Den-
          ver Museum of Natural History, Popular Series, No. 4.
   1961   *Prehistoric Indians of the Southwest.* 5th printing.
          Denver: Denver Museum of Natural History, Popular
          Series, No. 7.

PART I. THE INDIAN IN PREHISTORIC AMERICA

Chapter I: The Aboriginal Pioneer

ARNOLD, J. R., and W. F. LIBBY
   1950 *Radiocarbon Dates.* Chicago: University of Chicago
         Institute for Nuclear Studies.
BIRD, JUNIUS
   1938 "Antiquity and Migrations of the Early Inhabitants
         of Patagonia," *The Geographical Review,* 28:250–75.
BOYD, WILLIAM C.
   1951 "The Blood Groups and Types," *The Physical An-
         thropology of the American Indian,* William S. Laugh-
         lin, ed., pp. 127–37. Ann Arbor, Michigan: Viking
         Fund.
HAAG, WILLIAM G.
   1962 "The Bering Strait Land Bridge," *Scientific American,*
         206 (1):112–23.
KURTZ, EDWIN B., JR., and ROGER Y. ANDERSON
   1955 "Pollen Analysis," *Geochronology; with Special Ref-
         erence to Southwestern United States,* Terah L.
         Smiley, ed., pp. 113–25. Tucson: University of Arizona
         Press. Physical Science Bulletin No. 2.
LIBBY, WILLARD F.
   1955 *Radiocarbon Dating,* 2nd ed. Chicago: University of
         Chicago Press.
SELLARDS, E. H.
   1952 *Early Man in America.* Austin: University of Texas
         Press.
SWADESH, MORRIS
   1962 "Linguistic Relations Across Bering Strait," *American
         Anthropologist,* 64 (6):1262–91.

Chapter II: Rise of the Stone Boilers

KROEBER, THEODORA
   1961 *Ishi.* Berkeley: University of California Press.

Chapter III: The Farmers and the Potters

CUSHING, F. H.
1886   "A Study of Pueblo Pottery as Illustrative of Zuni Culture Growth," 4th Annual Report of the Bureau of American Ethnology, pp. 473–521. Washington.

HARRINGTON, M. R.
1960   *The Ozark Bluff Dwellers*. Indian Notes and Monographs, Vol. 12. New York: Museum of the American Indian, Heye Foundation.

MACNEISH, R. S.
1960   "Agricultural Origins in Middle America and Their Diffusion into North America," *Katunob* 1 (1):24–28.

THOMPSON, STITH
1929   *Tales of the North American Indians*. Cambridge: Harvard University Press.

WEBB, WILLIAM S., and W. D. FUNKHOUSER
1936   *Rock Shelters in Menifee County, Kentucky*. University of Kentucky Reports in Archaeology and Anthropology, Vol. III, No. 4. Lexington: Department of Anthropology and Archaeology, University of Kentucky.

Chapter IV: The Builders

GRIFFIN, JAMES B.
1952   *Archaeology of Eastern United States*. Chicago: University of Chicago Press.

SHETRONE, HENRY CLYDE
1936   *The Mound Builders*. New York: D. Appleton-Century.

Chapter V: The Coming of the Grand Pipe

BROOKS, JEROME E.
1937   *Tobacco: Its History Illustrated by the Books, Manuscripts, and Engravings in the Library of George Arents, Jr*. New York: The Rosenbach Company.
1952   *The Mighty Leaf*. Boston: Little, Brown & Co.

HENRY, ALEXANDER, and DAVID THOMPSON
1897 *New Light on the Early History of the Greater North-west*. 3 vols. Elliott Coues, ed. New York: Francis P. Harper.

LAUFER, BERTHOLD
1924 *The Introduction of Tobacco into Europe*, Chicago: Field Museum of Natural History, Leaflet No. 19.

ROBERT, JOSEPH CLARKE
1952 *The Story of Tobacco in America*. New York: Alfred A. Knopf.

WALKER, J. R.
1917 "The Sun Dance and Other Ceremonies of the Oglala Division of the Teton Dakota," Anthropological Papers of the American Museum of Natural History, Vol. 16, Pt. 2. New York.

Chapter VII: The Grand Old Algonkin Family

BRINTON, DANIEL G.
  1885 *The Lenâpé and Their Legends.* Philadelphia: D. G.
       Brinton.
HOFFMAN, W. J.
  1891 "The Midewiwin or 'Grand Medicine Society' of the
       Ojibwa," 7th Annual Report of the Bureau of Ameri-
       can Ethnology, pp. 143–300. Washington: Smith-
       sonian Institution.
JOSEPHY, ALVIN M., JR.
  1961 *The Patriot Chiefs.* New York: The Viking Press.
LEACH, DOUGLAS EDWARD
  1958 *Flintlock and Tomahawk.* New York: Macmillan.
RADIN, PAUL
  1914 "Religion of the North American Indians," *Journal of
       American Folklore,* 27:335–73.
SYLVESTER, HERBERT MILTON
  1910 *Indian Wars of New England.* 3 vols. Boston: W. B.
       Clarke Company.
UNDERHILL, RUTH M.
  1953 *Red Man's America. Op. cit.*
VOEGELIN, C. F., *et al*
  1954 *Walam Olum, or Red Score; The Migration Legend
       of the Lenni Lenape or Delaware Indians.* Indian-
       apolis: Indiana Historical Society.
WALLACE, ANTHONY F. C.
  1949 *King of the Delawares: Teedyuscung.* Philadelphia:
       University of Pennsylvania Press.

Chapter VIII: The Old Northwest

BLACK HAWK
  1955 *Black Hawk, an Autobiography,* Donald Jackson, ed.
       Urbana, Illinois: University of Illinois Press.

HAGAN, WILLIAM T.
   1958   *The Sac and Fox Indians.* Norman: University of Oklahoma Press.
PARKMAN, FRANCIS
   1868   *History of the Conspiracy of Pontiac.* 4th revised ed. Boston: Little, Brown & Co.
PECKHAM, HOWARD H.
   1947   *Pontiac and the Indian Uprising.* Princeton: Princeton University Press.
TUCKER, GLENN
   1956   *Tecumseh: Vision of Glory.* Indianapolis: Bobbs-Merrill.
UNDERHILL, RUTH M.
   1953   *Red Man's America. Op. cit.*

Chapter IX: The Western Buffalo Hunters

GRINNELL, GEORGE BIRD
   1915   *The Fighting Cheyennes.* New York: Scribner.
   1923   *The Cheyenne Indians: Their History and Way of Life.* 2 vols. New Haven: Yale University Press.
HOEBEL, E. ADAMSON
   1960   *The Cheyennes: Indians of the Great Plains.* (Case studies in cultural anthropology.) George and Louise Spindler, eds. New York: Holt, Rinehart & Winston, Inc.
JENNESS, DIAMOND
   1932   *The Indians of Canada.* Bulletin 65, Canada Department of Mines. Ottawa: National Museum of Canada.
LOWIE, ROBERT H.
   1963   *Indians of the Plains.* American Museum Science Book. Garden City, New York: Natural History Press.
MAXIMILIAN, PRINCE OF WIED
   1843   *Travels in the Interior of North America.* English Edition.
NEWCOMB, WILLIAM W., JR.
   1956   *The Culture and Acculturation of the Delaware Indians.* Anthropological Papers, No. 10. Ann Arbor: University of Michigan, Museum of Anthropology.

STEWARD, JULIAN
  1934 *The Blackfoot.* Berkeley, California: U. S. Depart-
        ment of the Interior, National Park Service. Field
        Division of Education.

Chapter X: The Northern and Western Algonkin

BARNETT, HOMER G.
  1955 *The Coast Salish of British Columbia.* Eugene, Ore-
        gon: University of Oregon Press.
BOAS, FRANZ
  1909 "The Kwakiutl of Vancouver Island." New York:
        American Museum of Natural History, Memoirs,
        8:307–515.
COOK, J.
  1785 *A Voyage to the Pacific Ocean,* II:269–340. London.
DRUCKER, PHILIP
  1963 *Indians of the Northwest Coast.* American Museum
        Science Book. Garden City, New York: Natural His-
        tory Press.
GOLDSCHMIDT, WALTER
  1960 "The Ethical Prescriptions of Yurok Society," *Explor-
        ing the Ways of Mankind,* pp. 544–53. New York:
        Holt, Rinehart & Winston, Inc.
HOFFMAN, W. J.
  1891 "The Midewiwin or 'Grand Medicine Society' of the
        Ojibwa." *Op. cit.*
JENNESS, DIAMOND
  1932 *The Indians of Canada. Op. cit.*
JOSEPHY, ALVIN M., JR.
  1961 *The Patriot Chiefs. Op. cit.*
KROEBER, A. L.
  1925 *Handbook of the Indians of California.* Bureau of
        American Ethnology, Bulletin 78. Washington: Smith-
        sonian Institution.
RADIN, PAUL
  1914 "Religion of the North American Indians." *Op. cit.*
SMITH, MARIAN W.
  1949 *Indians of the Urban Northwest.* New York: Columbia
        University Press.
TEIT, JAMES A.
  1930 *The Salishan Tribes of the Western Plateaus,* Franz

Boas, ed. 45th Annual Report of the Bureau of American Ethnology. Washington: Smithsonian Institution.

Chapter XI: The Iroquois Family

COLDEN, CADWALLADER
1958   *The History of the Five Nations of Canada.* Ithaca, New York: Cornell University Press.
FENTON, WILLIAM N.
1940   "Problems Arising from the Historic Northeastern Position of the Iroquois," *Essays in Historical Anthropology of North America,* pp. 159–251. Washington: Smithsonian Miscellaneous Collections, Vol. 100.
GILBERT, WILLIAM HARLEN, JR.
1943   *The Eastern Cherokees.* Bureau of American Ethnology, Bulletin 133. Washington: Smithsonian Institution.
1957   "The Cherokees of North Carolina: Living Memorials of the Past," Annual Report of the Smithsonian Institution, pp. 529–55. Washington.
GOREMAN, GRANT
1934   *The Five Civilized Tribes.* Norman: University of Oklahoma Press.
1938   *Sequoyah.* Norman: University of Oklahoma Press.
GULICK, JOHN
1960   *Cherokees at the Crossroads.* Chapel Hill: Institute for Research in Social Science, University of North Carolina.
HEWITT, J. N. B.
1918   *A Constitutional League of Peace in the Stone Age of America.* Annual Report of the Smithsonian Institution, pp. 527–45. Washington.
HUBBARD, J. NILES
1886   *An Account of Sa-Go-Ye-Wat-Ha, or Red Jacket and His People.* Albany.
HUNT, GEORGE T.
1960   *The Wars of the Iroquois.* Madison: University of Wisconsin Press.
JEFFERSON, THOMAS
1955   *Notes on the State of Virginia,* William Peden, ed. Williamsburg, Virginia: Institute of Early American

History and Culture, by the University of North Carolina Press.

JOSEPHY, ALVIN M., JR.
  1961 *The Patriot Chiefs. Op. cit.*

MOONEY, JAMES
  1900 "Myths of the Cherokee," 19th Annual Report of the Bureau of American Ethnology, pp. 3–548. Washington: Smithsonian Institution.

MORGAN, LEWIS HENRY
  1954 *League of the Ho-De-No-Sau-Nee, or Iroquois.* 2 vols. New Haven: Human Relations Area Files. (1901, New York: Dodd Mead & Co.)

STONE, WILLIAM L.
  1841 *The Life and Times of Red-Jacket, or Sa-Go-Ye-Wat-Ha.* New York and London: Wiley and Putnam.
  1865 *Life of Joseph Brant.* 2 vols. Albany: J. Munselle.

WOODWARD, GRACE STEELE
  1963 *The Cherokees.* Norman: University of Oklahoma Press.

Chapter XII: The Family of the Caddo

DORSEY, GEORGE A., and JAMES R. MURIE
  1940 "Notes on Skidi Pawnee Society," Anthropological Series 27 (2):65–119. Chicago: Field Museum of Natural History.

DUNBAR, JOHN B.
  1880 "The Pawnee Indians, A Sketch," *Magazine of American History,* 4 (4):241–81, 5 (5):321–45. Also 1883, New York.

HODGE, F. W.
  1950 "Pitalesharu and His Medal," *The Masterkey,* 24:111–19.

HYDE, GEORGE E.
  1951 *Pawnee Indians.* Denver: University of Denver Press.

PARSONS, ELSIE CLEWS
  1941 "Notes on the Caddo," Memoirs of the American Anthropological Association, 57:1–76.

SWANTON, JOHN R.
  1942 *Source Material on the History and Ethnology of the Caddo Indians.* Bureau of American Ethnology, Bulletin 132. Washington: Smithsonian Institution.

WILLIAMS, STEPHEN
1964 "The Aboriginal Location of the Kadohadacho and Related Tribes," *Explorations in Cultural Anthropology*, Ward Goodenough, ed. New York: McGraw-Hill.

Chapter XIII: The Southeastern Tribes

BOLTON, HERBERT E.
1916 *Spanish Explorations in the Southwest, 1542–1706*. Original Narratives of Early American History. New York: Scribner.
BOURNE, EDWARD G.
1904 *Narratives of the Career of Hernando de Soto*. 2 vols. New York: A. S. Barnes & Co.
CATLIN, GEORGE
1848 *Illustrations of the Manners, Customs, and Conditions of the North American Indians*. Several editions.
McREYNOLDS, EDWIN C.
1957 *The Seminoles*. Norman: University of Oklahoma Press.
SWANTON, JOHN R.
1911 *Indian Tribes of the Lower Mississippi Valley and Adjacent Coast of the Gulf of Mexico*. Bureau of American Ethnology, Bulletin 43. Washington: Smithsonian Institution.

Chapter XIV: The Siouan Family

HYDE, GEORGE E.
1937 *Red Cloud's Folk*. Norman: University of Oklahoma Press.
1961 *Spotted Tail's Folk: A History of the Brulé Sioux*. Norman: University of Oklahoma Press.
KENNEDY, MICHAEL STEPHEN, ed.
1961 *The Assiniboines: From the Accounts of the Old Ones Told to First Boy (James Larpenteur Long)*. Norman: University of Oklahoma Press.
LOWIE, ROBERT H.
1909 *The Assiniboine*. Anthropological Papers, Vol. IV, Pt. 1. New York: American Museum of Natural History.
1935 *The Crow Indians*. Revised 1956. New York: Rinehart.
1963 *Indians of the Plains. Op. cit.*

MACGREGOR, GORDON
  1946   *Warriors Without Weapons.* Chicago: University of Chicago Press.

McCARY, BEN C.
  1957   *Indians in Seventeenth-Century Virginia.* Williamsburg, Virginia: 350th Anniversary Celebration Corp.

ROBINSON, DOANE
  1904   "A History of the Dakota or Sioux Indians," *South Dakota Historical Collections,* Vol. 2.

SANDOZ, MARI
  1942   *Crazy Horse.* New York: Alfred A. Knopf.

Chapter XV: The Penutian Families

CHITTENDEN, HIRAM MARTIN, and ALFRED TALBOT RICHARDSON
  1905   *Life, Letters and Travels of Father Pierre Jean de Smet, S.J.* New York: Francis P. Harper.

EELLS, MYRON
  1894   "The Chinook Jargon," *American Anthropologist,* VII:300–12.

HAINES, FRANCIS
  1955   *The Nez Percés; Tribesmen of the Columbia Plateau.* Norman: University of Oklahoma Press.

HALE, HORATIO
  1890   *An International Idiom. A Manual of the Oregon Trade Language or "Chinook Jargon."* London: Whittaker & Co.

HEIZER, ROBERT F., and M. A. WHIPPLE
  1951   *The California Indians.* Berkeley & Los Angeles: University of California Press.

HOWARD, HELEN ADDISON
  1941   *War Chief Joseph.* Caldwell, Idaho: The Caxon Printers.

HOWARD, GENERAL OLIVER O.
  1881   *Nez Percé Joseph* (an account of his ancestors, his lands, his confederates, his enemies, his murders, his war, his pursuit, and capture). Boston: Lee and Shepard.

KROEBER, A. L.
  1925   *Handbook of the Indians of California. Op. cit.*

KROEBER, THEODORA
1959 *The Inland Whale.* Bloomington: Indiana University Press.
1961 *Ishi. Op. cit.*
MURRAY, K. A.
1959 *The Modocs and Their War.* Norman: University of Oklahoma Press.
RAY, VERNE F.
1963 *Primitive Pragmatists; the Modoc Indians of Northern California.* Seattle: University of Washington Press.
SPIER, LESLIE
1930 *Klamath Ethnography.* University of California Publications in American Archaeology and Ethnology, Vol. 30. Berkeley: University of California Press.
SPINDEN, H. J.
1908 *The Nez Percé Indians,* Memoirs of the American Anthropological Association, Vol. II, Pt. 3, pp. 165–274.

Chapter XVI: The Nadene Families

BOATRIGHT, MODY C.
1949 *The Sky is My Tipi.* Austin & Dallas, Texas Folklore Society, XXII: 1–243.
DRUCKER, PHILIP
1963 *Indians of the Northwest Coast. Op. cit.*
FORBES, JACK D.
1960 *Apache, Navaho, and Spaniard.* Norman: University of Oklahoma Press.
HEARNE, SAMUEL
1911 *A Journey from Prince of Wales's Fort in Hudson's Bay to the Northern Ocean,* J. B. Tyrrell, ed. Toronto: Publications of the Champlain Society, VI.
JENNESS, DIAMOND
1932 *The Indians of Canada. Op. cit.*
1938 *The Sarcee Indians of Alberta.* National Museum of Canada, Bulletin 90, Anthropological Series, No. 23.
KLUCKHOHN, CLYDE, and DOROTHEA LEIGHTON
1946 *The Navaho.* Cambridge: Harvard University Press. Revised ed. Garden City, New York: Anchor Natural History Library.

OPLER, MORRIS E.
  1938 "A Chiricahua Apache's Account of the Geronimo Campaign of 1886," *New Mexico Historical Review*, 13 (4):360–86.
SONNICHSEN, C. L.
  1958 *The Mescalero Apaches*. Norman: University of Oklahoma Press.
UNDERHILL, RUTH M.
  1956 *The Navajos*. Norman: University of Oklahoma Press.

Chapter XVII: The Aztec-Tanoan Families

BOURKE, J. G.
  1884 *The Snake Dance of the Moquis of Arizona*. New York: Scribner.
CASTETTER, E. F., and W. H. BELL
  1942 *Pima and Papago Indian Agriculture*. Inter-American Studies, I. Albuquerque: University of New Mexico Press.
COLTON, HAROLD S.
  1949 *Hopi Kachina Dolls*. Albuquerque: University of New Mexico Press.
COLTON, MARY RUSSELL F. and HAROLD S.
  1951 "An Appreciation of the Art of Nampeyo and her Influence on Hopi Pottery," *Hopi Indian Arts and Crafts*, reprinted from the publications of the Museum of Northern Arizona, Museum Notes and Plateau. Flagstaff: Northern Arizona Society of Science and Art. Reprint Series, No. 3, pp. 91–93.
DORSEY, GEORGE A. and H. R. VOTH
  1902 *The Mishongnovi Ceremonies of the Snake and Antelope Fraternities*. Chicago: Field Columbian Museum of Natural History, Anthropological Series, III:159–261.
HEBARD, GRACE RAYMOND
  1930 *Washakie. An Account of Indian Resistance of the Covered Wagon and Union Pacific Railroad Invasions of Their Territory*. Cleveland: The Arthur H. Clark Company.
  1933 *Sacajawea*. Glendale, California: The Arthur H. Clark Company.

JOSEPH, ALICE, ROSAMOND B. SPICER, and JANE CHESKY
1949 *The Desert People.* Chicago: University of Chicago Press.

LEWIS, MERIWETHER, and WILLIAM CLARK
1904–6 *Original Journals of the Lewis and Clark Expedition, 1804–1806,* Reuben Gold Thwaites, ed., 7 vols. New York: Dodd, Mead & Co.

LUTTIG, JOHN C.
1920 *Journal of a Fur-Trading Expedition on the Upper Missouri, 1812–1813,* Stella M. Drumm, ed. St. Louis: Missouri Historical Society.

MARRIOTT, ALICE LEE
1948 *Maria: The Potter of San Ildefonso.* Norman: University of Oklahoma Press.

MAYHALL, MILDRED P.
1962 *The Kiowas.* Norman: University of Oklahoma Press.

MORGAN, DALE L., ed.
1953–58 "Washakie and the Shoshoni," *Annals of Wyoming,* Vols. 25–30, misc. pp.

MORLEY, SYLVANUS G.
1946 *The Ancient Maya.* Stanford: Stanford University Press.

NEQUATEWA, EDMUND
1951 "Nampeyo, Famous Hopi Potter," *Hopi Indian Arts and Crafts,* reprinted from the publications of the Museum of Northern Arizona, Museum Notes and Plateau. Flagstaff: Northern Arizona Society of Science and Art. Reprint Series, No. 3, pp. 88–90.

OPLER, M. E.
1939 "The Ute Indian War of 1879," *El Palacio,* 46:255–62.

SHIMKIN, DIMITRI B.
1947 *Wind River Shoshone Ethnography.* Anthropological Records, Berkeley and Los Angeles: University of California Press, V:245–88.

STEPHEN, A. M.
1936 *Hopi Journal of Alexander M. Stephen,* Elsie Clews Parsons, ed. New York: Columbia University Press.

STEWARD, JULIAN H.
1955 "The Great Basin Shoshonean Indians," *Theory of Culture Change,* pp. 101–21. Urbana: University of Illinois Press.

TITIEV, MISCHA
 1943   "Hopi Snake Handling," *Scientific Monthly*, 57:44–
        51.
UNDERHILL, RUTH M.
 1940   *The Papago Indians of Arizona and their Relatives
        the Pima.* Indian Life and Customs Pamphlets, No.
        III. Lawrence, Kansas.
 1946   *First Penthouse Dwellers of America.* 2nd ed. Santa
        Fe: Laboratory of Anthropology.
VAILLANT, GEORGE
 1941   *Aztecs of Mexico.* Garden City, New York: Double-
        day, Doran & Co.
WALLACE, ERNEST, and E. ADAMSON HOEBEL
 1952   *The Comanches.* Norman: University of Oklahoma
        Press.

PART III. INDIAN LIFE IN GENERAL

Chapter XVIII: *The Indian Way of Life*

MASON, OTIS T.
  1895 *Woman's Share in Primitive Culture.* New York: Macmillan.
MOONEY, JAMES
  1928 *The Aboriginal Population of America North of Mexico,* John R. Swanton, ed. Smithsonian Institution, Miscellaneous Collections, 80, No. 7. Washington.

Chapter XIX: *When the White Man Went Indian*

DARLINGTON, WILLIAM M.
  1893 *Cristopher Gist's Journals.* Cleveland: The Arthur H. Clark Company.
HANNA, CHARLES A.
  1911 *The Wilderness Trail.* 2 vols. New York: G. P. Putnam's Sons. Knickerbocker Press.
KEPHART, HORACE
  1916 *Captives among the Indians.* New York: Outing Publishing Co.
SMITH, WILLIAM
  1868 *Historical Account of Bouquet's Expedition Against the Ohio Indians, in 1764.* Cincinnati: Robert Clarke.

Chapter XX: *Three Strange Gifts from the White Man*

HENRY, ALEXANDER, and DAVID THOMPSON
  1897 *New Light on the Early History of the Greater Northwest. Op. cit.*
HORNADAY, WILLIAM T.
  1889 "The Extermination of the American Bison; with a sketch of its discovery and life history," United States National Museum, Report for 1887, pp. 367–548. Washington.

MACLEOD, WILLIAM CHRISTIE
  1928 *The American Indian Frontier.* New York: Alfred A. Knopf.

ROE, FRANK GILBERT
  1951 *The North American Buffalo; a Critical Study of the Species in Its Wild State.* Toronto: University of Toronto Press.
  1955 *The Indian and the Horse.* Norman: University of Oklahoma Press.

Chapter XXI: The Mystery of the Indian Mind

HENRY, ALEXANDER, and DAVID THOMPSON
  1897 *New Light on the Early History of the Greater Northwest. Op. cit.*

KURZ, RUDOLPH FRIEDERICH
  1937 *Journal of Rudolph Friederich Kurz; an Account of His Experiences among the Fur Traders and American Indians along the Mississippi and Upper Missouri Rivers During the Years 1846–52,* J. N. B. Hewitt, ed. Myrtis Jarrell, trans. Washington.

Index

Abnaki tribe, 68, 80

Aboriginals. *See* Prehistory, prehistoric Indians; specific places, tribes

Acoma Pueblo, 42, 239

Acorns, use of, 21–23, 202–4, 329

Adena Indians, 36

Adobe dwellings, 41–44, 229, 243

Adobe Walls, Texas, 112

Adolescents. *See* Children

Africa, 4

Aged, the, 17, 265, 273, 289; appearance of, 299; liquor and, 303

Agents and agencies, 107, 194, 210, 247, 294, 312–17. *See also* Reservations

Agriculture. *See* Farming; Plants; specific crops, tribes

Ahtena (or Copper River Indians), 214

Alabama (state), 159, 168, 171

Alabama River, 168

Alaska, 52, 263 (*see also* specific tribes); basketry, 18; Nadene, 213, 214, 215–23; prehistoric Indians and, 4, 5, 6, 10, 263; stone boilers in, 16, 18, 21

Alaska, University of, 6, 7

Albany, N.Y., 129, 130, 284

Alberta, Canada, 102, 286

Albinos, 198

Alcohol. *See* Liquor

Aleuts, 67, 263

Algonkin family, 69–87, 135, 142, 166, 173, 213, 262, 285, 286 (*see also* specific places, tribes); characteris-

tics, mode of life, 72–77, 121–25, 135, 285, 298; chiefs, leaders, 71, 84–86, 91, 94–100; contributions, 223; Dakota (Sioux) and, 173–74, 178, 182–85, 187, 189; dress and fashions, 72, 75–77; Eastern, 69–87, 278; and Iroquois (*see under* Iroquois); lake tribes, 114–17; Northern and Western, 113–25, 221; Old Northwest, 88–100; Pacific Coast, 118–21, 221; Plains, 101–12; population, 78 ff., 122

Algonkin-Wakashan language group, 67, 68, 118–21. *See also* specific families, places, tribes

Alibamu tribe, 160

Allegheny Mountains, 93

Alphabets, Indian, 150, 176

Amarillo, Texas, 245

America, prehistoric. *See* Prehistory, prehistoric Indians

American Geographical Society, 82

American Horse, Chief, 175

American Indian Frontier (Macleod), 295 n

Ammunition, 117, 285, 289. *See also* Guns; Weapons

Anasazi culture, 40–41

Ancient Man in North America (Wormington), 12 n

Andaman Islands, 52

Andes, 44, 328

Animal gods, 74. *See also* Totemism

Animal life, 266–72, 327 (*see also* Hunting; specific kinds); aboriginal Indians

Animal life (*cont'd*)
and, 3–15, 26; beliefs concerning, 305, 306; cooking, stone boilers and, 16; furs, 285 (*see also* Fur trappers and trading)

Anne, Queen, 53, 81

Apache tribes, 214, 224–28, 240, 275, 290, 296 (*see also* specific divisions); divisions listed, 214; Kiowa, 213, 214, 215, 224; Western, 214

Apartment dwellings, 40–43, 208, 237, 243

Appalachians, 69, 70, 83, 91, 127

Apple orchards, 136

Arabia, 51

Arapaho tribes, 68, 69, 101, 102, 108–11, 123, 198; and Blackfoot, 103; Shoshoni and, 246; symbolic designs, 322

Archaeology, 18, 20, 78, 120, 221; and builders, 35, 37, 39, 42, 44; and early farming, 25–26, 30, 204; and language, 66–67 (*see also* Language); and origin of Indians, 5–15; and pottery, 31, 32; and smoking, 48, 54

Architecture, 40–43, 208 (*see also* Dwellings); Natchez, 160–62, 163–65; Navaho (hogan), 228–29; Pawnee, 157; Pueblo, 41–43, 243; temple, 160–62; Tlingit, 217, 219

Arctic area, 3, 213, 221, 222. *See also* Alaska

Argentina, 10

Arikara (Ree) tribe, 151, 152, 153, 183, 186

Aristocracy, 163, 220

Arizona, 200, 234, 235, 263, 290, 296; early corn cultivation, 28, 266, 268; Na-

dene families, 213, 214, 215, 224–33; Pima and Papago, 248; pottery, 31–33; Pueblos, 42, 237–44, 273

Arkansas (state), 154

Arkansas River, 111

Arm bands, 223

Army, U. S., 142, 286, 290, 291 (*see also* Treaties; Wars and warfare; specific events, individuals, places); Algonkin and (Old Northwest), 93; Apache and, 224–27; Caddo and, 154; Cherokee and, 147; Cheyenne and, 111–12; Dakota (Sioux) and, 186–89 ff.; Modoc and, 205–6; Navaho and, 232, 233; Nez Percé and, 209–12; Pawnee and, 153, 155, 156; Piegan and, 108; Seminole and, 171–72

Arrows, sacred, 109, 124. *See also* Bows and arrows

Art, arts and crafts, 110, 123, 178, 179, 215, 219–20, 223, 230–32, 274–75, 329 (*see also* Architecture; Pottery; specific items, tribes); of the builders, 36–40; symbolic, 110, 123, 322

Artifacts, prehistoric, 6–15

Artillery, 112, 134, 189. *See also* Guns; Weapons

Asia, 5–14 *passim*, 25, 31, 215, 302

Assiniboin (Dakota-Assiniboin) tribe, 108, 174, 177, 178, 181; and Blackfoot, 104; mode of life, 196, 197–98; Waneta and, 185

Astronomy, 152, 236

Athapascan family, 102, 214, 220–23 (*see also* specific tribes); *babiche*, 220–23;

Athapascan family (*cont'd*)
mode of life, 220–23; tribes,
divisions, 214, 222–23

Atlantic Coast, 55, 68–87,
134, 166, 173, 199, 322
(*see also* East Coast; New
England; specific places,
tribes); farming, 27–31

Atlantis, lost continent of, 4

Atsina (Gros Ventre) tribe,
68, 101, 102, 103, 108, 197

Auburn, N.Y., 138

Auk tribe, 214

Australia, 52, 283

Aztec Pueblo, 41, 43, 244

Aztec-Tanoan language families, 67, 234–58 (*see also*
specific divisions, tribes);
tribes and divisions, list of,
235, 236

Aztecs (or Nahuatlan), 234–
36, 295. *See also* specific divisions

Babiche, 220–23

Baggage, transportation of,
13, 102, 180, 272, 273

Bags, 73, 207

Bakersfield, Calif., 202

Balsam, 328

Bands, woven, 223

Bands and communities, Indian, 261–62, 263–75

Bannock tribe, 235

Barks, use of, 72, 164, 329
(*see also* Birchbark); clothing, 154, 217, 329; cooking
utensils, 18, 19, 20; dwellings, 36, 144; for horse
feed, 290–91; pottery, 32;
smoking, 52

Barter, 323

Basketmaker periods, 28, 40,
41

Basket making, basketry, 16–
24, 27, 32, 40, 45, 243, 248,
322; Algonkin, 72; Apache,

228; Nez Percé, 206–7;
Tlingit, 218; Zuni, 32

Basswood fiber twine, 116

Bat Cave, N.M., 27

Bathing, washing, 75, 125

Bayonets, use of, 290

Beads and beadwork, 42, 110,
180, 230, 329

Bean Festival, 137

Beans, 28, 37, 41, 136

Bear fat, use of, 76

Bear Lake tribe, 214

Bear Society, 137

Beaver tribe, 214, 222

Bella Coola tribe, 68, 120

Bering Strait, 5, 6

Berries, dried, 23, 207

Big Bellies, 197

Big Belly River, 108

Big Horn country, 191, 192

Billings, Mont., 211

Biloxi tribe, 174

Birchbark: canoes, 69, 114,
116, 178, 223; dwellings,
72, 116; paper, 116; utensils, 20, 116

Bird gods, 74. *See also* Totemism

Birth rate, 265

Bismarck, N.D., 197, 253

Bison. *See* buffalo

Bison americanus, 8

Bison taylori, 7

Bitterroot Valley, 121

Blackfeet Teton-Dakota
(Sioux), 174, 177

Blackfoot tribes, 68, 101, 102–
8, 119, 121, 124, 249 (*see
also* specific tribes); Algonkin, 223; blood types, 12;
guns, 286; North, 101, 102,
108, 286, 300; Plains, 68,
275; smoking, 57, 300

Black Hawk, Chief, 68, 98–99

Black Hills, 108, 189, 192–93,
245

Detroit, 88, 89, 91, 92, 97; Huron in, 133; Red Jacket at, 142

De Vargas. *See* Vargas, Diego de

Dialects. *See* Language

Diet, 26, 40, 116. *See also* Food; specific kinds, tribes

"Digger Indians," 234, 247

Dindjie tribe, 214

Disease and epidemics, 79, 106, 107, 108, 153, 178, 198 (*see also* specific diseases, tribes); magic beliefs, 304, 307, 308–9 (*see also* Medicine: men); on reservations, 311, 316

Doctors, Indian, 74 (*see also* Medicine: men); root, 74

Dogrib tribe, 214, 222

Dogs, 13, 40, 44, 102, 136, 165, 326; travois, 124, 180, 273, 329

Dolls, wooden, 238

Domestic animals, 13, 136, 188, 290–91, 327. *See also* Dogs; Sheep

Donkeys, use of, 290

Dreams, 125, 306, 329

Dress. *See* Clothing

Drinking, drunkenness. *See* Liquor

Drummond Island, 185

Dunmore, Lord Governor, 139

Du Pratz, on Natchez temples, 160–62

Duquesne, Fort, 90

Dutch, the. *See* Holland and the Dutch

Dutch Reformed Church, 226

Dwellings, 32, 116, 118, 119, 198, 248, 272, 291, 330 (*see also* Architecture; Tipis; specific kinds, places); Algonkin, 72, 85; Apache, 228; beehive-shaped, thatched, 154;

Caddo, 154, 157; cave, 6, 10, 13, 26; cliff, 28, 29, 40; Delaware, 85; Iroquois, 144; Navaho (hogan), 229; Pawnee, 154, 157, 291; pit, 40, 41; Pueblo, 40–43, 208, 238, 243; reservations, 312, 315, 316; Tlingit, 216, 219, 220

Eagle-feather headdresses, 175, 200

Eagle Society, 137

Early Woodland period, 36

Ear spools, 38

Earthen pots and vessels, 21, 30, 33

Earth houses, 198, 291, 330

Earth sculpture; earthworks, 35–40, 44–45

East Coast, 49, 52, 69–87, 263, 274 (*see also* Atlantic Coast; specific places, tribes); early farming, 27–31; prehistoric builders, 35–36, 39

Eastern Dakota tribe, 174, 182–89, 199

Eastern Woodland area. *See* Woodland Indians

Education, 324. *See also* Alphabets; Literacy; Writing

Egypt, 21, 31, 33, 153

Elbow pipes, 49, 50, 51, 54

Electricity, use of, 316

Elephants, 3

Elk, 3, 266–71

Embankments, building of, 37, 39

England and the English, 43, 65, 79, 105, 264, 276–81 (*see also* Colonies and colonists; specific events, individuals); Algonkins and, 69, 83, 93, 94, 95, 97; Cherokee and, 146; Dakota (Sioux) and, 184–85, 186,

England and English (*cont'd*)
187; and France, Indians,
and wars between, xvii, 70,
81, 88–92, 132, 133, 136,
144, 146, 286; Iroquois and,
132, 133, 136, 141–43, 144;
and liquor, 295; smoking
and, 52, 53; and Southeastern tribes, 166, 168
Epidemics. *See* Disease and
epidemics
Episcopal Church, 143
Erie, Lake, 97, 132–33
Erie tribe, 126, 127, 132–33,
134
Eskimos, 12, 67, 114, 213,
217, 284, 327; blood types,
12; population, 263; smoking, 52
Eskimo-Aleut language group,
67
Estevanico, 239
Etowah Mound (Ga.), 39–40,
44
Europe and the Europeans, 4,
13, 43, 51, 53, 65, 326 (*see
also* Old World; specific
countries, events, individuals); and "going" Indian,
276–81
Evergreens, 14. *See also* Conifers; Forests
Eyak tribe, 214

Fairbanks, Alaska, 6
Fallen Timbers, battle of, 93–
94, 95, 97, 133
Fall Indians, 197. *See also* At-
sina tribe
False Face Society, 137, 144,
302
Families, language. *See under*
Language
Family organizations, relation-
ships, 118; Iroquois, 136–
37; maternal, 137
Farming, 21, 25–34, 194, 234,

266, 273, 326, 329, 330 (*see
also* Corn; Food; Plants;
specific crops, places); Algonkin, 72; Caddo, 154;
early, 25–34; Iroquois, 137,
144; Natchez, 165; Navaho,
231, 233; Pawnee, 152;
prayers and rituals, 124–25,
152–53, 237–38, 320 (*see
also* Ceremonies; Religious
beliefs); Pueblo, 237, 243;
on reservations, 315, 316–
21; Sioux, 194, 198–99
Farms and farm buildings,
raids on, 82
Fashions, 72, 75–77. *See also*
Clothing; specific items
Fatalities, 82–84. *See also*
Death
Fats, use of, 76, 165
Feasts, festivals, 137, 218. *See
also* Ceremonies; Potlatch
Feather headdresses, 175, 200,
321, 330
Federations, 79, 99, 128–30,
158, 169, 263. *See also* specific groups
Fell's Cave, Chile, 6, 10, 17,
33
Fibers, plant, use of, 40, 73,
116, 165. *See also* Cloth;
specific items
Finger Lakes, N.Y., 128
Firearms. *See* Guns; Weapons
Fired vessels, 32
Fires: ceremonial, 30, 130,
161–62; indoor, 42, 72, 157,
165, 217
Fish and fishing, 116, 118,
121, 217, 268, 271; prehis-
toric, 23, 38; salmon, 21,
23, 121, 207–8, 271–72
Five Civilized Tribes, 160,
169–72
Five Nations, 129–45. *See also*
Six Nations; specific tribes
Flathead tribes, 68, 121, 209

Massasoit (Wampanoag sachem), 68, 71

Mastadons, 3, 5, 9, 11

Maternal family organization, 137

Mathematics, 182, 236–37, 328

Matotope, Chief, 197

Mattole tribe, 214

Maumee, Ohio, 93

Maximilian, Prince of Wied, 197

Maya Indians, 31, 234, 235, 326, 328. See also specific tribes

Meal, acorn, 22–23, 203, 329

Meat eating, 266–72. See also Animal life; Food; Hunting

Medicine, 74–75, 304, 328; bundles (see Bundles); men, 77–78, 158, 218, 304, 307 (see also Magic); pipes, 57, 109; Society, 137, 158

Melbourne, Fla., 12

Men (see also specific places, tribes): as hunters, 266–71, 272; population figures, 263–65, 271; role in way of life, 261–75

Menifee County, Ky., 26

Menomini tribe, 68, 73, 114–16

Mesa Verde, Colo., 40, 41, 43, 243

Mescalero Apache, 227

Mesoamerica, 27. See also Central America

Messiah, belief in, 195

Metallurgy, metal working, 327–28. See also specific metals

Mexican War, 246

Mexico, 150, 187, 234, 245–46, 248, 296, 326, 327; Apache, 224–26, 296; Hopi, 238–43; Navaho, 232–33; Penutian tribes, 203; prehistoric Indian, 5, 6, 10, 27, 30, 31, 39, 44, 49; Pueblos, 239–43

Mexico City, 239

Mexico, Gulf of, 7, 173, 200, 287

Mexico, Valley of, 6, 11, 326, 327

Miami tribes, 68, 86, 133; at Fallen Timbers, 94; French and, 89, 91; land claims and settlements, xi–xii

Mica ornaments, 38

Michigan (state), 88, 114–15, 135, 142; Huron in, 131, 132

Michigan, Lake, 114, 115, 132

Middle Woodland period, 36

Midé (Midéwin) Society, 75, 116

"Midland Man," 12

Miles, General Nelson A., 211–12, 226

Mingo Indians, 85, 137–39

Miniconjou Teton-Dakota, 174, 177

Minnehaha, 175

Minnesota, 96, 101, 176; Dakota (Sioux), 183, 187, 188, 190, 200

"Minnesota Man," 11

Minnesota River and Valley, 189

Minnitari, 197. See also Hidatsa

Mishongnovi (Hopi village, Arizona), 238

Missions and missionaries, 228, 314, 324. See also Christianity; specific individuals, places

Mission tribe, 235, 248

Mississippi period, 36, 39

Mississippi River and Valley, 99, 146, 152, 159, 183, 253, 269 (see also specific places, tribes); builders, 38, 46;

Pueblos (*cont'd*)
302, 330 (*see also* Hopi; Zuni; specific divisions); Navaho and, 232; villages, 42-43, 237-44, 263 (*see also* specific villages)
Puget Sound, 19, 119, 120, 268
Pulque, 295, 296
Purification ceremonies, 125

Quakers, 134, 147
Quapaw tribe, 174
Quebec, 88, 90, 91; Huron in, 134
Queen Anne's War, 81
Quillwork, porcupine, 180, 223, 329

Rabbitskin blankets, 207
Radiocarbon dating, 6, 8-10, 15, 27, 43
Raids and raiding, xvi-xviii, 63, 70, 135, 158, 271, 291 (*see also* Massacres; Wars and warfare; specific places); Apache, 225-27; Comanche, 245-46; Dakota (Sioux), 181, 186-87, 194; Navaho, 232; New England, 82 ff. (*see also* specific places, tribes); Old Northwest, 88, 91 (*see also* specific places, tribes); Western plains, 105, 111-12 (*see also* specific places, tribes)
Railroads, 187, 191, 311
Rain gods, 231, 233, 238
Rattles, 269
Rattlesnakes, 238
Red Cloud, Chief, 174, 191-92, 193
Red Jacket, Chief, 126, 136, 141-43, 144
Red stone pipes, 175, 200
Red Wing, Chief, 185

"Red Wing" (song), 175
Ree (abbreviation of Arikara). *See* Arikara
Reindeer, 222
Religious beliefs, 38, 45, 49, 110, 123-25, 152-64 *passim*, 179-82, 195, 200. *See also* Ceremonies; Christianity; Gods; Mythology; Supernaturalism; specific places, tribes
Republican Pawnee. *See* Kitkehahkis
Reservations, 259, 281, 294, 310-25; Arapaho, 108; Blackfoot, 103, 108; Cheyenne, 111; Dakota (Sioux), 189, 192, 193, 195; Iroquois, 136; Klamath and Modoc, 205; life on, xii, 310-25; Menomini, 115; Navaho, 231-33; Nez Percé, 210; number of, 312; Ontario, 86; Sauk and Fox, 99; Shoshoni, 250-52; Ute, 247
Revolt of 1680, 240
Revolution, American, 133, 136, 141 (*see also* specific individuals, tribes); Cherokee and, 146-47; Dakota (Sioux) and, 184
Rhode Island, 78, 79
Rice. *See* Wild rice
Rifles, 112, 188, 286, 289. *See also* Guns; Weapons
Rio Grande River, 239, 240
Rituals and ritualism. *See* Ceremonies and ceremonialism
Ritwan language group, 68, 118
Road building, 234, 314
Robes, 40-41, 135, 179, 180, 217, 270
Robinson, Doane, 185 n, 194 n
Rock River, 99

Sunflower (*Helianthus an-nuus*), 26
Sun worship, 161–64, 181
Superior, Lake, 114, 115
Supernaturalism, 28–29, 57–58, 73–75, 85, 179–82, 303–9. *See also* Gods, Mythology; Religious beliefs; specific tribes
Supreme Court, U. S., 147
Susquehanna (Conestoga) tribe, 83, 126, 127, 134
Susquehanna River and Valley, 134
Swadesh, Morris, 7, 66, 337
Swanton, John, 154, 162 n, 336
Sweat baths, 125
Symbolic designs, 110–11, 123, 322; Arapaho, 322
Symbolism, 153, 197, 200, 322; Aztec, 236

Taciturnity, Indian trait, 298
Taensa tribe, 159 ff., 166
Taft, Lorado, 99
Tahltan tribe, 214
Takulli tribe, 214
Taku tribe, 214
Tales of the North American Indians (Thompson), 28–29
Tama, Iowa, 98
Tamenend (Tammany), Chief, 84, 85
Tammany, 84, 85
Tanana (or Lower Tanana) tribe, 214
Tanaina tribe, 214
Tanner, John, 277
Tannin, methods of removing from acorn meal, 22, 203–4
Tanoan family, 67, 235, 236, 239. *See also* specific divisions, tribes
Taos Pueblo, 235, 239

Tapage. *See* Pitahuerat
Tapioca, 25
Tapirs, 11
Tatsanottine tribe, 214
Tattooing, 76
Tawakoni tribe, 151
Tecumseh, Chief, 68, 95, 133, 166, 184; and Tippecanoe battle, 96–97
Temples, 37, 39; Aztec, 236; Natchez, 159–62, 166; Pawnee, 154
Tenas, 214
Tenino tribe, 203, 225
Tennessee, 36, 148, 159, 173
Tenskwatawa (the Prophet), 96
Tepees (*see also* Tipis): meaning of word, 176–77
Tesuque Pueblo, 235
Teton Dakota tribe, 174, 176, 177, 178–82, 189–96, 197; economic depression, 194–96; history of, 189–96; mode of life, 178–82, 197, 198, 199
Teton Mountains, 177, 189
Tewa Pueblos, 235, 236. *See also* specific divisions
Texas, 112, 200, 245; Caddo, 154; Comanche and Kiowa, 244, 245–46; Delaware in, 87; early corn cultivation, 27; prehistoric Indians in, 8, 12, 27
Textiles, 17, 27, 42, 123, 165, 229–30, 269, 322. *See also* Weaving
Thlingchattine tribe, 214
Thompson, David, 58 n, 293 n, 301 n, 339
Thompson, Stith, 28–29, 338
Three Forks, Mont., 252, 254
Thunder, 57–58, 73, 124
Thunderbird, 74, 330
Ticonderoga, 90
Tigers, saber-toothed, 5

Women (*cont'd*)

271–74 (*see also* Cooking; Food; specific tribes); as gardeners, 33, 72, 273 (*see also* Farming); Iroquois, 137; Maria Martinez, 242; marriage, 137, 157, 164, 253, 273, 280–81 (*see also* Intermarriage); and maternal family organization, 137; medicine (magic), 78; Nampeo, 242; Natchez, 164–65; Navaho, 229–32; Pawnee, 155, 157; Pocahontas, 71, 134, 176, 252; population figures for, 264–65, 271; Pueblo, 42, 237, 242; Sacajawea, 235, 252–58; Sioux, 179, 180; textile and pottery designs by, 322 (*see also* Pottery; Textiles); weaving, 230, 243, 273–74, 322 (*see also* Weaving)

Woodcraft, wood-working, 19, 43, 123, 215–17, 219–20, 238, 283. See *also* specific objects, tribes

Woodland Indians, 69–87 ff., 123 (*see also* specific places, tribes); Early, 36; Eastern, 274

World War II, effects on Indians of, 323–24

Wormington, H. M., 12 n

Writing, 75, 149–50, 169, 176, 234; invention of, 326, 329;

picture, 75, 116

Wyandot (Huron) tribe, 94, 126, 127, 131–33, 138, 144

Wyoming, 108, 111, 235, 236, 266; Dakota (Sioux), 189, 190, 191; Shoshoni, 244–46, 249–52, 258

Yakima tribe, 203, 206

Yakutat tribe, 214

Yampa Utes, 247

Yams, 223

Yana tribe, 200

Yanktonai, 185

Yankton Dakota, 174

Yaqui tribe, 235

Yellowknife tribe, 214, 222

Yellowstone Park, 211

Yellowstone River, 190, 191, 254

Yokuts tribe, 202, 275

Young, Brigham, 249

Yucatan, 235, 326

Yucca plant fibers, 40

Yuchi tribe, 200, 275

Yuki tribe, 200

Yukon, 7, 222

Yuma tribe, 200

Yurok tribe, 68, 118

Zero, use of, 236

Zoos, 236

Zoque tribe, 203

Zuni Pueblos, 31–32, 42, 204, 237, 239–44, 275

CLARK WISSLER was born in Indiana in 1870. A graduate of Indiana University, he received his Ph.D. in anthropology from Columbia University, and was Curator Emeritus of the Department of Anthropology at The American Museum of Natural History until his death in 1947. Recognized as a world authority on the American Indian, Dr. Wissler is also the author of *The American Indian, Man and Culture,* and *Indian Cavalcade.*